How to Access
the Government's
ELECTRONIC
BULLETIN
BOARDS

WASHINGTON
ONLINE

How to Access
the Government's
ELECTRONIC
BULLETIN
BOARDS

1996

BRUCE MAXWELL
bmaxwell@netcom.com

Congressional Quarterly
Washington, D.C.

For Barbara

Library of Congress Cataloging-in-Publication Data

in process

SUMMARY CONTENTS

CONTENTS

Business, Trade, and Economics   63

Business   64

Economic Data   72

Foreign Trade   87

Government Contracts and Grants   90

.

PREFACE

Until a few years ago, if you needed federal government information your options were limited. You could visit your local library, and if the library was large enough you might—or might not—find what you sought. Or you could call Washington and hope that after getting transferred eighteen times you might find a person who could send you the information. Or you could try to gain access to a commercial database that might contain what you wanted—for a price.

Today, your options for obtaining federal government information have vastly expanded with the proliferation of federal government bulletin board systems (BBSs). BBSs operated by federal agencies, departments, and courts offer everything from presidential speeches to lists of federal job openings to consumer publications about how to buy a home.

BBSs are electronic libraries that you dial into with a computer and modem. You can browse through the information, read whatever you like, and download anything you need into your own computer.

Best of all is the price for accessing this information: free. All you pay for is the phone call—and even that's free if you live within a board's local calling area or if the board has a toll-free number. You also can save on long-distance charges if you have an Internet account, since many of the boards are accessible through the Internet.

How to Access the Government's Electronic Bulletin Boards: Washington Online provides detailed descriptions of more than 200 federal BBSs. It describes how to reach them, how to navigate through them, what they offer, and any quirks you should know about to use them successfully. I've spent hundreds of hours online examining the boards listed in this book, so each description is written from a user's perspective.

A companion book, *How to Access the Federal Government on the Internet: Washington Online,* describes federal government Internet sites, which are proliferating even more rapidly than BBSs. Together, the two books provide a detailed guide to the vast resources that the federal government offers online.

While the Internet's technical complexity intimidates some people, BBSs are easy to use. Most of the BBSs have menus that help you find your way around. Nearly all of them also have online help if you get stuck. Thus, you need very little computer knowledge to use a federal BBS successfully. The few technical matters you need to understand are fully explained in the Introduction. And if you run across an unfamiliar technical word, you can turn to the Glossary at the back of this book for a quick explanation.

Federal BBSs change rapidly. Boards are born or die seemingly overnight, software upgrades alter the appearance and operation of boards, and new files are added and old ones deleted. I've worked hard to make this book as current as possible, but the rapid pace of change makes it inevitable that some of the information will be outdated by the time you read it. To guide you through the changes since the last edition, I have added three appendixes: (1) boards added since the 1995 edition; (2) boards deleted since the 1995 edition; and (3) boards with changed names.

Because things are changing so rapidly, I'm writing new editions of this book annually. If you learn about new boards or significant changes in those listed here, please send me an e-mail message. My e-mail addresses are:

Internet: bmaxwell@netcom.com
FedWorld: Bruce Maxwell

I would like to thank many people for their contributions to this book. To begin with, my thanks go to Mark Leff and, at FedWorld, to Bob Bunge and Carol Wilson. They compiled lists of federal BBSs that were very helpful in preparing this book. I'd also like to thank all the sysops who patiently answered my questions about their BBSs.

I'm also indebted to those who directly worked on this book. I especially thank Debra Naylor for her beautiful design work, Pat Ruggiero for creating the superb index, Ann Davies for her excellent work on the organization and final presentation, Carolyn Goldinger for editing the 1996 edition, and Jackie Davey, Joni Berkley, and Elizabeth Ashley for their publicity efforts. I'm especially indebted to Jeanne Ferris, former acquisitions editor at CQ, whose graciousness and encouragement helped keep me sane during the writing process.

And saving the most important for last, I'd like to thank my wife, Barbara, whose love has made this book—and so much else in my life—possible.

Bruce Maxwell

INTRODUCTION

This book provides all the information you need to access more than 220 bulletin board systems (BBSs) operated by federal agencies, departments, and courts. The definition of BBS used here is a broad one. Most of the systems are traditional BBSs with information you can download and messaging features, but a few are not. They are databases, dial-in systems that provide a stream of information, or Internet sites that offer dial-in access to people who lack Internet accounts.

To be included in this book, a board had to meet four requirements. It had to be (1) accessible with a computer and modem; (2) available to the public; (3) accessible at no cost; and (4) operated by the federal government, funded in significant part by the federal government, or a source of large amounts of federal government information.

Certain types of federal government BBSs are not included in this book: (1) those that are closed to the public; (2) those that charge a fee for access; and (3) those that are unusable because they are so unstable.

WHAT'S NEW IN THIS EDITION

The second edition of *Washington Online: How to Access the Government's Electronic Bulletin Boards* has descriptions of 67 new BBSs and other types of dial-in computer systems. Here are some highlights from among the new sites:

- CDC WONDER/PC provides access to Centers for Disease Control databases about subjects such as mortality, cancer incidence, hospital discharges, AIDS, behavioral risk factors, and diabetes, among others.

- The Department of Energy Home Page connects you with the Department of Energy's World Wide Web site, which has links to dozens of Internet sites operated by DOE laboratories and field offices and a database containing references to more than 250,000 declassified documents about human radiation experiments and nuclear testing.

- GPO Access, a collection of databases created by the Government Printing Office, provides the full text of the *Congressional Record*, the *Federal Register*, bills being considered by Congress, and reports from the General Accounting Office, which is the investigative arm of Congress.

- IRIS (Internal Revenue Information Services) has hundreds of IRS forms and publications for individuals, businesses, and nonprofit organizations.

- LingNet, operated by the Defense Language Institute, has a huge collection of programs and files to help users learn foreign languages ranging from Arabic to Chinese to Spanish.

- The MEDLARS AIDS Databases, which are operated by the National Library of Medicine, provide thousands of bibliographic references to materials about HIV/AIDS, information about clinical trials of AIDS drugs, and a directory of thousands of organizations and resources that offer biomedical information.
- The Nuclear Regulatory Commission (NRC) at FedWorld has daily reports about unexpected events at nuclear power plants, NRC reports about problems at nuclear plants, and related documents.
- The U.S. Postal Service's Rapid Information Bulletin Board System (RIBBS) has information about postal rates, how to detect mail bombs, various types of mail fraud, and lots more.
- RTK NET, which is operated by OMB Watch and The Unison Institute, provides access to more than a dozen federal databases containing information about toxic chemicals, home mortgages, and other subjects.
- The U.S. Arms Control and Disarmament Agency BBS has documents about nuclear, chemical, and biological weapons and efforts to control their proliferation.
- VA ONLINE, operated by the Department of Veterans Affairs, offers information about benefits available to active duty military personnel and veterans and a database that includes all of the names inscribed on the Vietnam Memorial in Washington, D.C.
- Five different BBSs operated by federal courts of appeals provide opinions, rules, and docket sheets.
- The Automated Vacancy Announcement System (AVAS) provides listings of job openings at the National Institutes of Health.

Some of the new systems are not traditional BBSs. Instead, they provide dial-in access to Gophers or World Wide Web sites on the Internet. This is especially nice for people who don't have Internet accounts, since it gives them a chance to try the Internet easily and inexpensively.

Nearly all federal courts run BBSs, but none were listed in the first edition of this book. The reason was that at the time, the courts were forced to charge hefty fees for access. The decision to impose fees was made by the Judicial Conference of the United States, an advisory body to the federal courts. The initial fee was $1 per minute, although that fee generated so much revenue it was later reduced to 75 cents per minute.

Some judges rebelled against imposing fees, and issued blanket orders waiving fees for anyone using their boards. This edition contains listings for the five federal court BBSs that refuse to charge fees.

The most strongly worded opposition to fees was issued in January 1995 by the judges of the Seventh Circuit Court of Appeals. They wrote: "Charging a fee for this previously free public information amounts to a confiscatory tax on public information. If we had charged nongovernmental users a fee during the last year, they would have paid $10,800. When compared with the costs to the court of about $468 per year, it is obvious that such a charge is not a user fee, but a tax on previously free court information."

The Judicial Conference continues to pressure the rebel judges to charge fees, but so far most are still resisting.

BULLETIN BOARDS AND THE INTERNET

Reports of the death of BBSs are greatly exaggerated.

Some misguided souls claim that with the profusion of government Internet sites, there is no reason to continue operating BBSs. They could not be more wrong. Here are five reasons why BBSs continue to play a critical role in providing government information:

1. Many provide valuable information that isn't available on the Internet.

2. BBSs are more accessible than Internet sites, since anyone with a computer, a modem, communications software, and a telephone line can access them.

3. Most BBSs are easy to use because they are menu driven. They are much simpler to learn than the Internet, making them less intimidating for some people.

4. BBSs can be started for next to nothing, which in these days of government budget cuts makes them appealing. Virtually any computer can run a BBS, and BBS software is available for free.

5. Most BBSs have message capabilities that allow users to share ideas and ask questions. Gophers and World Wide Web sites don't have these capabilities.

Today, government agencies that are truly committed to electronic dissemination offer the same information on both BBSs *and* Internet sites. This is the ideal situation because it allows the broadest possible access to government information.

THE HARDWARE AND SOFTWARE YOU NEED

To access a BBS, you need two pieces of hardware: a computer and a modem. You also need one piece of software: a communications program.

You can use virtually any kind of computer—an IBM, an IBM compatible, a Macintosh, an Amiga, or whatever—as long as it can connect to a modem. You don't need anything fancy.

A modem is the device that lets two computers exchange data over ordinary telephone lines. There are two types: internal and external. Internal modems go inside your computer, while external ones sit on your desktop.

The other factor that differentiates modems is the speed at which they transfer data. The higher the number, the speedier the modem. Today, modems are commonly available at speeds ranging from 14,400 to 28,800 baud. Currently, 14,400-baud modems cost about $100, while 28,800-baud models cost about $200. It makes sense to buy the fastest modem you can afford. However, there are two caveats. First, high-speed modems (defined as 9600-baud and above) are slightly less stable than lower-speed models, leading to more connection problems. Second, many federal BBSs (and other online services) currently support modem speeds only up to 14,400 baud.

The last item you need—a communications program—is the tool that allows your computer to "talk" to another computer. Commercial communications software costs about $100. Many good shareware communications programs also exist. With shareware, you get to try the program before deciding whether to send in your fee. Fees for communications programs generally run between $25 and $50. You can find shareware programs through computer user groups, commercial services such as CompuServe and America Online, and the Internet. In addition, many of the government BBSs listed in this book have copies of shareware communications programs. For the Macintosh, Zterm is the favorite program. For IBM and compatible computers, Procomm is popular. Just don't confuse it with Procomm Plus, its commercial cousin.

To get the full benefit of BBSs, you will find two other pieces of software helpful: a decompression program and a file translation program. Many files on BBSs are compressed. Compression makes them smaller and quicker to download. However, you can't use the file on your computer until you decompress it back to its original size.

Compressed files have extensions on their names that indicate what program was used to compress them. Two of the most common extensions are ZIP and EXE. For example, a file named BBSGUIDE.ZIP has been compressed with a program called PKZIP.

Many decompression programs are available, mostly as shareware. For IBM and compatible computers, by far the most popular software is a shareware program called PKUNZIP. For Macintosh computers, the various commercial and shareware versions of StuffIt are popular.

Finally, it's useful to have a file translation program. Text and graphics files on BBSs are created with a wide variety of programs. Frequently, you'll have to translate the files so you can read them. For example, let's say you use

WordPerfect as your word processor. If you download a file created in Word-Star, you must translate the file from WordStar into WordPerfect before you can read it.

Some word processing and graphics programs have built-in translators that allow them to read certain "foreign" files. For information about what your program can do, check your manual. However, if you are planning to download many files, you should invest in a translation program. A translation program is especially important for Macintosh users because nearly all files on government computers are created with DOS programs.

WHAT TO DO BEFORE YOU CALL

After you hook up your computer and modem and install your communications software, you must do three things before calling a BBS:

1. Set your communications software at 8 data bits, 1 stop bit, and no parity. These are the default settings in most communications programs, and they are also the settings used by most federal government BBSs. Boards that use different settings are noted in this book. You don't need to worry about the technical meaning of these settings.

2. Choose the highest baud rate in your communications software that your modem can support. Check your modem manual for details.

3. Turn off Call Waiting if it has been installed on the telephone line used by your modem. Otherwise, you will be disconnected if a call comes in while you're online with a BBS. In most areas, the easiest way to turn off Call Waiting is to place a prefix before the BBS number you're calling. If you have tone dialing, use the prefix *70. Thus, if you want to call telephone number 123-4567, have your software dial *70123-4567. Doing so turns off Call Waiting for the duration of the call and restores it when you hang up. If you have pulse dialing, use the prefix 1170 instead of *70. Call your local telephone company if you have any questions about turning off Call Waiting.

A fourth action is optional. Before calling, turn on the "capture" or "log" feature in your communications software. If you do, your entire online session will be saved as a text file that you can review later with your word processing software.

WHAT HAPPENS WHEN YOU CALL A BBS

When the BBS answers, you'll hear an electronic buzz if your modem's speaker is turned on. If all goes well, you'll get a message that a connection has been made. What happens next varies from board to board, since each one is slightly different. Frequently, an opening message will welcome you to the board.

Warning Messages

You also may get a warning message, which varies from board to board. Here's a warning from one federal BBS:

> NOTICE!!! You are connected to a U.S. Government Bulletin Board System. Unauthorized access to this system is prohibited by Public Law 98-473. Punishment for offense can be up to $100,000 or up to 20 years prison or both.

The warnings can be intimidating. Don't worry about them, as long as you plan to use the computer properly. However, if you're a hacker who delights in harming computers, you should take them dead seriously.

If you call a federal BBS not listed in this book, you may get an opening message saying the board is not open to the public. All of the boards listed in this book were public when it was written, but some other federal BBSs are not. If the message says the computer is only available to certain people and you aren't one of them, log off.

Registering

Next, you'll be asked to register. At a minimum, registering involves providing your name, address, and telephone number. Be sure to use your real name. Some commercial BBSs allow the use of aliases or handles, but nearly all federal BBSs require real names. If you use an alias on a federal BBS, you will probably lose your privileges on the board.

The BBS will also ask you to choose a password. You can use the password the next time you log on to avoid going through the registration process again. When choosing a password, make sure it isn't something obvious like your name or city. For added security, some people use passwords that include a combination of letters and numbers.

On many boards, after you provide your name, address, telephone number, and password, you have full access. However, some boards also ask for some or all of the following information:

- Whether you want graphics. If you don't know if your terminal supports graphics, choose "no."

- Whether you want to use color.

- What kind of computer you're using.

- How many characters your monitor can display per line. The usual answer is 80.

- How many lines of text you want displayed before you get a prompt. The usual answer is 24.

- Where you learned about the board.

- What transfer protocol you want to use when downloading files. The board will tell you which protocols it supports. If both the board and your communications software support the Zmodem protocol, choose it. Zmodem is fast and secure, and supports downloads of multiple files in one batch. The second-best choice is Ymodem, and the third-best choice is Xmodem.

- Your mother's maiden name. Some boards ask this so they can confirm your identity if you forget your password.

Once you register, many boards present you with the Main Menu. The Main Menu is the heart of each board. Figure 1 is the Main Menu for RBBS-PC, a popular BBS program used by many federal government boards.

Figure 1. Main Menu

	*>>>	RBBS-PC	MAIN MENU	<<<*	
MAIL		SYSTEM		UTILITIES	ELSEWHERE
[E]nter Messages		[A]nswer Questions		[H]elp (or ?)	[D]oors
[K]ill Messages		[B]ulletins		[J]oin Conferences	[F]iles
[P]ersonal Mail		[C]omment to Sysop		[V]iew Conf. Mail	[G]oodbye
[R]ead Messages		[I]nitial Welcome		[X]pert on/off	[Q]uit
[S]can Messages		[O]perator Page			[U]tilities
[T]opic of Msgs		[W]ho's on		* = unavailable	[*]Library

Current time: 12:25 PM   Minutes remaining: 70   Security: 5

MAIN: 70 min left
MAIN command <?, A, B, C, D, E, F, G, H, I, J, K, O, P, Q, R, S, T, U, V, W, X> ? f

Federal BBSs use many types of operating software. Although these programs differ somewhat in how they look and operate, they all follow certain conventions. All require that you type a single letter (or rarely a few letters) to select an item from a menu. And all require that after entering any command, you press your Enter (or Return) key. The only exceptions are boards where you can elect to use Turbokeys. If you choose this option, you just have to type the command.

All BBS software packages used by federal government boards have similar features. For example, on most boards you'll find bulletins, files, and messages. In addition, nearly every board requires that you type **g** (for goodbye) to log off. The similarities in features and commands make it easy for you to explore new boards once you get the hang of BBSing.

The first time you see a Main Menu, however, the multitude of choices can be daunting. Following are brief explanations of the major areas you can access from the RBBS-PC Main Menu:

- [R]ead Messages   Allows you to read messages written by other users of the board. As you can see, there are many other message options as well.

- [B]ulletins   Brief text files that typically explain how to use the BBS, list upcoming conferences and meetings, and provide news updates. You can read bulletins online, and some BBSs allow you to download copies to your computer.

- [C]omment to Sysop   Allows you to leave a message for the system operator, commonly known as the "sysop."

- [O]perator Page   Allows you to page the sysop if you have a question while you're online. If the sysop is available, he or she will type a message that will appear on your screen, and the two of you can then type messages back and forth.

- [H]elp   Provides information about how to use various commands on the board.

- [J]oin Conferences   Allows you to join conferences, which offer collections of messages on a specific topic. On a few federal BBSs, conferences also have files.

- [D]oors   A gateway to other programs available on the BBS. On federal boards, doors usually lead to searchable databases.

- [F]iles   Written documents, graphic images, and computer programs that you can download to your computer.

- [G]oodbye   Provides a clean break from the BBS and resets the board for the next caller. Choose this option when you want to leave the BBS.

- [U]tilities   Allow you to change how the BBS interacts with your computer. For example, if you're getting garbage characters from the BBS, you can go to the Utilities Menu and turn off the board's graphics.

Other Menus

What happens when you type a letter at the Main Menu prompt? Usually, you get another menu that takes you deeper into the board. In the Figure 1 example, the user typed **f** at the prompt and hit the Enter key. Doing that brought up the File Menu.

As with the Main Menu, you simply type a letter for the function you want. You can type **d** to download a file, **l** to list the files that are available, **s** to search the files, **h** for help, and so on. In Figure 2, the user has typed **g**, the command for signing off the board.

Figure 2. File Menu

	>>> RBBS-PC FILE MENU <<<		
TRANSFER	INFORMATION	UTILITIES	ELSEWHERE
[D]ownload file	[L]ist files	[H]elp (or ?)	[G]oodbye
[P]ersonal dwnld	[N]ew files	[X]pert on/off	[Q]uit
[*]pload file	[S]earch files		
	[V]iew archives	* = unavailable	
Current time: 12:25 PM		Minutes remaining: 70	

MAIN: 70 min left
FILE command <?, D, G, H, L, N, P, Q, S, V, X>? g

When logging into a new board, it's usually best to begin by reading the bulletins. They frequently provide basic information about the BBS, how it operates, and what kinds of files it contains. Next, you may want to download the user's manual. Most boards have manuals that provide detailed information about how they operate.

Many boards also have master lists of every file they contain. It's useful to download these lists so you can examine them at your leisure without running up long-distance charges. The master file list usually includes the file name, a few words of description, the file size (so you can estimate how long it will take to download), and the date the file was created (so you can see if it's current).

Exploration is the best way to get to know a BBS. Feel free to browse and try anything that looks interesting. Don't worry about hurting the board. Harming a BBS is virtually impossible (unless you are a sophisticated computer user with a malicious intent). Most boards have advanced features that are too numerous to explain in this book. For example, if you are looking for a specific file or piece of information, many boards have sophisticated search functions that let you search all the files by keywords.

HOW TO GET HELP

There are many ways to get help using BBSs in general or a specific BBS in particular. General help is always available from members of your local computer user group, from people on commercial services such as CompuServe and America Online, and from users of the Internet. In addition, several excellent books about computer telecommunications are available at your local bookstore or library.

If you'd like to save money, two government boards have user's manuals that are excellent general introductions to BBSs. Both manuals are geared toward specific boards, but they contain lots of generic information as well. You can download them from the following boards:

- The Nonpoint Source Program Electronic Bulletin Board, which is listed in the Environment section of this book (p. 199). The manual includes a guided tour through a sample BBS session that you can read and then try online. It also describes commands you're likely to see on most BBSs.

- The Technology Transfer BBS is also listed in the Environment section (p. 203). The manual provides clear, detailed explanations of the major commands found on BBSs.

For help in using a specific board, download the user's manual (if one is available) and read it. Most boards also have extensive online help if a question arises while you're connected. On most boards, you can reach online help by typing **h** or **?** at a prompt. When you do so, the board will present information about using the area you're in at the time. Some boards also allow you to page the sysop while you are online if you have a question. You should not abuse this privilege. Sysops of federal boards don't have time to answer basic computer questions, so you should page them only if you have a specific question about their board.

COMMON PROBLEMS AND SOME SOLUTIONS

If you spend much time online, you're bound to experience occasional problems. Connecting to a BBS involves lots of intricate equipment—two computers, two modems, two sets of communications software, and a telephone line—and glitches can develop anywhere. Human error—most likely by you, although BBS operators also make occasional mistakes—can cause problems, too.

If you have a problem, first check the settings in your communications software. To access most boards, the software should be set at 8 data bits, 1 stop bit, and no parity. Also check that the modem speed set in your software works with your modem. If you have questions, check the manual for your modem.

The following list outlines some of the most common problems you can experience when using a federal BBS and suggests solutions. This list of potential problems is not exhaustive, nor is the list of suggested solutions. If you run into a problem not mentioned here, consult one of the sources of help described earlier in this Introduction or your computer manuals.

The BBS's telephone is always busy when I call. Busy signals are fairly common on federal BBSs, since many boards have only one or two phone lines. Even boards with many lines are sometimes busy because they're so popular. Try calling back another time, especially at night or on a weekend.

The BBS doesn't answer when I call. Failures to respond usually occur because either the board has ceased operating or it has temporarily crashed. "Temporary" crashes can last from a few minutes to a few weeks, depending on the extent of the problem and how much time the sysop has for repairs. If a board doesn't answer on your first call, try calling back several times over a period of a few weeks. If it still doesn't answer, you can assume it has stopped operating. To confirm this assumption, you can call the voice number listed for the board.

The BBS answers when I call, but I can't establish a connection. Make sure your communications software is set properly. Also check the description of the board in this book to see whether any special settings are required.

If you're using a high-speed modem (defined as 9600 baud or above), your problem could lie there. High-speed modems can be unstable, particularly if there is noise anywhere on the telephone line. Try connecting at a lower speed, such as 2400 baud.

After I connect to the board, nothing happens. Try hitting your Enter key once or twice. This usually will get you to a menu. If it doesn't, hang up and try calling again.

I can establish a connection to the board, but I only get garbage characters. "Garbage" can be caused by a number of things. Basically, either the board has crashed or the board and your computer aren't communicating properly. If you get garbage, try each of the following solutions in order until you find one that works:

1. From the Main Menu, choose the Utilities Menu (some boards call it the User Settings Menu). Turn off the board's graphics capabilities for your session.

2. Log off the BBS and try calling back at a lower modem speed, such as 2400 baud.

3. Log off and change the terminal setting in your communications software so that you emulate a VT100 terminal (don't worry about what this means technically). Then try calling again.

4. Log off, and in your communications software change your settings to 7 data bits, one stop bit, and even parity. Then try calling back.

5. Try solutions 3 and 4 in combination.

The board looks different from its description in this book. You may find variations from the descriptions in this book if the sysop has upgraded the BBS software, changed software packages, or overhauled the board in some other way. Use this book as a general guide to a board, not as a catalog of every feature and file.

Sometimes in the middle of an online session, my connection suddenly goes dead. There are two possible causes of this problem. First, most boards have time limits. If you exceed your time limit on the board, you will automatically be disconnected. The limits vary widely, but typically run about an hour per call.

Second, your modem may have had a momentary technical problem. This happens most commonly with high-speed modems, which can be finicky. It's possible that a little noise got in the telephone line and caused your modem to burp, leading to a dropped connection. Try calling back the BBS.

I was interrupted during an online session and had to leave for a while. When I returned to the computer, I found that I had been disconnected from the BBS. Most boards will automatically disconnect if you don't issue a command for a few minutes. They do this so that people who wander away from their computers won't tie up all of the telephone lines.

I'm stuck in a board, and can't get where I want. Simply press your Enter (or Return) key until you get a prompt.

Something froze in either the BBS or my communications software, and the board will not respond to my commands. Wait five minutes to see if whatever is stuck manages to unstick itself. If it doesn't, press the key that your communications software uses as a "break" key. This key varies among programs. If you still get no response, follow the procedures in your communications software for disconnecting from the board. If your communications software is frozen, follow any emergency shutdown procedures that may exist for your computer. And if that doesn't work, turn off your computer and your modem, let them rest for a couple of minutes, turn them back on, and try calling back the board. Be aware that if you were saving your online session to a capture file, you'll lose it when you turn off the computer.

The board contains files similar to what I want, but not exactly what I need.   Leave a message on the board for the sysop explaining what you're looking for and asking whether it can be provided. Most sysops will do everything possible to get what you need.

A FEW GUIDELINES FOR SUCCESSFUL BBSING

Your experiences with federal BBSs can be more satisfying and productive if you follow five simple guidelines:

Be sure to install an anti-virus program on your computer.   Sysops of most federal BBSs carefully check files for viruses before posting them on their boards. However, it's always possible for a virus to slip through. Both commercial and shareware anti-virus programs are available for every type of computer. Many federal BBSs have copies of the most popular shareware programs available for downloading. If you want to learn more about viruses and anti-virus programs, log into the NIST Computer Security Resource Clearinghouse described on page 126.

Always carefully read the information that scrolls on your screen from a BBS.   This information will answer many of your questions about using the board. Be especially attentive to the bottom line of each page displayed. That's where you'll see the prompt asking what you want to do next. In many cases, this prompt will ask a question and then give you various options.

Don't abuse a federal BBS.   This guideline seems obvious, but the bad experiences of some federal BBSs make it worth repeating. A few federal boards have experienced so many problems with callers that they have shut down. Other boards now restrict access to their toll-free telephone numbers. For example, one major BBS in the Washington, D.C., area started out widely publicizing its toll-free number. Soon the bill for the toll-free line was running thousands of dollars every month. Too many of the callers were like the two kids from Kansas City who called the BBS to leave messages for each other about what videos they should watch at night. The kids had no interest in the board itself—they just used it to send messages to each other instead of picking up the telephone and making a local call. All of the abuse caused the board to stop publicizing its toll-free number.

Don't bother sysops with basic computer questions. Most sysops of federal boards have many other duties besides running the BBS. They simply don't have time to answer basic questions about computers or telecommunications. However, if you have a specific question about a board, most sysops are happy to help.

Follow the proper logoff procedure when you want to disconnect from a BBS. On most federal BBSs, logging off simply involves typing **g** at a prompt. Some boards will ask if you're sure you want to disconnect. Type **y** for yes. Using the proper procedure disconnects you cleanly and prepares the board for the next caller. If you disconnect by turning off your modem or using your communications software to hang up, you can cause problems for the next caller to the board.

CONNECTING TO FEDERAL BOARDS THROUGH THE INTERNET

You can access some federal BBSs directly through the Internet. If a BBS described in this book is connected to the Internet, its Internet address is listed.

Many federal BBSs that lack Internet connections can be accessed indirectly through FedWorld's Internet connection. FedWorld (see p. 22) is a gateway to more than 100 federal government BBSs. Once you connect to FedWorld through the Internet, you can then transfer to any BBS on FedWorld's gateway. You can determine whether a BBS is included on FedWorld's gateway by looking for a FedWorld gateway number in the box that gives basic information about each board.

You can access some of the boards that have Internet connections using file transfer protocol (FTP). To log into these sites, when asked for your name or login, type **anonymous** and when asked for your password, type your e-mail address.

HOW TO USE THIS BOOK

The boards in this book are arranged alphabetically by subject as logically as possible. However, many boards cover multiple subjects. You may find just the information you need in places that you might not think to look. Please be sure to check the index for topics of interest.

Each entry in this book lists the board's name and its postal address. The address is included because federal government telephone numbers tend to change frequently. With the address, you should be able to track down a federal BBS even if its phone numbers have changed.

The basic connection information for each board is set off in a box. This information varies from board to board, but you will find the following whenever applicable:

Data   The telephone number to call with your communications software to connect with the board.

Voice   The telephone number where you can reach the sysop if you have questions.

FedWorld gateway   The board's number on the FedWorld gateway.

Internet   The board's Internet address.

Manual   The file name of the user's manual.

File list   The file name of the master list of all files.

To access files   Instructions for reaching the files.

Time limit   The board's time limit, either per call or per day.

Available   The hours during which the board is available. Boards are available twenty-four hours a day unless noted otherwise.

Note   Special instructions for accessing or using the board.

The description of each board provides details about what kinds of information are available and notes particular strengths and weaknesses. Two conventions are followed throughout the descriptions:

1. Commands or other text that you must type are shown in **bold type**. You don't need to type the commands in bold type when you enter them on a BBS.

2. File names appear in UPPERCASE letters.

In addition, one piece of shorthand is used. References made to DOS and Windows computers actually refer to computers that run DOS or Windows operating software.

THE
BULLETIN
BOARDS

ACCESS TO INFORMATION

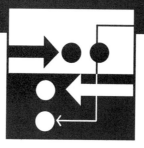

FedWorld

National Technical Information Service
5285 Port Royal Rd.
Springfield, VA 22161

FedWorld is the granddaddy of federal BBSs. Its most popular feature is a gateway to more than 100 other federal BBSs, but FedWorld also offers IRS tax forms, hundreds of White House documents, files from the Office of Management and Budget, cancer information from the National Cancer Institute, publications for investors from the Securities and Exchange Commission, lists of federal job openings, and lots, lots more.

If you access FedWorld through the World Wide Web, FedWorld also provides a gateway to dozens of federal government Web sites. All the sites are arranged by subject. This gateway is a great starting place for an exploration of government resources on the Internet.

Unfortunately, in late 1994 FedWorld's managers redesigned the system's menus and made a mess of things. They took what had been a simple, intuitive system and made it quite difficult. Fortunately, they also left a way for users to access most—though not all—of the system's features through the old menu structure. I strongly recommend that you use the old structure, which you can access by typing **u** at the opening menu.

The following details only touch on FedWorld's highlights, since the system is too extensive to fully describe here:

Gateway The gateway provides links to more than 100 federal government BBSs. The boards are operated by the Agriculture Department, Environmental Protection Agency, Library of Congress, Interior Department, Food and Drug Administration, Nuclear Regulatory Commission, Defense Department, NASA, Small Business Administration, Energy Department, Federal Aviation Administration, Patent and Trademark Office, and other agencies.

To access the gateway, at the Main Menu type **ud** and hit your Enter key. Once you reach the gateway, type **l** to get a list of all the BBSs. To access a BBS, type **d** at the Gateway Menu and at the "Select a system #" prompt, type the number of the BBS you want.

VITAL STATS

Data: 703-321-3339

Voice: 703-487-4608

Login (dial-in and Telnet only): **new**. You must then register.

Manual: FEDUSER.DOC (uncompressed) or FEDUSER.ZIP (compressed)

File list: ALLFILES (uncompressed) or ALLFILES. ZIP (compressed)

Internet: telnet fedworld. gov *or* http://www. fedworld.gov *or* ftp ftp. fedworld.gov

Login (FTP only): **anonymous**

Password (FTP only): your e-mail address

Files   FedWorld has more than 8,000 files. Here are some highlights:

- Hundreds of documents issued by the White House, including press releases, transcripts of news conferences and background briefings for reporters, speeches by the president and vice president, and the full text of selected documents. These include the federal budget, the North American Free Trade Agreement, and the National Information Infrastructure report. Files are available dating back to January 1993. You can search the White House documents by keywords, date, and other variables.

- Numerous brochures and handbooks for investors from the Securities and Exchange Commission. Some sample titles include "Invest Wisely: Introduction to Mutual Funds," "What Every Investor Should Know," "Opening an Account With a Stockbroker," "Fraud in the Sale of Unregistered Securities," "Replacing Lost or Stolen Securities," and "Registration of Securities Professionals."

- The daily *SEC News Digest* from the Securities and Exchange Commission.

- Hundreds of files from the National Cancer Institute that provide information about prevention, diagnosis, and treatment of specific types of cancer; side effects frequently experienced by cancer patients; new drugs being tested with cancer patients; how to access information from the National Cancer Institute; scientific misconduct in cancer trials; cancer information sources; risk factors and possible causes of cancer; and unconventional treatment methods, among other topics. Many of the files are available in both English and Spanish.

- Hundreds of files about the regulation of nuclear power plants from the Nuclear Regulatory Commission. To get a full description of these files, see Nuclear Regulatory Commission (NRC) at FedWorld (p. 162).

- Images from weather satellites, which are updated daily.

- Documents from the National Highway Traffic Safety Administration about child safety seats, drunk driving, and safety standards for cars and trucks.

- Numerous documents from the Office of Management and Budget, including Circular A-130 about federal information policy.

- Hundreds of files related to computer-aided acquisitions and logistic support.

- An excellent list of federal government BBSs.

- The National Performance Review report and related documents.

- Information about hundreds of products available from the National Technical Information Service.

- Job information, including a list of Office of Personnel Management offices nationwide, the optional application form for federal employment, information about placement assistance and reduction in force benefits for federal employees, and information about the Department of Defense Outplacement Referral System.

Federal job openings   These documents list federal jobs available in the United States and overseas. The lists are provided by Office of Personnel Management offices nationwide. To reach the job lists, type **j** at the Main Menu.

GPO Access

Government Printing Office
North Capitol and H Sts., N.W.
Washington, DC 20401

The GPO Access system, which is operated by the Government Printing Office, offers free access to the full text of the *Congressional Record,* the *Federal Register,* bills introduced in Congress, and reports issued by the General Accounting Office, the watchdog arm of Congress. This is a tremendous service, since annual subscriptions to some of these databases previously cost $375 each from the GPO.

When this book was being written, fifteen sites offered gateways to GPO Access through dial-in and Internet connections. Eventually, the GPO hopes to have a gateway in every state.

Besides providing GPO Access, some of the gateways also offer links to dozens or even hundreds of federal government Internet sites. But be forewarned that these gateways undergo frequent changes and updating, so the login procedures may change slightly from those listed in the box on the next pages.

GPO Access offers seven searchable databases:

VITAL STATS
Data: See box on the next three pages for access information

Congressional Bills Database   This database has the published versions of all bills introduced in or acted upon by Congress. It has bills dating back to the 103d Congress.

Congressional Record   The *Congressional Record* contains the full text of statements made in Congress, along with information about congressional activities. The database contains issues dating back to January 1994, the beginning of the second session of the 103d Congress. The database is updated between 9 a.m. and 11 a.m. EST each day that the *Congressional Record* is published.

Federal Register   The *Federal Register* database contains proposed and final federal regulations, presidential documents, meeting and grant notices, and other official documents. The database contains daily issues of the *Federal Register* dating back to January 3, 1994. The database is updated at 6 a.m. EST each day that the *Federal Register* is published.

GAO Reports   This database contains the full text of reports issued by the General Accounting Office. Reports are available dating back to October 1994, with a few earlier reports also online.

Congressional Record Index   This database is an index of the *Congressional Record* dating back to 1992.

Unified Agenda   The Unified Agenda, otherwise known as the Semi-Annual Regulatory Agenda, summarizes pending regulatory actions by federal agencies. The database is updated semi-annually.

History of Bills Database   This database is an index of every action taken on a bill as reported in the *Congressional Record.*

GPO Access Gateways

Alaska

Statewide Library Electronic Doorway (SLED)

Data: Users within Alaska can dial into SLED through the AlaskaNet node nearest their city or village

Voice: 800-478-4667

Internet: telnet sled.alaska.edu

Path: *Government Information/Federal Government Information/GPO Access*

E-mail: ffwh@aurora.alaska.edu

Note: After connecting, hit your Enter key to reach a menu

Arizona

Arizona Telecommunication Community (AzTeC)

Data: 602-965-4151 (2400 baud) or 602-965-6699 (9600 baud and above)

Voice: 602-965-5985

Login: **guest**

Password: **visitor**

Internet: telnet aztec.asu.edu

Path: *Government/Federal/GPO Access Online Services*

E-mail: joe.askins@asu.edu

Colorado

Pueblo Library District

Data: 719-542-7629

Voice: 719-543-9600

Internet: telnet pldvax.pueblo.lib.co.us

Login: **library**

Path: *Government Databases/GPO Access*

E-mail: bob@pueblo.lib.co.us

Note: After connecting, hit your Enter key to get a prompt

Georgia

Georgia Southern University

Data: 912-681-0005 (see the detailed login instructions below)

Voice: 912-681-5032

Internet: telnet gsvms2.cc.gasou.edu

Path: *Government Printing Office Access*

E-mail: soliblw@gsvms2.cc.gasou.edu

Note: After you connect, hit your Enter key twice. At the "GSnet" prompt, type **connect gsvms2** and hit your Enter key. Type **info** when prompted for a username.

Missouri

Columbia Online Information Network (COIN)

Data: 314-884-7000

Voice: 314-443-3161

Internet: telnet 128.206.1.3

Login: **guest**

Path: *Government Center/Access the Government Center/United States of America/ GPO Access*

E-mail: mmcleod@mail.coin.missouri.edu

North Carolina

University of North Carolina—Chapel Hill

Data: 919-962-9911

Voice: 919-962-1151

Login: **library**

Internet: telnet library.unc.edu

Path: *U.S. Government Databases/ GPO Access*

E-mail: kessler.davis@mhs.unc.edu

Note: When you connect, choose *UNC-CH Library Services*

Ohio

Case Western Reserve University

Data: 216-368-3888

Voice: 216-368-6512

Internet: telnet catalog.cwru.edu

Path: *The Library/CWRU Libraries/University Library/EuclidPLUS/GPO Access*

E-mail: gdb2@po.cwru.edu

Note: If you use a dial-in connection, you must register online before you can access the system. Also, it is extremely difficult to connect to this site with dial-in access because the phone number is almost always busy.

Oregon

Portals

Data: 503-227-3962

Voice: 503-725-5049

Internet: gopher portals.pdx.edu

Path (dial-in only): *Portals/Databases/Federal Government Documents*

Path (Gopher only): *Databases/Federal Government Documents/GPO Access*

E-mail: zendog@lib.pdx.edu

Note: If you use a dial-in connection, after connecting choose VT100 as the terminal type

Pennsylvania

Pennsylvania State University

Data: 814-865-5427 (see the detailed login instructions below)

Voice: 814-863-1345

Internet: telnet lias.psu.edu

E-mail: dlc@psulias.psu.edu

Note: After you connect, hit your Enter key and then respond to the prompts about terminal emulation. When prompted "Penn State ID Number," hit your Enter key. At the LIAS Welcome Screen, type **select** and at the Selection Menu choose *GPO Access.*

Ursinus College
Data: 610-409-3616
Voice: 610-489-4111, ext. 2460
Internet: telnet lib.ursinus.edu
Login (Telnet only): **library**
Path: *Library Catalog and other Services/GPO Access*
E-mail: dmalone@lib.ursinus.edu
Note: If you use dial-in access, after connecting hit your Enter key once or twice

Rhode Island

Ocean State Free-Net
Data: 401-946-9810, 401-658-3995, 401-683-4550, 401-348-9330, 401-789-9764 (see the detailed login instructions below)
Voice: 401-863-2522
Internet: telnet osfn.rhilinet.gov
Login: **guest**
Password: **guest**
Path: *Government Center/U.S. Government/ Government Printing Office (GPO)*
E-mail: ap201159@brownvm.brown.edu
Note: After you connect through dial-in access, type **telnet osfn.rhilinet.gov** at the prompt. Also, if you use the 401-789-9764 number, you must set your com-

munications software to even parity, seven data bits, and one stop bit.

Tennessee

University of Memphis
Data: 901-678-3600
Voice: 901-678-2206.
Internet: telnet msuvx1.memphis.edu
Login (dial-in only): **guest**
Login (Telnet only): **library**
Path: *library/Find/Choose Database/GPO Access*
E-mail: willias@cc.memphis.edu

Texas

Texas State Library
Data: 512-475-4444
Voice: 512-463-5426
Internet: telnet link.tsl.texas.gov
Login: **link**
Path: *Find a Menu Item in the Electronic Library by Keyword.* Type **gpo** in the resulting box.
E-mail: diana_houston@tsl.texas.gov

Virginia

University of Virginia
Data: 804-982-5966 (see the detailed login instructions below)
Voice: 804-924-4963
Internet: telnet gwis.virginia.edu
Path: *Library Services/Social Science Data Center/Government Printing Office/ GPO Access*

CapAccess

P.O. Box 2626
Washington, DC 20013-2626

CapAccess offers a variety of federal government information. It has some unique resources, such as a daily list of reports issued by the General Accounting Office, in addition to information that is difficult to find elsewhere. CapAccess also offers lots of other information that's not related to the federal government.

Following are highlights from the major subdirectories available under the Federal Government Center Menu:

Legislative Branch Information   It has:

- The *GAO Daybook,* which lists reports and testimony issued each day by the General Accounting Office, the investigative arm of Congress. This area also has the most recent issue of GAO's monthly list of reports and testimony and a link to another site that offers the full text of GAO reports.

- Links to Senate and House of Representatives Gophers.

- Telephone numbers for recorded information from the Democratic and Republican cloakrooms in the House and Senate.

Executive Branch Information   A list of postal addresses and telephone numbers for former U.S. presidents and a link to the White House's World Wide Web site.

Judicial Branch Information   Biographies of Supreme Court justices and fact sheets on new justices.

Communicating with Federal Officials   Information about sending e-mail to the White House and to the House of Representatives, details about electronic access to White House publications, and lists of phone numbers and fax numbers for the House and the Senate.

VITAL STATS

Data: 202-785-1523

Voice: 703-824-7300

Login: **guest**

Password: **visitor**

Path: At the "Your Choice" prompt, type **go federal**

Internet: telnet capaccess.org

E-mail: help@capaccess.org

Consular Affairs Bulletin Board (CABB)

Overseas Citizens Services
U.S. Department of State
Room 4800
Washington, DC 20520

If you are planning a trip to a foreign country, the Consular Affairs Bulletin Board (CABB) is the place to check first. It offers everything from details about how to get a passport to extensive information about every country in the world to information about adopting foreign-born children. The CABB also serves as a gateway to another BBS that offers current reports about security incidents in foreign countries and profiles of terrorist groups. The CABB files are updated daily.

Information on the BBS is arranged in hundreds of files and searchable databases, but everything is easy to find because the BBS is well designed and menu driven. Here are three quick tips you may find useful:

1. To stop information that's scrolling on your screen, type **s**

2. If you get lost in the menu hierarchy and want to return to the Main Menu, type **o**

3. If you want to back up one level to the previous menu, press the Escape key

The Main Menu presents seven sub-menus, which you can select by typing the appropriate number:

1. **Passport information for U.S. citizens** Files about passport eligibility, how to obtain a passport, passport fees, what to do about lost and stolen passports, and how to obtain a passport quickly.

2. **Emergency services available to U.S. citizens abroad** Files provide contact information and explain various emergency services provided by the Citizens Emergency Center. The center helps Americans abroad who die, become destitute, get sick, disappear, have accidents, or get arrested. The center is also the State Department's focal point for major disasters involving Americans abroad such as plane crashes, hijackings, and natural disasters.

VITAL STATS

Data: 202-647-9225

Voice: 202-647-1488

FedWorld gateway: 82

To access files: At the Main Menu, choose the sub-menu you want

Time limit: 60 minutes per call

3. **Nonemergency information for U.S. citizens** Information about acquiring U.S. citizenship, dual nationality, loss of U.S. citizenship, marriages abroad, marriages to foreigners, receipt of federal benefits abroad, Romanian adoptions, international adoptions, and international parental child abduction. The sub-menu also contains the text of the Hague Convention on the Civil Aspects of International Child Abduction.

4. **Consular information sheets and public announcements** Consular information sheets replace the former travel advisories. They're available for every country in the world, and list the location of U.S. embassies or consulates in the country, immigration practices, health conditions, minor political disturbances, currency and entry regulations, crime and security information, and drug penalties. Any areas of instability in the country are also listed. Separate travel warnings are posted for countries where the State Department believes a threat exists to American travelers.

5. **Travel information on specific subjects or regions** The subject files provide information on travel abroad in general, how to have a safe trip, tips for Americans residing abroad, travel tips for older Americans, foreign entry requirements, HIV testing requirements for entry into foreign countries, and medical information for Americans abroad. The region files provide information on traveling to the Caribbean, Central and South America, China, Eastern Europe, Mexico, the Middle East and North Africa, South Asia, Subsaharan Africa, and Russia.

6. **Visa information** Information for U.S. citizens who wish to travel abroad and for foreigners who wish to visit the United States. You can search the database of foreign entry requirements by country name.

7. **OSAC bulletin board** A gateway to the Overseas Security Advisory Council Electronic Bulletin Board, which provides information about incidents in foreign countries that could affect travelers. The information is arranged in nine sub-menus:

   - *Alert messages* A database of travel alert messages that you can search by country.

   - *Daily highlights* A database of news briefs about events that may affect travel safety. You can search the database by country.

   - *Current security/incident reports* A database with information about security incidents that may affect travel. You can search it by country.

- *Consular information phone numbers* A database, searchable by country, with telephone numbers for U.S. embassies and consulates and local police.

- *Special topics* Lists of State Department publications and travel information telephone numbers.

- *Group profiles* A database containing profiles of terrorist groups operating around the world. You can search the database by the group's name or by region.

- *Anniversary dates* A database, searchable by country, of anniversaries that may affect the safety of travel. For example, the database lists the anniversary of the Tienanmen Square massacre in China.

- *Consular information sheets and public announcements* The same consular information sheets and travel warnings available through the main CABB BBS.

- *General crime information* A database of reports about crime in foreign countries. You can search it by country.

Consumer Information Center (CIC) BBS

General Services Administration
18th and F Sts., N.W. (XC)
Washington, DC 20405

The Consumer Information Center (CIC) BBS has a wealth of consumer information, including electronic copies of hundreds of publications prepared by federal agencies and departments. The publications discuss topics such as understanding food additives, buying a house, choosing a nursing home, and helping your child do better in school, among many others. (The box on the next page lists some of the available titles.)

The publications are divided into nearly three dozen file areas. You can browse through titles by topic or by the issuing agency.

One publication, the *Consumer's Resource Handbook,* is especially notable. This book describes how to get the most for your money, how to avoid consumer problems, and how to write complaint letters when problems arise. It also lists addresses for government and private agencies that can help you with problems and for consumer affairs representatives at hundreds of major companies. The book is split into two files on the BBS.

In addition to the publications, the BBS offers:

- An electronic version of the Consumer Information Center's latest catalog.

- Press releases geared toward newspaper reporters about Consumer Information Center publications.

- Scripts of public service announcements for radio and TV stations about publications listed in the Consumer Information Catalog.

VITAL STATS

Data: 202-208-7679

Voice: 202-501-1794

FedWorld gateway: 6

File list: ALLFILES.ZIP

To access files: At the Main Menu type **f**

Internet: http://www.gsa. gov/staff/pa/cic/cic.htm *or* gopher gopher.gsa. gov *or* ftp ftp.gsa.gov

Login (FTP only): **anonymous**

Password (FTP only): your e-mail address

Path (FTP only): *pub/cic*

Path (Gopher only): *Staff Offices/Public Affairs/ Consumer Information Center*

Selected Consumer Information Center Publications

66 Ways to Save Money
AIDS and the Education of Our Children
The Americans with Disabilities Act: Q & A
Books for Children
Child Health Guide
Civil War at a Glance
Condoms and Sexually Transmitted Diseases
Consumer Tire Guide
Consumer's Guide to Life Insurance
Consumer's Handbook on Adjustable Rate Mortgages
Consumer's Resource Handbook
Contact Lenses
Diet, Nutrition, and Cancer Prevention
Eating to Lower High Blood Cholesterol
The Fair Credit Reporting Act
Food Additives
Funerals: A Consumer Guide
Gas Mileage Guide
Growing Up Drug Free
Guide to Choosing a Nursing Home
Guide to Federal Government Sales
Helping Your Child Do Better in School
Helping Your Child Learn to Read

A Home of Your Own
Homebuyer's Guide to Environmental Hazards
How to File a Claim for Your Benefits
How to Protect Yourself
Job Outlook in Brief: 1992-2005
Lesser Known Areas of the National Park System
Lista de Publicaciones Federales en Espanol
Mortgage Money Guide
National Park System Map and Guide
Nine Ways to Lower Your Auto Insurance
Plain Talk About Wife Abuse
Protect Yourself from Telemarketing Fraud
Q & A About Breast Lumps
Repairing Your Flooded Home
Second Hand Smoke
Small Business Handbook
Staying Healthy & Whole: A Consumer Guide
Stress
Stripping Paint From Wood
Thrifty Meals for Two
Tips on Preventing AIDS
Understanding Social Security
Where to Write for Vital Records

Federal Bulletin Board

Office of Electronic Information Dissemination Services (EIDS)
U.S. Government Printing Office
Washington, DC 20401

The Federal Bulletin Board is a very strange—and almost useless—BBS. The Government Printing Office (GPO) deserves forty lashes for foisting this travesty upon the public. What's really strange is that the GPO has done a fantastic job of making government information available over the Internet, yet its BBS is awful.

There is some good news: the BBS has been redesigned, and is now much easier to navigate than it used to be. Previously, the board was virtually impossible to use and was the worst-designed BBS operated by any federal agency or department. It isn't great now, but it's better than it was.

The bad news is there's little reason to call this board because its offerings are so slim. The few useful files it does have usually cost money—and are frequently available elsewhere for free. To make matters worse, many of the files are woefully outdated. And still on a negative note, some of the files are compressed in a self-extracting format that makes them unusable on most Macintosh computers.

What's most surprising is what the board *does not* have: a full catalog of GPO publications. You can download some subject catalogs from the board, but if you want the full catalog you have to order a paper copy. Very strange.

Here are some examples of what's available (the files are free unless otherwise noted):

VITAL STATS
Data: 202-512-1387
Voice: 202-512-1530
FedWorld gateway: 22
Internet: telnet federal.bbs.
gpo.gov 3001

- A list of libraries that offer free dial-in and Internet access to GPO Access (p. 25), a GPO database system that offers the full text of bills introduced in Congress, the *Congressional Record,* the *Federal Register,* and reports issued by the General Accounting Office. However, the GPO Access databases are not available through this BBS—at least not for free.

- Various congressional directories for the 103d Congress, which was in session from 1993 to 1994. These were being offered in mid-1995, in the midst of the 104th Congress, which makes absolutely no sense. And GPO was charging for them!

- *Federal Register* notices for selected federal agencies. What's strange is that the full text of the *Federal Register* is available through GPO Access for free, yet these files cost money.

- Reports from the General Accounting Office. Again, these documents are available for free on GPO Access, yet cost a few dollars per file on the BBS.

- A few old White House reports, but nothing at all current. FedWorld (p. 22) is a far better source for White House documents.

- The full text of the federal budget—but for the previous fiscal year. If you want the budget for the current year, you have to pay $22. The full text of the current federal budget is available for free at FedWorld and other sites on the Internet.

- Supreme Court opinions, which typically cost $2 or $3. These same opinions are available for free on SEARCH-BBS (p. 302), and at a number of Internet sites.

- A database listing all Federal Depository Libraries that includes the address, telephone number, congressional district, and other information.

- A few hearing documents from the Senate Rules Committee and the Subcommittee on Regulation and Government Information of the Senate Committee on Governmental Affairs.

- Lists of CD-ROMs and computer disks available for purchase from the GPO.

Federal Register Electronic News Delivery (FREND)

Office of the Federal Register
National Archives and Records Administration
Washington, DC 20408

FREND provides limited information about federal laws and regulations. It has Public Law numbers for bills recently signed by the president, lists of documents that will appear in the next day's edition of the *Federal Register,* and tables of contents from recent editions of the *Federal Register.* The board does *not* provide the full text of bills or of the *Federal Register.* The full texts of bills and of the *Federal Register* are available from GPO Access (p. 25).

FREND's Top Menu has three major areas:

1. **News and Announcements** A schedule of public briefings about how to use the *Federal Register,* a list of *Federal Register* publications, and a list of all volumes of the Code of Federal Regulations available from the Government Printing Office.

2. **Public Law Finding Aids** Lists of bills passed by Congress and signed by the president that have been assigned Public Law numbers. Each listing includes the bill number, Public Law number, name of the act, approval date, U.S. Statutes at Large page citation, and the number of pages in the published law. This area also offers tables showing how recent Public Laws affect the U.S. Code.

3. **Federal Register Finding Aids** A list of documents that will appear in the next day's edition of the *Federal Register.* The lists normally are posted shortly after 8:45 a.m. each day the *Federal Register* is published, and are updated during the afternoon. This area also offers tables of contents from the *Federal Register.* Entries are alphabetized by the name of the agency, and are then grouped as rules, proposed rules, and notice documents. The first posting, which occurs about mid-afternoon of the day before publication, does not include page numbers. A second posting after publication updates the file to include page numbers.

VITAL STATS

Data: 202-275-1538 or
202-275-0920

Voice: 202-523-3447

FedWorld gateways: 87 and
88 (they are identical)

Time limit: 60 minutes per
call

IITF (Information Infrastructure Task Force) Gopher

National Telecommunications and Information Administration
U.S. Department of Commerce
Room 4092
14th and Constitution Ave., N.W.
Washington, DC 20230

The IITF (Information Infrastructure Task Force) Gopher contains information about efforts to develop the National Information Infrastructure (NII). The NII is supposed to become a system of thousands of interconnected computer networks, televisions, fax machines, and telephones that will provide information cheaply and easily.

If you access the site with a dial-in connection, you are connected to a Gopher. This makes the site extremely easy to use. Here are some highlights of what's available:

VITAL STATS

Data: 202-501-1920

Voice: 202-482-1407

FedWorld gateway: 119

Internet: gopher iitf.doc.gov
or telnet iitf.doc.gov

Login (dial-in and Telnet
only): **gopher**

- Answers to frequently asked questions about the NII.

- Numerous documents about the NII, including congressional testimony, speeches, and White House papers.

- Selected legislation.

- Information about the U.S. Advisory Council on the NII, including a list of members, press releases, and meeting notices.

- Names and telephone numbers of contacts.

- A fact sheet about the Information Infrastructure Task Force.

- News about upcoming meetings of various groups working on the NII.

- Press releases.

- Minutes and reports from various committees.

NTIA Information Stores

National Telecommunications and Information Administration (NTIA)
U.S. Department of Commerce
Herbert C. Hoover Building, Room 4090
Washington, DC 20230

Two types of files are available on NTIA Information Stores: highly technical documents about spectrum requirements and more general documents about telecommunications policy issues such as development of the National Information Infrastructure (NII). The National Telecommunications and Information Administration (NTIA), which serves as the president's chief adviser on telecommunications policies, is the lead agency in developing the NII.

Here are some highlights of what's available:

- *The National Information Infrastructure: Agenda for Action,* a report about the NII.

- Information about where to send Freedom of Information Act requests pertaining to the NTIA or the Department of Commerce.

- An NTIA telephone directory.

- A list of documents published by NTIA, along with ordering information.

- Transcripts of hearings, speeches, testimony, and committee meetings about the NII.

- A calendar of upcoming public events involving the NII.

- Press releases.

- An administration white paper on reform of the Communications Act.

- Notices about the availability of grants for NII projects.

- NTIA reports about spectrum requirements.

VITAL STATS

Data: 202-482-1199

Voice: 202-482-3999

FedWorld gateway: 109

Internet: gopher gopher.ntia.doc.gov *or* http://www.ntia.doc. gov *or* ftp ftp.ntia.doc. gov *or* telnet ntiabbs. ntia.doc.gov

Login (FTP only): **anonymous**

Password (FTP only): your e-mail address

E-mail: nschroeder@ntia. doc.gov

Automated Library Information Exchange (ALIX)

FEDLINK
Library of Congress
Washington, DC 20540-5110

Although the Automated Library Information Exchange (ALIX) is aimed at librarians in federal government agencies, it offers information of interest to other librarians and the public as well. However, the board has a major problem with many of its files being seriously out of date.

Here are some highlights of what's available:

- A calendar of training classes.

- Lists of job openings in federal and nonfederal libraries.

- Copies of announcements published in the *Commerce Business Daily* by the Library of Congress Contracts and Logistics Service that seek bids from vendors that can supply services to federal libraries under the FEDLINK program.

- A number of guides to the Internet (all of which are at least a couple of years old).

- Shareware and freeware computer programs to help librarians automate their work.

- Library-oriented applications of hypertext and hypermedia software, expert systems, and other systems that use artificial intelligence.

- Library-oriented templates in Lotus 1-2-3 and SuperCalc formats.

- Library job standards established by the Office of Personnel Management.

- Proceedings from a meeting titled "Federal Librarians in the 21st Century."

- A handbook titled *Managing Information Resources for Accessibility,* published by the General Services Administration Clearinghouse on Computer Accommodation.

VITAL STATS

Data: 202-707-4888

Voice: 202-707-4800

FedWorld gateway: 3

Time limit: 40 minutes per call

Internet: telnet alix.loc.gov 3001

Note: When this book was being written, the Internet connection was very buggy

E-mail: flicc@mail.loc.gov

- Copies of a newsletter titled *ALCTS Network News.*

- A searchable database containing addresses of federal libraries around the country.

- Forums where users can exchange messages about archives and records management, CD-ROM products, services to the disabled, government information, libraries and technology, library management, preservation issues, reference issues, and technical services, among other topics.

LC News Gopher

Public Affairs Office
Room LM105
Library of Congress
Washington, DC 20540-8610

The LC News Gopher provides dial-in access to a wide range of information about the Library of Congress and its programs. The files come from LC MARVEL, a Gopher operated by the Library of Congress that is not available through dial-in access.

Here are some highlights of what's available:

- Calendars of current events, upcoming exhibits, and forthcoming conferences at the Library of Congress.

- A link to an Internet site that offers images and text from Library of Congress exhibits, including "1492: An Ongoing Voyage," "Revelations from the Russian Archives," "Rome Reborn: The Vatican Library and Renaissance Culture," "Scrolls from the Dead Sea," "The African-American Mosaic," and "The Russian Church and Native Alaskan Cultures."

- Information about facilities at the Library of Congress.

- Information about Library of Congress publications and products.

- Press releases.

- Information about the Center for the Book.

- Information about services to blind and physically handicapped people.

- A history of the Library of Congress.

VITAL STATS
Data: 202-707-3854
Voice: 202-707-9217

AGRICULTURE

AgEBB (Agricultural Electronic Bulletin Board)

325 Mumford Hall
University of Missouri-Columbia
Columbia, MO 65211

The AgEBB (Agricultural Electronic Bulletin Board) presents a wealth of information for farmers in Missouri and other states. It is sponsored by the Commercial Agriculture Extension Program at the University of Missouri.

Connecting to the board can be tricky because it's run on an old computer that supports connections only at 9600 baud or lower. Fortunately, the sysop is a master at solving connection problems, so call the voice number if you have difficulties.

The most current information is provided in bulletins, which you can access by typing **b** at the Main Menu. The bulletins, which you can read online, offer information about farm management, farm marketing, pest management, agricultural law, horticulture, dairy science, animal science, occupational medicine, and no-till cropping systems, among other subjects. They also provide agricultural weather forecasts for Missouri, updates about government programs, and press releases from the U.S. Department of Agriculture.

Some of the bulletins are also available as files that you can download. You can save on long-distance charges by downloading the files instead of reading them online.

The board also offers:

- Files, including farm-related spreadsheet programs, which you can access by typing **f** at the Main Menu.

- Market listings, where farmers seeking to buy or sell hay can list their offers. You can access the market listings by typing **l** at the Main Menu.

- Plant disease information, which you can access by typing **i** at the Main Menu. The files, which cover topics such as restricted use pesticides, pesticide safety, greenhouse insecticides and miticides, field crops, alternative crops, trees, fruit, vegetables, and indoor flowers, are taken from the *Plant Disease Management Guide*. The guide includes disease management information for the major plant species in Missouri.

VITAL STATS

Data: 314-882-8289

Voice: 314-882-4827

Internet: gopher
etcs.ext.missouri.edu

Path: *AgEBB - Agricultural
Electronic Bulletin Board*

Note: You must connect to
the board at 9600
baud or less

- Crop performance testing information, including results for corn, soybeans, grain sorghum, oats, soft red winter wheat, hard red winter wheat, alfalfa, cotton, sunflowers, and rice. You can access the crop testing results by typing **t** at the Main Menu.

- An events calendar, which you can access by typing **e** at the Main Menu.

Agricultural Library Forum (ALF)

National Agricultural Library
U.S. Department of Agriculture
10301 Baltimore Blvd.
Beltsville, MD 20705-2351

The greatest strength of the Agricultural Library Forum (ALF) is its bibliographies on subjects as diverse as alternative agriculture, catfish farming, diet and cancer, food irradiation, and crime in rural America. The bibliographies are compiled from AGRICOLA, a fee-based database. Many can be downloaded from ALF, while others can be ordered for free from the National Agricultural Library (NAL).

ALF has three major areas:

VITAL STATS

Data: 301-504-6510
Voice: 301-504-5113
FedWorld gateway: 2
Manual: ALFGUIDE.TXT
E-mail: kschneid@nalusda.
gov

Bulletins ALF's bulletins describe the NAL, explain how to download files from ALF, list agriculture-related BBSs around the country, list upcoming agricultural events, describe how to download and use compressed files, list telephone numbers for NAL contacts, and list telephone numbers for contacts at land-grant colleges, state colleges of agriculture, and USDA field libraries. They also describe and list contacts for NAL's Information Centers on agricultural trade and marketing, alternative farming, animal welfare, aquaculture, biotechnology, food and nutrition, global change, plant genome data, rural information, technology transfer, water quality, and youth development. You cannot download most of the bulletins, but you can save them using your communications software's capture feature.

Conferences ALF has more than two dozen public conferences on various subjects, including the AGRICOLA database, animal welfare, biotechnology, rural development and health, and water quality. Each conference also has bulletins that you can save using your communications software's capture feature.

Files ALF has hundreds of files, including newsletters, other publications, software, and the full text of bibliographies prepared by the NAL. Two documents are particularly valuable for new users:

- ALFGUIDE.TXT — This user's guide is extremely helpful, especially for people who expect to spend lots of time on ALF.

- NALQBLST.TXT — This file lists all of the bibliographies produced by the NAL. Many can be downloaded from ALF, and others can be ordered for free from the NAL.

ALF has more than twenty file areas. Here are highlights from some of the major areas (you can get a list of files in an area by typing the letters that appear in caps):

AFS (Alternative Farming Systems)   Numerous publications about raising and marketing alternative crops such as shitake mushrooms, herbs, specialty vegetables, wildflowers, and asparagus, in addition to exotic livestock, cashmere goats, and other types of livestock. This area also has a list of publications produced by the Alternative Farming Systems Information Center, a list of periodicals about alternative farming, a calendar of upcoming events related to sustainable agriculture, a bibliography of books about sustainable agriculture, and a list of educational and training opportunities in sustainable agriculture. Finally, the area has numerous issues of a newsletter called *Small-Scale Ag Today*.

AGRICOLA database   Documents about the fee-based AGRICOLA database. However, this area does not provide access to the database itself. It has a list of journals indexed in AGRICOLA, a keyword index to NAL publications, information on searching AGRICOLA, AGRICOLA training schedules, and utilities for using CD-ROM versions of AGRICOLA.

AGRITOPics   Background information, extensive bibliographies, and contact lists on a wide range of subjects, including production and marketing of cut flowers, greenhouses, doing business overseas, organic farming, gardening books, and making cheese and yogurt at home.

Information ALERTS   Information about activities and publications of the NAL.

ANIMAL welfare   A list of publications available from the Animal Welfare Information Center, center newsletters, bibliographies on animal welfare issues, descriptions of animal welfare legislation considered by Congress, and contacts for information on animal welfare.

AQUA—Aquaculture files   A calendar of aquaculture meetings and shows, a list of publications available from the Aquaculture Information Center, a directory of state aquaculture coordinators and contacts, a huge guide to aquaculture information, a report titled *The Status and Potential of Aquaculture in the United States: An Overview and Bibliography,* and bibliographies about fish farming, shrimp farming, salmon and trout farming, catfish farming, crawfish farming, restoring aquatic ecosystems, and controlling aquatic vegetation.

ARS—Agriculture Research Service A list of job openings in the Agriculture Research Service, the *ARS Quarterly Report of Selected Research Projects,* and a list of patents issued to the ARS.

Bulletin BOARDS Lists of environmental and technology BBSs, BBSs with Internet access, and BBSs in the Washington, D.C., area. Most of them are outdated.

COMPUTER stuff Communications and decompression shareware for DOS computers.

DCRC Reference Center files Keyword indexes to USDA Agriculture Handbooks and Agricultural Information Bulletins, along with user's guides to various CD-ROM versions of the AGRICOLA fee-based database.

FAS Extensive information about foreign markets, trade policy, and outlooks. The file area includes newsletters from the Agricultural Trade and Marketing Information Center and food market reports for fifty-five countries. The reports discuss the market overview, U.S. position in the market, competition, trends, opportunities, distribution systems, and domestic food processing. They are written by U.S. agricultural attachés posted in the countries. The file area also has dozens of files about agricultural markets and prices in Mexico.

FOOD Bibliographies of books and articles about diet and cancer, diet and dental health, nutrition and the handicapped, nutrition and the elderly, nutrition and cardiovascular disease, nutrition and diabetes, nutrition and behavior, nutrition and adolescent pregnancy, sports nutrition, vegetarian nutrition, anorexia nervosa and bulimia, food allergies, and weight control. The area also has a bibliography of children's books on food and nutrition, information about food and nutrition activities for children, and a calendar of food and nutrition meetings.

FORESTs Files about timber management programs and bibliographies about water quality and forestry, the effect of air pollution on crops and forests, and deforestation.

GENERAL Reference A little bit of everything, including lists of hundreds of NAL bibliographies and other publications, many of which can be downloaded from ALF or obtained free from NAL. There are also keyword indexes to NAL publications, USDA Agricultural Handbooks, and Agriculture Information Bulletins; lists of job openings at the U.S. Department of Agriculture; descriptions of the NAL's Information Centers; lists of publications available from the Agricultural Trade and Marketing Information Center, the Aquaculture Information Center, and the Alternative Farming Systems Information Center; newsletters of the Agricultural Trade and Marketing Information Center and the Plant Genome Research Program; a guide to NAL services; a calendar of events related to aquaculture; a calendar of agriculture-related meetings and events for the year; a list of agriculture-related resources on the Internet and BITNET; and issues of the *Agricultural History Newsletter*.

QBSERIES Numerous bibliographies about such topics as tourism development, animal welfare legislation and regulations, laboratory animal facilities, housing and husbandry of beef cattle, animal models of disease, and anesthesia and analgesia for farm animals. The bibliographies list books, reports, audiovisual materials, and articles from journals, newspapers, and newsletters. The listings are derived from online searches of the fee-based AGRICOLA database.

RURAL Information about the Rural Information Center, a list of rural development contacts by state, calendars of rural events, a list of Rural Health Research Center activities, rural health news and announcements, information about federal grants for rural health, a rural health bibliography, a list of rural development resources in the NAL, and information about health care reform in various states.

SEEDS A list of protected plants, information about seed import laws, and lists of noxious weed seeds by state.

SPECIAL reference briefs Annotated bibliographies on a wide range of subjects, including nutrition and AIDS, growing and using herbs, sustainable agriculture, exercise for dogs, animal euthanasia, aging, the meat industry, substance abuse, and food irradiation.

WATER A calendar of water meetings, a list of water resources hotlines, a list of water-related publications produced by the NAL, and bibliographies about drinking water standards for various contaminants, wetland construction to treat livestock wastes, water quality and forestry, and streambank protection.

Aquaculture Network Information Center (AquaNIC)

3-104 Lilly Hall
Animal Sciences Department
Purdue University
West Lafayette, IN 47907-1151

If you are interested in aquaculture—better known as fish farming—the Aquaculture Network Information Center (AquaNIC) is a gold mine. The service is sponsored by Purdue University libraries, the Purdue University Cooperative Extension Service, the U.S. Department of Agriculture Extension Service, and the Illinois-Indiana Sea Grant Program.

Accessing the system through a dial-in connection requires four steps:

1. At the "Enter username" prompt, type **lynx**

2. At the prompt that has several letters and numbers and ends with >, type **rlogin lib.purdue.edu**

3. At the resulting menu, choose *Purdue University Databases*

4. At the next screen, choose *AquaNIC*

This takes you to AquaNIC's home page on the World Wide Web, which provides an easy-to-use interface to the system.

Here are some highlights of what's available:

- Publications with titles such as "Channel Catfish Production," "Financial Sources for Aquaculture," "Information on Methods for Raising Oysters," "Managing Sport Fish Populations in Farm Ponds," "Status and Potential of Aquaculture in the U.S.: Overview and Bibliography," and "Wisconsin Aquaculture Resource Guide."

- A directory of state aquaculture coordinators and contacts.

- A document titled *Guide to Drug, Vaccine, and Pesticide Use in Aquaculture.*

- Information about the National Aquaculture Information Center.

- The *Resource Guide to Aquaculture Information* from the National Agricultural Library.

VITAL STATS

Data: 317-496-1440

Voice: 317-494-4862

Internet: gopher thorplus.lib.purdue.edu *or* http://thorplus.lib. purdue.edu/AquaNIC/

Path (Gopher only): *Scholarly Databases/AquaNIC*

E-mail: meinstei@hub2. ansc.purdue.edu

Note: See the special login instructions for the BBS

- Situation and outlook reports about aquaculture from the U.S. Department of Agriculture.

- Various newsletters about aquaculture.

- Links to other sources of aquaculture information on the Internet.

- Information about Internet mailing lists related to aquaculture.

- Lists of e-mail addresses for aquaculture contacts, divided by state for United States addresses and by country for foreign addresses. The lists do not have any information about a particular individual's area of expertise.

- A calendar of aquaculture events.

Call-ERS/NASS

Economic Research Service
U.S. Department of Agriculture
1301 New York Ave., N.W.
Washington, DC 20005-4788

Call-ERS/NASS, which is operated by the Economic Research Service (ERS) and the National Agricultural Statistics Service (NASS), offers a wealth of statistics and other information about agricultural economics and rural America.

Here are some highlights of what's available:

- The full text of ERS *Situation & Outlook* reports about vegetables, livestock, dairy, poultry, international agriculture and trade, feed, oil crops, wheat, rice, cotton and wool, the agricultural outlook, and aquaculture.

- NASS reports about crop progress, agricultural prices, and crop production.

- Descriptions and ordering information for new paper reports from ERS on topics such as U.S. agricultural exports and economic indicators of the farm sector.

- Samples of data files available from ERS.

- Catalogs of ERS data products, monographs, magazines, periodicals, and videotapes.

VITAL STATS

Data: 800-821-6229 or
  202-219-0377 or
  202-219-0378

Voice: 202-219-0304

FedWorld gateways: 113
  and 114 (they are the
  same)

Manual: At the Main Menu
  type **u**

To access files: At the Main
  Menu, type the letter
  for the file area you
  want

Time limit: 20 minutes per
  call

Consolidated Farm Service Agency
Bulletin Board System (CFSA-BBS)

USDA/TD/CSB-BBS
8390 Ward Parkway
Kansas City, MO 64114

The Consolidated Farm Service Agency Bulletin Board System (CFSA-BBS) provides current market prices for various commodities, including corn, barley, oats, wheat, soybeans, and peanuts, among others.

The board also has details about commodity purchases by the U.S. Department of Agriculture's Kansas City Commodity Office. Each listing describes the product and lists the company it was purchased from and the price.

VITAL STATS

Data: 816-823-1521 or
816-823-1894

Voice: 816-823-1910

Internet: telnet bbskc.kcc.usda.gov *or* http://bbskc.kcc.usda.gov *or* ftp bbskc.kcc.usda.gov

Login (FTP only): **anonymous**

Password (FTP only): your e-mail address

E-mail: wlehotz@mail.coin.missouri.edu

EXNET

110 EES Building
Haber Road
Iowa State University
Ames, IA 50011

EXNET is aimed at farmers in Iowa and surrounding states. It's operated by the Cooperative Extension Service at Iowa State University.

Accessing EXNET is needlessly complicated. There are three different sets of procedures, depending on how you access the system:

1. Dial-in at 2400 to 9600 baud: To access the system, dial 515-294 and your modem speed. For example, if you have a 2400-baud modem you should dial 515-294-2400. Once you connect, follow these steps:

   Press your Enter key to reach the "DIAL" prompt

   At the "DIAL" prompt, type **exnet**

   At the "login" prompt, type **guest**

2. Dial-in at modem speeds above 9600 baud: Call 515-268-3638 with your communications software, and after connecting follow these steps:

   At the Welcome to the Xyplex Terminal Server Menu, choose item 1, *Telnet host*

   At the "Telnet host" prompt, type **exnet**

   At the "login" prompt, type **guest**

3. Telnet: After you connect, at the "login" prompt type **guest**

Here are some highlights of what the system offers:

VITAL STATS

Data: See text for details

Voice: 515-294-8658

Login: See text for details

Internet: telnet exnet.
   iastate.edu *or*
   http://exnet.iastate.edu

E-mail: exnet@exnet.
   iastate.edu

- Detailed weather forecasts for Iowa from the National Weather Service. There also are less detailed forecasts for Minnesota, Wisconsin, Illinois, Missouri, Nebraska, Kansas, the Dakotas, the Northeast, the Southeast, the Southwest, the Rocky Mountains, the Pacific Northwest, and Canada.

- Commodity market reports.

- Information about how weather is affecting Iowa crops.

- Results from yield tests for corn, soybeans, oats, and other crops.

- Newsletters about horticulture, integrated crop management, and other topics.

- A database called QUERRI that contains bibliographic information for more than 12,000 resources produced by Cooperative Extension Service specialists in the North Central Region. The database, which you can search by keywords, includes information about printed resources and more than 800 videotapes regarding agriculture, families, 4-H and youth, and community resource development. Ordering details are included for each item.

Hay Locator Service

Department of Agronomy
Purdue University
LILY
West Lafayette, IN 47907-1150

Farmers can use the Hay Locator Service to learn about hay and straw for sale or to advertise their own crops. Most of the listings are for hay and straw in Indiana, but there also are listings for crops nationwide. You can search the listings, enter a new listing, or delete old listings.

When you start a search, the board takes you through a series of questions to narrow your request. It asks whether you want:

- Buyers, sellers, or both.

- Hay, straw, or both.

- Listings nationwide, in Indiana, in a specific Indiana county, or in a state other than Indiana.

The listings of crops available for sale generally include the type of crop, when it was cut, where it's located, how it's baled, the quantity available, the chemical analysis, whether it's stored inside, whether it has suffered any rain damage, and the name, address, and telephone number of the seller. Buyers and sellers must contact each other directly because they cannot negotiate through the board.

Illinois Dialup Extension Access (IDEA)

Illinois Cooperative Extension Service
528 Bevier Hall
905 S. Goodwin
University of Illinois
Urbana, IL 61801

IDEA specializes in information about recovering from floods, preserving foods at home, and horticulture. It also offers current market news for Illinois farmers.

If you access IDEA with a dial-in connection, you'll be presented with a modified Gopher interface. This makes the system quite easy to use, although some parts of the interface are non-standard.

Here are some highlights of what's available:

- Dozens of files about recovering from floods. Some are aimed at farmers, while others also apply to non-farmers. Sample titles include "Flooded Grain Needs Attention," "Adding Up Crop Losses," "Helping Kids Deal With a Flood," "Food Safety for Flood Victims," "Rodents After the Flood," "Cleaning Carpet and Floors," and "Restoring Flooded Appliances."

- Illinois flood contacts, listed by county and by keyword.

- Detailed information about preserving foods at home. There are documents about drying food at home, freezing fruits, freezing sweet corn, blanching foods for freezing, canning peaches, canning tomatoes, problems with home-canned foods, sources of canning equipment, and similar topics.

- More than 100 files about horticulture, separated by season. Some sample titles include "Preserving Flowers," "Safety Precautions for Yard Work," "Controlling Insects in the Home," "Fall Lawn Care," "Protecting Plants from Winter Injury," "Spring Bulb Planting," "Understanding Grass Seed Labels," "Yard Pests," "Weather Stress on Plants," "When to Use Pesticides," "Annual Fruit Tree Pruning," "Christmas Trees—Choosing," and "Feeding Birds During the Winter."

VITAL STATS

Data: 217-244-5158

Voice: Telephone support is not provided

Login (dial-in and Telnet only): **guest**

Internet: gopher cesgopher. ag.uiuc.edu *or* http://www.ag.uiuc.edu *or* telnet idea.ag.uiuc. edu

E-mail: idea@idea.ag.uiuc. edu

National Biological Impact Assessment Program (NBIAP)

Virginia Polytechnic Institute & State University
120 Engel Hall
Blacksburg, VA 24061

The National Biological Impact Assessment Program (NBIAP) system, which is operated by Virginia Tech under a grant from the U.S. Department of Agriculture, offers news, files, and searchable databases about agricultural and environmental biotechnology. The dial-in system used to be hard to use, but the sysop recently switched to a Gopher interface that's clean and simple.

The files provide the biotechnology policy of the federal Office of Science and Technology Policy, the Environmental Protection Agency's policy on microbial products, and the Food and Drug Administration's policy on foods derived from new plant varieties. In addition, files list free publications on biotechnology, articles from industry publications, reports from the U.S. Department of Agriculture, databases and BBSs about biotechnology, biotechnology directories, newsletters about agricultural biotechnology, videocassettes and slide sets on biotechnology, and meetings, symposia, and workshops.

The system also offers access to searchable databases that contain listings of biotechnology companies, state biotechnology centers, state regulators and state laws, and institutional biosafety committees. You can search each database by a number of variables.

The site also offers numerous links to other agricultural biotechnology Gophers and to other agricultural Gophers.

VITAL STATS

Data: 800-624-2723 or 540-231-3858

Voice: 540-231-3747

Login (dial-in and Telnet only): **gopher**

Internet: gopher nbiap.biochem.vt.edu *or* http://ftp.nbiap.vt.edu *or* telnet nbiap.biochem.vt.edu or ftp ftp.nbiap.vt.edu

Login (FTP only): **anonymous**

Password (FTP only): your e-mail address

Path (FTP only): *pub/nbiap*

E-mail: problems@nbiap.biochem.vt.edu

NBCI BBS

National Biological Control Institute
U.S. Department of Agriculture, APHIS, OA
Unit 5
4700 River Rd.
Riverdale, MD 20737

The NBCI BBS, which is operated by the National Biological Control Institute, offers information about sustainable agriculture, biological control of pests and weeds, and integrated pest management. The board is aimed primarily at researchers.

Most of the information on the board is duplicated. You can read a file online by choosing a particular category from the Main Menu, or you can download the file by typing **d** at the Main Menu and then choosing a category from the Library System Menu.

Here are examples of what's available:

- Calendars of events relating to biological control, entomology, integrated pest management, sustainable and organic agriculture, plant pathology, weed science, nematology, and invertebrate pathology.

- Lists of jobs in biology, primarily at universities.

- Newsletters about biological control. Some of the titles available include *Alternative Agriculture News, Association of Applied Insect Ecologists News, ExSel Newsletter, Natural Enemy News, The Ladybeetle Flyer, Tachinid Times, Association of Natural Bio-control Producers Newsletter, Biocontrol Flash, International Bioherbicide Group News, Plant Protection News, STING: Newsletter on Biological Control in Greenhouses, The Entomophagus (Mexico),* and *Pesticides Coordinator Report.*

- Minutes from professional meetings of the Coordinating Committee for Russian Wheat Aphid Biology and other groups.

- Summaries of newspaper articles about biological control.

- Detailed information about training and grant opportunities.

VITAL STATS

Data: 800-344-6224 or 301-734-4792

Voice: 301-734-4329

FedWorld gateway: 129

Time limit: 30 minutes per call

Internet: http://www.aphis.usda.gov/nbci/nbci.htm/

- Information about databases, hotlines, and other BBSs about sustainable agriculture.

- Results of surveys by various organizations.

- Forums on the sweet potato whitefly, Russian wheat aphid, Aphis BC operations, quarantine operations, and other subjects.

TEKTRAN (Technology Transfer Automated Retrieval System)

Agricultural Research Service
Office of Technology Transfer
U.S. Department of Agriculture
Building 005, BARC-West, Room 415
Beltsville, MD 20705

The TEKTRAN database contains more than 12,000 summaries of research results obtained by scientists at the Agricultural Research Service (ARS). The research covers topics such as genetic engineering, safeguarding crops and animals from disease, biological control of pests, and human nutrition, among others. The database also contains information about more than 1,000 ARS inventions that are available for licensing.

Entries typically include a brief summary of the research, a technical abstract, and the name, address, and telephone number of the ARS scientist who conducted the research. You can search the database by keyword, multiple keywords, scientist's name, commodity, and date, among other variables.

To access TEKTRAN, you must call the TEKTRAN office. The staff will send you an ID, password, modem number, and user's manual.

TEKTRAN is designed to be accessible with VSterm and Crosstalk, two communications programs for DOS computers. It may not be accessible with some other programs, especially those designed for Macintosh computers. If you cannot access the database, you can call the TEKTRAN office and ask the staff to run a search. They will send you a printout with the results.

VITAL STATS

Data: Number must be obtained from TEKTRAN office

Voice: 301-504-5345

Manual: Can be obtained by calling TEKTRAN office

BUSINESS, TRADE, AND ECONOMICS

Office of Economic Conversion Information

Economic Development Administration
Room 7231
U.S. Department of Commerce
Washington, DC 20230

The Office of Economic Conversion Information BBS has tons of information for people, businesses, and communities affected by the closing of military bases and defense conversion. The BBS is a joint project of the U.S. Department of Commerce and the U.S. Department of Defense.

Here are some examples of the information that's available:

- A list of the most recent military base closures.

VITAL STATS

Data: 800-352-2949 or
      202-377-2848
Voice: 800-345-1222
FedWorld gateway: 130
Internet: gopher ecix.doc.
      gov
E-mail: epages@doc.gov

- Extensive bibliographies of government reports, books, and newspaper and magazine articles about base closings and defense conversion.

- An annotated list of private voluntary organizations that are active on defense conversion issues.

- Press releases about federal defense conversion initiatives.

- Speeches by President Clinton on defense conversion.

- Employment statistics by major industry for each state.

- Information about federal conversion assistance programs for military and civilian employees, businesses, and communities.

- The text of the Defense Base Closure and Realignment Act of 1990.

- The text of the National Historic Preservation Act, the Resource Conservation and Recovery Act, the Clean Air Act, Superfund legislation, the McKinney Act, the Clean Water Act, the National Environmental Policy Act, and the Endangered Species Act.

- Guidelines for the disposal of surplus property.

- Policies for fast-track cleanup of closed and realigned bases.

- A list of contacts for each of the closed or realigned bases.

- Lists of contacts in various federal offices.

- Case studies of defense conversion in selected cities.

- The text of the "Governor's Guide to Economic Conversion."

- Information about technology centers in various states.

PTO Bulletin Board System

U.S. Patent and Trademark Office
OEIPS CP2
Room 9D30
Washington, DC 20231

The PTO Bulletin Board System contains more than 40,000 files that provide extensive information about patents and trademarks, although it does not have registration documents for patents and trademarks.

Here are some highlights of what's available:

- Lists of all patents issued during a particular week that include the name of the inventor and an abstract describing the invention.

- Lists of expired patents.

- Front pages of the *Official Gazette of the United States Patent and Trademark Office* and the *Trademark Official Gazette.*

- The *Manual of Patent Examining Procedure.*

- Information about how to use the Patent and Trademark Office's public search room.

- Booklets about patent information on CD-ROM, other electronic products produced by the PTO, and publications about patents.

- A telephone directory for the Patent and Trademark Office.

- Press releases.

Rapid Information Bulletin Board System (RIBBS)

U.S. Postal Service
National Customer Support Center
Suite 101
6060 Primacy Parkway
Memphis, TN 38188-0001

Information about postal rates, how to detect mail bombs, numerous types of mail fraud, bulk mailings, and new stamps is available from the Rapid Information Bulletin Board System (RIBBS), which is operated by the U.S. Postal Service.

Most of the information on the board is free. However, you must subscribe and pay a fee to access a few areas that offer technical information for commercial mailers.

Following are some highlights of what's available for free:

- Postal rates.

- Information about services such as certified mail, money orders, post office boxes, postal insurance, and return receipt service.

- Information for people who are moving.

- News releases about new stamps.

- Information about how to order stamps by phone.

- A security plan for suspected letter and parcel bombs.

- Information about how to identify mail bombs and what to do if you think you've received one.

- Details about the jurisdiction of the U.S. Postal Inspection Service.

- Information about numerous types of mail fraud, including free prize schemes, lotteries, free vacation schemes, investment schemes, real estate swindles, oil and gas well swindles, phony job opportunities, work at home schemes, pyramid marketing schemes, chain letters, prison pen pal money order scams, false billing schemes against consumers, charity scams, scams that charge for services the government offers for free, receipt of unsolicited

VITAL STATS

Data: 800-262-9541

Voice: 800-238-3150

FedWorld gateway: 29

Manual: RIBBUSER.DOC (uncompressed) or RIBBUSER.ZIP (compressed)

Time limit: 30 minutes per day for non-subscribers

merchandise, credit repair schemes, scams against business, the Nigerian prince swindle, and many others.

- A guide to products, services, and publications available from the National Customer Support Center.

- Information about address correction services available to commercial mailers.

- Rules for telephone solicitations and characteristics of telemarketing fraud schemes.

- Posters of people wanted by the U.S. Postal Inspection Service, in PCX format.

- Mailing tips for consumers.

- A directory of offices for business mailers.

- A lengthy history of the Postal Service.

- Information about Postal Service publications.

- Press releases.

- Speeches by Postal Service officials.

- Santa Claus's address and details about how to receive North Pole cancellations.

- A biography of the postmaster general.

- Details about disruptions of mail service to various foreign countries.

SBA Online

Small Business Administration
409 Third St., S.W.
Washington, DC 20416

SBA Online is primarily aimed at helping people start and run small businesses. It has hundreds of files and computer programs for small businesses.

The Small Business Administration has made things a little complicated by granting different levels of access depending on what number you use to call the board. The box lists the three options.

SBA Telephone Options

202-401-9600   Provides full access to the board. You can download any files, use the gateway to dozens of other federal government BBSs, and send e-mail to other users.

900-463-4636   Also provides full access. However, the first minute costs thirty cents and each additional minute is ten cents. For example, a thirty-minute call costs $3.20.

800-697-4636   Toll-free, but provides somewhat limited access. You can download all SBA files and send e-mail to the sysop. You cannot access the gateway to other federal BBSs, download software, or exchange e-mail with other users.

The Main Menu offers ten numbered choices, most of which lead to sub-menus. Here are highlights for each choice:

1. **General Information**   Information about the SBA, employment opportunities at the SBA and other federal agencies, and federal job programs.

2. **Services Available**   Information about services available from the SBA, articles from the *Small Business Advo-*

VITAL STATS

Data: 800-697-4636
    (limited access),
    202-401-9600 (full
    access), 900-463-4636
    (full access for a fee)

Voice: 202-205-6400

FedWorld gateway: 40
    (full access)

Internet: telnet sbaonline.
    sba.gov

File list: SBAFILES.TXT

To access files: At the Main
    Menu type **f**

Time limit: 90 minutes
    per call

Available: 24 hours a day
    except from 6:30 a.m.
    to 8:30 a.m. EST

cate newsletter, information about government contracting opportunities, and a huge list (divided by state) of large government contractors that work with sub-contractors.

3. **Local Information** Lists of local SBA offices, SBA Disaster Area Offices, Small Business Development Centers, and offices of the Service Corps of Retired Executives (SCORE). In addition, this area has extensive overviews of the small business situation in individual states, including economic projections.

4. **Outside Resources** A gateway to dozens of other BBSs operated by federal agencies and departments, limited information about Internal Revenue Service programs to help small businesses, information about patents and trademarks from the U.S. Patent and Trademark Office, and information from the Census Bureau, including business statistics, telephone numbers for key contacts at the Census Bureau, and articles from the *Census and You* newsletter.

5. **Quick Search Menu** Allows searching of the files in the Main Menu areas by topics and full-text searching by keywords.

6. **White House Information** Various documents from the White House, including the National Information Infrastructure report and the National Performance Review report.

7. **Talk to Your Government** A list of more than 150 federal government BBSs, an area where users can offer suggestions about how the federal government can improve services to citizens, the text of the Americans with Disabilities Act, a list of members of Congress by state that includes addresses, telephone numbers, and fax numbers, and a list of state chambers of commerce that includes contact names, addresses, telephone numbers, and fax numbers.

8. **Small Business Success Stories** Stories about small businesses that have received SBA assistance.

9. **Business Cards** Business card information provided by other users of the BBS.

0. **New Items** New files on the BBS.

SBA Online also has a Files Area that you can reach by typing **f** at the Main Menu. The files, which offer everything from White House documents to business-related shareware programs for DOS and Windows computers, are separated into more than two dozen directories. All callers can access the first eighteen directories and directory 27, but those using the toll-free number cannot access directories 19-26 and 28-29 (see box).

File Directories in SBA Online

1. Women
2. International trade
3. Veterans
4. General business development files
5. Business initiatives, education, and training
6. Service Corps of Retired Executives (SCORE)
7. Government contracting
8. Minority small business
9. Small business innovation and research
10. Surety guarantee
11. Small business investment companies
12. Financial assistance
13. Disaster assistance
14. Legislation and regulations
15. Small Business Development Center files
16. Miscellaneous files
17. White House files
18. Talk to your government files
19. Offline mail readers and help
20. Files for starting up a business
21. Files for managing a business
22. Files for financing a business
23. Files for marketing your business
24. Files that help run your business
25. Miscellaneous file uploads
26. New files
27. List of all SBA Online files
28. Access to SBA Online information
29. Internet information

Census-BEA Electronic Forum

Bureau of the Census
Data Users Services Division
State and Regional Program Staff
U.S. Department of Commerce
Washington, DC 20233

The Census-BEA Electronic Forum contains a wealth of statistical information about the U.S. population and economy. The BBS has exchange rates, highlights from the 1992 Census of Agriculture, data about imports and exports, economic data, housing and construction data, state rankings and demographic profiles, reports about numerous industries, and demographic information for every country in the world.

The board's name is somewhat misleading because the Bureau of Economic Analysis (BEA) files aren't available to the public. They can be accessed only by members of the BEA's users group, which includes people at state universities, state government agencies, and similar institutions. The BEA files, which provide regional economic statistics, are available to the public on the fee-based Economic Bulletin Board (see p. 75).

Nonetheless, the census files are extremely valuable. After logging in, you will be asked to join a special interest group (SIG). You have to join a SIG before you can access the files. SIG titles include Open Forum, 1990 Census, TIGER, Census Economic, CD-ROM, Agriculture, and Population Estimates and Projections. At some point, the board plans to add a SIG on the 2000 Census. If you just want to download files, it doesn't matter which SIG you join because they all access the same files. But if you want to exchange messages with other users or ask questions of Census Bureau employees, make sure you join the relevant SIG.

Once you join the SIG, type **f** to go to the Files Transfer Menu. The files are separated into eighteen areas. Downloading a file is cumbersome because you have to be in the area where the file is located to download it. This gets to be a nuisance if you want to download several files from different areas.

VITAL STATS

Data: 301-457-2310

Voice: 301-457-1242
   (Census)

Voice: 202-606-5360 (BEA)

FedWorld gateway: 64

Manual: Several files are
   available on the
   Tutorial Menu

File list: FILELIST.ZIP

To access files: Join any
   special interest group
   (SIG), then type **f**

Time limit: 60 minutes
   per call

Here are highlights of what's available:

- Press releases, including information about new Census Bureau reports.

- Descriptions of machine readable data available from the Census Bureau.

- Help in using CD-ROMS produced by the Census Bureau.

- A table with exchange rates for the last decade.

- Descriptions of electronic products available from the Census Bureau.

- Highlights from the 1992 Census of Agriculture by state and county.

- Tips about upcoming Census Bureau reports and activities.

- Telephone directories for the Census Bureau, the Bureau of Economic Analysis, the Bureau of Labor Statistics, the Office of Business Analysis, and the Office of the Under Secretary for Economic Affairs.

- Monthly data on U.S. imports and exports.

- The *Final Report of the GATT Uruguay Round of Multilateral Trade Negotiations.*

- Several major presidential reports, including the Health Security Plan, the National Export Strategy, and the National Performance Review.

- Data on monthly retail sales; durable goods manufacturers' shipments and orders; manufacturers' shipments, inventories, and orders; manufacturer and trade inventories and sales; finances of manufacturing, mining, and trade corporations; large retailers' profits; wholesale trade sales and inventories; and plant and equipment expenditures and plans.

- Extensive housing and construction data.

- State rankings on population, schools, educational attainment, civilian labor force, nonfarm employment, poverty status, farms, and other areas. The numbers are taken from the *Statistical Abstract of the United States.*

- State profiles taken from the *Statistical Abstract of the United States.* The files contain statistics on population, housing units, low-weight births, hospital beds and physicians per 100,000 population, average teacher salaries, educational attainment, federal defense spending, Social Security recipients, civilian labor force, disposable income, number of persons below the poverty level, average value of farmland, number of hazardous waste sites, and motor vehicle deaths, among other subjects.

- Reports on a wide range of industries, including flour milling, fats and oils, titanium dioxide, glass, aluminum ingot and mill products, steel mills, civil aircraft and aircraft engines, truck trailers, fabrics, apparel, inorganic chemicals, fertilizer, footwear, carpet and rugs, industrial air pollution control equipment, computers and office and accounting machines, major household appliances, and aerospace, among others. The reports typically include detailed data on inventories, unfilled orders, quantity and value of shipments, production, exports, imports, and consumption.

- National population projections through 2050 and state population projections through 2020.

- Detailed demographic information for every country in the world, including population statistics dating back for several decades and projections to 2000.

- Statistical briefs about topics such as the housing of American Indians on reservations, reducing toxins, mothers who receive AFDC payments, housing of the elderly, poverty, housing in New York City, health insurance coverage, college costs and financing, state population projections, condominiums, mobile homes, and other topics.

Economic Bulletin Board (EBB)

STAT-USA
U.S. Department of Commerce
Washington, DC 20230

The Economic Bulletin Board is a one-stop source for current economic information. It contains statistical data, trade leads, and press releases from the Bureau of the Census, Bureau of Economic Analysis, Bureau of Labor Statistics, Bureau of Export Administration, Federal Reserve Board, Department of the Treasury, Office of the U.S. Trade Representative, Economics and Statistics Administration, International Trade Administration, Department of Energy, and the Foreign Agricultural Service, among others.

Technically speaking, the EBB is not a free BBS. However, some parts of it can be accessed without charge, and the cost of using the rest is relatively low. If you have an Internet account, you can access all of the EBB's files for free on a Gopher operated by the University of Michigan library. Each day, the librarians call the EBB, download all the new files, and upload them to their Gopher. The Gopher's address is gopher.lib.umich.edu and the path to the files is *Social Sciences Resources/Business and Economics/Dept. of Commerce Economic Data.*

To explore the EBB before subscribing, type **guest** when the board asks for your user ID. Guests have very limited access to the board and are limited to twenty minutes per call, but can call back immediately when their time expires.

Subscribers have full access to all files. Subscriptions cost $45 annually, but come with $20 worth of connect time. At 300 to 2400 baud, connect time costs between $3 and $12 per hour, depending on the time of day. At 9600 baud, 14400 baud, or through the Internet, connect time costs between $6 and $24 per hour. Flat-rate annual subscriptions are also available. One hour of access daily costs $250 annually, and four hours of access daily cost $400 annually. You can subscribe by calling the voice number or by downloading and filling out a registration form.

So what can you get for free as a guest? Here are some of the most valuable resources, by area:

VITAL STATS

Data: 202-482-3870
(300-2400 baud),
202-482-2584 (9600
baud), 202-482-2167
(14400 baud)

Voice: 202-482-1986

FedWorld gateway: 13

To access files: Most files
available only to
subscribers

Time limit: 60 minutes
per call (subscriber),
20 minutes per call
(guest)

Internet: telnet ebb.
stat-usa.gov

Bulletins

- A description of the EBB and information about how to subscribe.

- The EBB QuickStart Manual, an excellent user's guide.

- A list of all the files on the board.

- A description of the types of files available by agency.

Files

- Lists of telephone contacts at the Bureau of Economic Analysis, Bureau of Labor Statistics, Bureau of the Census, Office of the Under Secretary for Economic Affairs, and the Office of Business Analysis.

- Schedules of document release dates for the Bureau of Economic Analysis and the Office of Management and Budget.

Trade Promotion

- A calendar of upcoming trade promotion events.

- An explanation of where to go for export assistance.

- A list of U.S. and Foreign Commercial Service district offices.

- A list of key officers at U.S. embassies.

- A description of U.S. and Foreign Commercial Service export assistance programs.

- A state-by-state list of export resources.

Presidential

- The full text of the federal budget, along with a publication titled *Citizen's Guide to the Federal Budget* and dozens of documents that analyze the budget.

- President Clinton's budget plan.

- The full text of the North American Free Trade Agreement (NAFTA).

News

- A list of reports to be issued during the upcoming week by the Commerce Department.

- News about the board's operation.

Subscribers can access thousands of files, including statements by administration officials, summaries of current economic conditions, national income data, economic indicators, employment statistics, price and productivity statistics, foreign trade data, industry statistics, fiscal and monetary policy data, Department of the Treasury auction results, regional economic statistics, energy statistics, daily trade opportunities from the U.S. and Foreign Commercial Service, current business statistics, press releases and reports from the Office of the U.S. Trade Representative, International Marketing Insight (IMI) reports from the U.S. and Foreign Commercial Service, trade leads in the former Soviet Union and eastern Europe, agricultural trade leads, and other information.

FED FLASH!

Federal Reserve Bank of Dallas
Research Department
2200 N. Pearl St.
Dallas, TX 75201

FED FLASH! offers economic and banking data for the southwestern United States and the entire country. It is operated by the Federal Reserve Bank of Dallas, which serves Texas and parts of Louisiana and New Mexico.

The files are separated into more than two dozen directories. Some of the more interesting directories include:

FEDPUB Electronic copies of publications produced by the Federal Reserve Bank of Dallas.

AGSVY Results of the agricultural survey conducted by the Federal Reserve Bank of Dallas.

REGION Regional economic indicators.

SALES Retail sales figures for Dallas, Houston, Texas, Louisiana, and the United States.

CONST Various kinds of construction data for Texas, Louisiana, and New Mexico.

AGLAND Values of agricultural land in the region served by the Federal Reserve Bank of Dallas.

ENERGY Oil drilling statistics for Texas, Louisiana, and New Mexico.

HHUNEMP Unemployment rates for Dallas, Fort Worth, the three states served by the Federal Reserve Bank of Dallas, and the United States.

BANKFIN A wide range of financial data for banks in the region served by the Federal Reserve Bank of Dallas, including assets, financial ratios, income and expenses, liabilities and capital, and nonperforming assets.

Federal Reserve Economic Data (F.R.E.D.)

Research and Public Information Department
Federal Reserve Bank of St. Louis
P.O. Box 442
St. Louis, MO 63166

F.R.E.D., which is operated by the Federal Reserve Bank of St. Louis, has hundreds of files of economic and financial data. It specializes in regional economic data for Missouri, Arkansas, Kentucky, Tennessee, Illinois, Indiana, and Mississippi, although it also has lots of current and historical national data as well.

The files are divided into more than two dozen directories. To get a directory list, type **f** at the Main Menu. To get a list of files in a directory, type its number at the prompt.

The first ten file directories offer historical numbers, many dating from decades ago to the present. For example, you can get figures for the Consumer Price Index from 1913 to the present, savings deposits at commercial banks from 1959, prime rate changes from 1929, federal government debt from 1953, the Gross National Product from 1946, and civilian employment from 1948.

Other files offer current data for the Gross Domestic Product, Consumer Price Index, Producer Price Index, employment and population, foreign exchange rates, and other economic indicators. The board also has many files that contain regional economic data.

VITAL STATS

Data: 314-621-1824

Voice: 314-444-8562

Manual: NEWUSER

File list: FILESEXE.EXE (self-extracting) or FILESZIP.ZIP

To access files: At the Main Menu type **f**

Time limit: One hour daily

Internet: http://www.stls.frb.org

FedLink

Public Affairs Department
Federal Reserve Bank of Chicago
230 S. LaSalle St.
Chicago, IL 60604

FedLink offers a huge quantity of regional and national economic data, much of it stretching back for decades. It is operated by the Federal Reserve Bank of Chicago, which serves all of Iowa and parts of Illinois, Indiana, Michigan, and Wisconsin.

Here are some highlights of what's available:

- Statistical releases that provide current data about industrial production and capacity utilization, consumer installment credit, foreign exchange rates, selected interest rates, factors affecting the reserves of depository institutions, and the assets and liabilities of banking institutions, among other subjects.

- Economic indicators, such as data on motor vehicle production from 1990 to the present, capacity utilization from 1967, the Consumer Price Index from 1945, the Gross Domestic Product from 1946, the Industrial Production Index from 1947, gross private domestic investment from 1946, the Midwest Manufacturing Index from 1973, sales of new one-family homes by region from 1973, the disposition of personal income from 1946, Gross Domestic Product price deflators from 1947, the Producer Price Index from 1948, the regional Consumer Price Index for Chicago, Detroit, and Milwaukee from 1980, and housing starts and building permits from 1960, among other data.

- Labor market data, including employment levels from 1967 to the present in the cities of Des Moines, Chicago, Indianapolis, Detroit, and Milwaukee and the states of Iowa, Illinois, Indiana, Michigan, and Wisconsin.

- Financial market data, including weekly corporate bond yields from 1982 to the present, daily certificate of deposit rates from 1968, weekly certificate of deposit rates in the secondary market from 1965, daily commercial paper rates from 1971, daily and weekly Treasury constant maturity

VITAL STATS

Data: 312-322-2137

Voice: 312-322-2378

File list: ALLFILE3.EXE (compressed) or ALLFILE3.TXT (uncompressed).

Internet: gopher gopher. great-lakes.net 2200 or http://www. greatlakes.net:2200/ glinhome.html

Path (Gopher only): ECONOMY: Industry and Commerce in the Great Lakes Region/Federal Reserve Bank of Chicago data

E-mail: harker@great-lakes. net

rates from 1962, daily Eurodollar deposits from 1971, daily foreign exchange rates from 1971, selected daily interest rates from 1962, and daily three-month Treasury bill rates from 1954.

- Banking data, including commercial and industrial loan growth in the Midwest and the United States from 1989 to the present, deposit growth for the region and the country from 1989, and return on assets from 1989.

- Lists of publications, videos, and films produced by the Federal Reserve Bank of Chicago.

- Federal Reserve publications about obtaining and using consumer credit, the structure and functions of the Federal Reserve System, the history of the nation's money and financial system, government securities, and how the value of the U.S. dollar relates to currencies in other countries.

- The *Agricultural Letter,* the *Chicago Fed Letter,* and *FedWire,* all of which are monthly newsletters.

- Numerous papers from a conference about bank structure.

- Results from Treasury Department auctions.

- Glossaries of terms related to financial regulators and institutions, monetary policy, payment mechanisms, foreign banking, consumer credit, and securities credit.

- A calendar of area events of interest to economic educators.

FedWest Online

Research Library
Mail Stop 1140
Federal Reserve Bank of San Francisco
P.O. Box 7702
San Francisco, CA 94120

FedWest Online provides regional economic and banking information from the Federal Reserve Bank of San Francisco, which serves Alaska, California, Hawaii, Idaho, Nevada, Oregon, Utah, and Washington.

A warning: When this book was being written, the system suffered from some technical problems that sometimes caused it to freeze in the middle of online sessions.

Here are some highlights of what's available:

- Earnings statistics for Federal Reserve banks.

- Articles from the Federal Reserve Bank of San Francisco *Weekly Letter*. Sample titles include "International Trade and U.S. Labor Market Trends," "The Recent Behavior of Interest Rates," "Regional Income Divergency in the 1980s," and "A Primer on Monetary Policy."

- Abstracts of articles from the Federal Reserve Bank of San Francisco *Economic Review*.

- A monthly publication titled *Western Economic Developments*.

- Speeches by officials of the Federal Reserve Bank of San Francisco.

- Weekly reports on the condition of large commercial banks within the district.

- A quarterly publication titled *FedWest*.

- Information about the Community Reinvestment Act.

- Lists of banks within the district, by state and then by city.

VITAL STATS

Data: 415-896-0272

Voice: Telephone support is not provided, although users can leave questions to the sysop on the BBS

Note: The BBS supports connections only at 9600 baud and lower.

KIMBERELY

Public Affairs Department
Federal Reserve Bank of Minneapolis
250 Marquette Ave.
Minneapolis, MN 55480

KIMBERELY offers tons of regional and national economic data, in addition to information about the Federal Reserve System. The Federal Reserve Bank of Minneapolis, which operates KIMBERELY, serves the Ninth Federal Reserve District. The Ninth District includes Minnesota, Montana, North Dakota, South Dakota, the upper peninsula of Michigan, and twenty-six counties in northwestern Wisconsin.

Information on the board is presented in hundreds of files. To download a list of all the files, type **f** at the Main Menu, type **k** at the File Menu, and then select a transfer protocol from among those listed.

Here are some highlights of what's available:

- National economic data regarding the gross national product, unemployment, disposable personal income, retail sales, housing starts, inventories, consumer prices, producer prices, the money supply, and other economic factors.

- District economic indicators such as money market rates, mortgage loan delinquency rates, home sales and prices, cash farm receipts, savings rates, crop prices, livestock prices, dairy and poultry prices, annual cash farm receipts, and other economic data for the Ninth District.

- Economic forecasts for the Ninth District and the United States, issued quarterly.

- Directories of district banks by state.

- Press releases about the upper Midwest economy, bank performance, and other issues.

- Background information about the Federal Reserve Bank of Minneapolis, a list of directors and advisory council members, and information about touring the building.

VITAL STATS
Data: 612-340-2489
Voice: 612-340-2443
To access files: At the Main Menu type **f**
Internet: http://woodrow.mpls.frb.fed.us

- Background information about the Federal Reserve System, a guide to Federal Reserve regulations, addresses and phone numbers for the twelve Fed district banks, and a history of the Federal Reserve.

- Glossaries of terms related to financial regulators and institutions, monetary policy, foreign banking, consumer credit, and securities credit.

- Polls of business and community leaders published in the *FedGazette,* a quarterly regional business and economics newspaper. The polls report opinions on the regional economy, new banking regulations, the quality of schools, health care, and other issues.

- Articles from the *FedGazette.* Sample titles include "When a 'Company Town' Loses Its Company, No Magic Formula for Recovery," "From the Ashes of Economic Crises, Jackson, MN, Builds Economic Diversity," "District States Struggle with Budgets," and "Banking 2000: More Technology and Fewer Banks."

- Information about agricultural credit conditions, reported quarterly. The file contains data going back four years.

- Abstracts of research reports prepared by Ninth District staff.

- Lists of various publications and audiovisual materials that can be ordered.

- The text of recent speeches by top Federal Reserve System officials.

- Biographies of governors of the Federal Reserve System, presidents of Federal Reserve banks, and senior officials at the Federal Reserve Bank of Minneapolis.

- Facts about U.S. coins and paper money, and detailed information about counterfeit detection.

- Information about consumer credit protection and Fed publications about consumer finance.

Liberty Link

Federal Reserve Bank of New York
33 Liberty St.
New York, NY 10045

Liberty Link provides foreign exchange rates and lots of very technical economic data. It is operated by the Federal Reserve Bank of New York, which serves New York, Puerto Rico, the Virgin Islands, the twelve northern counties of New Jersey, and Fairfield County, Conn.

Here are some highlights:

- Copies of the *Weekly Bulletin,* which lists applications by banks to create holding companies, merge with each other, acquire additional banks, and take similar actions.

- Foreign exchange rates, updated daily, for England, Canada, France, Germany, Switzerland, Japan, the Netherlands, Belgium, Italy, Sweden, Norway, and Denmark.

- Commercial paper data and rates.

- Reports about dealer transactions in government securities.

- Selected interest rates.

- Weekly monetary and reserve statistics.

- Money supply data.

- Treasury quotes.

- News releases.

- Speeches by officials from the Federal Reserve Bank of New York.

- Biographies of officers of the Federal Reserve Bank of New York.

VITAL STATS
Data: 212-720-2652
Voice: 212-720-6143
To access files: At the Main Menu type **l**

New England Electronic Economic Data Center

Department of Economics
University of Maine
Orono, ME 04469

The New England Electronic Economic Data Center provides information about the New England economy, along with some national data. The BBS is sponsored by the University of Maine, the Federal Reserve Bank of Boston, the U.S. Bureau of Economic Analysis, and the National Trade Data Bank.

The bulletins, which you can access by typing **b** at the Main Menu, provide general information about how to use the BBS and tips on using specific features.

The BBS also offers two doors that lead to databases, which you can access by typing **d** at the Main Menu. The first database contains economic data for states, counties, and metropolitan areas from the Bureau of Economic Analysis. The second database offers personal income estimates for 1969-1991, descriptions of economic developments in a geographic area over the previous year or previous decade, and journey to work data from the Bureau of the Census for 1960, 1970, and 1980.

Here are highlights from the files area, which you can reach by typing **f** at the Main Menu:

- Economic indicators from the Federal Reserve Bank of Boston.

- Gross state product data from the Bureau of Economic Analysis.

- Data on employment, retail sales, personal income, corporate income tax collections, construction, and housing.

- Aggregate financial statements for commercial banks and savings banks in Connecticut, Massachusetts, Maine, New Hampshire, Rhode Island, and Vermont.

- Gross state product data for regions nationwide from the Bureau of Economic Analysis.

VITAL STATS

Data: 207-581-1860 (9600 baud) or 207-581-1867 (2400 baud)

Voice: 207-581-1863

Internet: ftp neeedc. umesbs.maine.edu

Login (FTP only): **anonymous**

Password (FTP only): your e-mail address

To access files: At the Main Menu type **f**

E-mail: breece@maine. maine.edu

Customs Electronic Bulletin Board (CEBB)

U.S. Customs Service
Office of Information Management
1301 Constitution Ave., N.W.
Washington, DC 22209

The Customs Electronic Bulletin Board (CEBB) features information for importers and others interested in global trade issues. It also has currency conversion rates for fifty countries. The rates are updated daily.
  Here are examples of the information that's available:

- A glossary of abbreviations and acronyms used by the Customs Service.

- *Federal Register* notices.

- News about the North American Free Trade Agreement (NAFTA).

- A notice prohibiting the importation of specific merchandise from the People's Republic of China made by convict, forced, or indentured labor.

- Information about the availability of Customs rulings on computer disks.

- Notices about increased duties on a wide range of foreign goods.

- A notice about counterfeit visas on textile shipments from China.

- News about the awarding or withdrawal of most-favored-nation trading status.

- A list of Customs Service representatives at American embassies around the world, with addresses, telephone numbers, and fax numbers.

- A list of Customs Service regional and district offices, with addresses and telephone numbers.

- A telephone list for headquarters and regional Customs Service staff.

VITAL STATS
Data: 703-440-6155
Voice: 703-440-6236
FedWorld gateway: 47
To access files: At the Main Menu type **f**
Time limit: 75 minutes per day
Available: 24 hours a day except Mondays from 7 a.m. to 9 a.m. EST

Eximbank Bulletin Board

Marketing Division
Export-Import Bank of the United States
811 Vermont Ave., N.W.
Washington, DC 20571

The Export-Import Bank (Eximbank) is an independent federal agency that helps finance exports of U.S. goods and services. Its BBS is designed for exporters, bankers, government officials, and others involved in exporting.

An opening message says the BBS is a "subscription board." That is incorrect. The BBS is public, and there are no fees for using it.

Information on the BBS is separated into bulletins and files. The board has more than three dozen bulletins, which you can access by typing **b** at the Main Menu. The bulletins describe the Eximbank and its programs, provide news releases, list key telephone numbers, and list Eximbank seminars.

The files, which you can access by typing **f** at the Main Menu, are separated into more than a dozen directories:

1. Eximbank press releases

2. Bank referral list (available by state)

3. Country information guide

4. How to contact Eximbank

5. Selected program descriptions

6. Working capital guarantee program

7. Eximbank seminar schedule

8. Eximbank summary of board minutes

9. Master guarantee and funding agreement

10. Project financing

11. Credit guarantee facilities

12. Procedures for economic impact analysis

13. Russia

14. Reinventing Eximbank: The results

Export License Information Status Advisor (ELISA)

Defense Technology Security Administration
400 Army Navy Drive, Suite 300
Arlington, VA 22202

Exporters can use ELISA to check the status of their export license applications at the Department of Defense. General callers cannot use the license database, since it requires an export license application number.

The only information for general users is Bulletin 6, which describes export assistance available from the Department of Commerce's Trade Information Center.

VITAL STATS

Data: 703-604-5902

Voice: 703-604-5176

FedWorld gateway: 14

Available: 24 hours a day except weekdays from 7 a.m. to 8 a.m. EST

Automated Policy Issuance and Retrieval System (APIRS)

Children's Bureau
Administration for Children and Families
330 C St., S.W.
Washington, DC 20201

The Automated Policy Issuance and Retrieval System (APIRS) has hundreds of technical documents relating to federal programs that serve children and families. The documents are primarily of interest to states and organizations that receive federal grants to operate the programs. The files originate with the Children's Bureau, the Head Start Bureau, and the National Center for Child Abuse and Neglect, all of which are part of the Administration for Children and Families.

The board offers information about grants available for various programs that serve children, notices of proposed rulemaking, a history of Head Start, and the text of the Head Start Act, among other documents.

VITAL STATS

Data: 202-260-1861

Voice: 202-205-8713

FedWorld gateway: 136

To access files: Type **b** at the Main Menu and **l** at the APIRS Bulletin Board Functions Menu

BPHC ACCESS

Bureau of Primary Health Care
Seventh Floor
4350 East-West Highway
Bethesda, MD 20814

BPHC ACCESS is aimed at providers of primary health care to the underserved, state agencies, and students who receive scholarships in exchange for serving in community-based health programs.

The board has lots of technical information for organizations that receive grants from the Bureau of Primary Health Care (BPHC), a directory of BPHC staff members, notices about the availability of grants, a list of Public Health Service regional offices, federal poverty guidelines, and notices from the *Federal Register.*

The board also has a database called the EDRS Database Query System that drug manufacturers can use to determine which primary care providers qualify for discounted outpatient drugs.

VITAL STATS

Data: 800-596-6405

Voice: 301-594-4060

FedWorld gateway: 138

To access files: At the Main
  Menu type **f**

Criteria Bulletin Board System (CBBS)

Sacramento District
U.S. Army Corps of Engineers
CESPK-EB-A
1325 J St.
Sacramento, CA 95814-2922

The Criteria Bulletin Board System (CBBS) contains design criteria and technical specifications used by the Sacramento District of the U.S. Army Corps of Engineers, which serves California, Nevada, Utah, and part of Colorado.

The files are primarily of interest to contractors. They explain the specifications required for construction of both military installations and civil works projects.

Before using this board, you must register by calling the voice number.

VITAL STATS

Data: 916-557-7997

Voice: 916-557-7670

Internet: telnet cbbs.usace.mil *or* http://www.usace.mil/cbbs/cbbs.html

Note: You must register to use this board

Department of the Navy Acquisition BBS

Department of the Navy (SADBU)
2211 Jefferson Davis Highway
Arlington, VA 22244-5102

The Department of the Navy Acquisition BBS provides access to two boards that are useful to government contractors.

The first board, the Department of the Navy Marketing BBS, helps companies determine what supplies are being purchased at Navy and Marine Corps contracting centers around the country. Users can search a database on the board to find marketing contacts at each facility. For detailed information about how to use the database, at the Department of the Navy Marketing BBS Menu type **b** and then select Bulletin 1. The board also has a complete list of Department of the Navy small business specialists. However, the file is compressed in a self-extracting format that makes it unusable on most Macintosh computers.

The second board, the Long Range Acquisition Estimate (LRAE) BBS, has lists of planned procurements by the Department of the Navy from fiscal year 1996 through fiscal year 2000. These are not solicitations for bids, but simply provide basic information about expected purchases. The board also has a list of codes and descriptions used in *Commerce Business Daily.*

VITAL STATS
Data: 317-306-3413
Voice: 703-602-2700

Department of State Office of Small and Disadvantaged Business Unit Bulletin Board System (SDBU)

A/SDBU
SA-6
Room 633
Department of State
Washington, DC 20522-0602

The Department of State Office of Small and Disadvantaged Business Unit Bulletin Board System (SDBU) provides information about contracting opportunities with the State Department.

The board has the full text of two publications: *A Guide to Doing Business With the Department of State* and an annual forecast of contracting opportunities at the State Department. Both files are compressed in a self-extracting format that makes them unusable on many Macintosh computers.

VITAL STATS
Data: 703-875-4945
Voice: 703-875-6822

DITCO's Electronic Bulletin Boards

DISA Information Technology Contracting Organization
2300 East Drive
Scott AFB, IL 62225-5406

DITCO's Electronic Bulletin Boards are primarily of interest to government contractors. The system provides access to two BBSs: the Defense Information Systems Agency Acquisition Bulletin Board System (DABBS) and the Information Technology Acquisition Bulletin Board System (ITABBS).

DABBS is used to solicit bids from telecommunications companies for various products and services, while ITABBS is used to solicit bids for information technology equipment such as personal computers and printers.

To reach the boards, type **j** at the Main Menu. Each board has solicitations, award notices, and other procurement related information.
There are no files of interest to general users.

VITAL STATS
Data: 618-256-9200
Voice: 618-256-9380
Manual: BULL93.BBS

ED Board

U.S. Department of Education
400 Maryland Ave., S.W.
ROB Room 3616
Washington, DC 20202-4726

ED Board provides information about grants and contracts available from the Department of Education.

While most of the information is offered in files, there's also a searchable database of announced grant programs. You can search the database for grant information by announcement date, current availability, or sponsoring program office. To access the database, type **g** at the Main Menu and **3** at the Grant Information Menu.

The following files are among the board's highlights:

Guide to U.S. Department of Education Programs   Information about the purpose and eligibility requirements of every grant program. The guide also lists the name and telephone number of the office responsible for each program.

Combined Application Notice (CAN)   Information about certain Department of Education grant programs, including the purpose of the program, eligibility requirements, applicable regulations, selection criteria, program priorities, projected number of awards, and program contact names and telephone numbers.

Doing Business with the Department of Education   General information about the contract process.

ED's Bidder List   Information about the contract bidders list and an application to sign up.

RFP Information   A list of current contracting opportunities at the Department of Education. Callers can request an RFP (Request For Proposal) package through the BBS.

GAO-OGC Decision Bulletin Board

Office of General Counsel
General Accounting Office
441 G St., N.W.
Washington, DC 20548

The GAO-OGC (General Accounting Office-Office of General Counsel) Decision Bulletin Board has GAO decisions in cases where government contractors protest the awarding of contracts to their competitors. It also has a few decisions in cases involving appropriations, civilian government employees, and military personnel. The GAO issues about 4,000 decisions each year, which remain online for sixty days after being issued.

VITAL STATS

Data: 202-512-2908

Voice: 202-512-4465

To access files: At the Main Menu type **I**

NASA SBIR/STTR Bulletin Board

National Aeronautics and Space Administration
Mail Code: CR
Washington, DC 20546

The SBIR/STTR Bulletin Board provides information for businesses that want to participate in NASA's Small Business Innovation Research or Small Business Technology Transfer programs. It contains annual solicitations, award lists, procurement information, contact information, and news about both programs. The BBS does not contain general information about NASA or space flights.

The BBS is divided into three sections: the Main Board, the Small Business Innovation Research Conference, and the Small Business Technology Transfer Conference. You can join a conference by typing **j** at the Main Menu. Each section has its own bulletins, files, and e-mail functions.

Following are descriptions of each section:

Main Board   This section contains information about how the BBS operates. The bulletins describe the board and provide help in using it. The files include two manuals and decompression programs for both DOS and Macintosh computers.

Small Business Innovation Research Conference   Under the SBIR program, NASA provides competitive research contracts to businesses with fewer than 500 employees. NASA's SBIR program is aimed at developing technologies in more than a dozen areas, including aeronautical propulsion and power, materials and structures, teleoperators and robotics, instrumentation and sensors, spacecraft systems and subsystems, and human habitability and biology in space. Bulletin 1 in the SBIR conference provides a short description of the program.

Small Business Technology Transfer Conference   The SBTT program is designed to encourage the transfer of technology to commercial markets by teaming small businesses and research institutions. Teams that develop research proposals can receive research contracts. Bulletin 1 in the SBTT conference provides a short description of the program.

VITAL STATS

Data: 800-547-1811 or
 202-488-2939

Voice: Telephone support is not provided; you can leave questions on the board

FedWorld gateway: 36

Manuals: QUIKSTRT.TXT (short version) and MANUAL.TXT (long version)

Internet: ftp coney.gsfc.nasa.gov

Login (FTP only): **anonymous**

Password (FTP only): your e-mail address

NIH Grant Line

Division of Research Grants
National Institutes of Health
6701 Rockledge Drive MSC-7710
Bethesda, MD 20892-7710

If you are looking for a grant to support biomedical research, the NIH Grant Line from the National Institutes of Health is the place to check. Most of the files on this BBS are RFAs (Request for Application), which announce the availability of grants from various agencies of the Public Health Service. The BBS also has electronic copies of the weekly *NIH Guide to Grants and Contracts*, lists of grants that have been awarded, and an edited version of the NIH telephone directory.

There are three ways to access this BBS:

1. **Through FedWorld**   You must switch to a half duplex communications setting when you move from FedWorld. If your communications program doesn't have a half duplex setting, turn on local echo instead. You'll get a message telling you when to make the change. If you don't change the setting, what you type will be invisible on the screen.

2. **Through the dial-in connection**   This requires special settings in your communications software of even parity, 7 data bits, 1 stop bit, and half duplex. If your communications program does not have a half-duplex setting, turn on local echo instead. In addition, you will need to experiment with your terminal setting to see what works. A VT100 setting works well. After you connect, type **,gen1** (the comma is essential) and press your Enter key. You won't be prompted to do this. At the "Initials?" prompt, type **bb5** and press Enter. At the "Account?" prompt, type **ccs2** and press Enter.

3. **Through the Internet**   After you connect, type **,gen1** (the comma is essential) and press Enter. At the "Initials?" prompt, type **bb5** and press Enter. And at the "Account?" prompt, type **ccs2** and press Enter.

VITAL STATS

Data: 301-402-2221

Voice: 301-594-7270

FedWorld gateway: 70 (you must switch to a half duplex communications setting when you move from FedWorld)

To access files: At the Main Menu type **f**

Internet: telnet wylbur.cu.nih.gov

Note: Dial-in callers must set their communications software to even parity, 7 data bits, 1 stop bit, and half duplex (or local echo)

On-Line Schedules System (OSS)

Information Resources Management Services
U.S. General Services Administration
18th and F Sts., N.W.
Washington, DC 20405

The On-Line Schedules System is designed for federal government buyers and contract specialists who wish to purchase computers or telecommunications equipment. It has information from vendors who are authorized to participate in the General Services Administration (GSA) Multiple Award Schedule Program.

The BBS has information about thousands of products, electronic copies of hundreds of contracts, and GSA price lists. You can search the product information by manufacturer's part number, contract number, product category, and other variables.

The board also has:

- Information about changes in federal acquisitions regulations, as published in the *Federal Register*. To access these files, type **2** at the Main Menu.

- An extensive list of companies and people barred from selling goods to the federal government. The list includes the company name, its address, the names of the people involved, and a code about why the company is excluded from federal procurement programs. To access the list, type **4** at the Main Menu.

- Numerous files for vendors.

VITAL STATS

Data: 202-501-7254

Voice: 202-501-0002

FedWorld gateway: 23

Manual: At the Main Menu type * and at the Documentation Download Area type **1**

Internet: telnet oss.gsa.gov 2020

SAMHSA BBS

Substance Abuse and Mental Health Services Administration
Network Support Center
Attn: BBS sysop
Room 6C-12
5600 Fishers Lane
Rockville, MD 20857

The SAMHSA BBS, which is operated by the Substance Abuse and Mental Health Services Administration, is primarily aimed at organizations seeking contracts and grants. SAMHSA operates the Center for Mental Health Services, the Center for Substance Abuse Prevention, and the Center for Substance Abuse Treatment.

The BBS offers:

- Requests for Proposals, which are used to acquire goods and services from contractors.

- Information about grants and cooperative agreements available from SAMHSA.

- Lengthy documents titled "Mental Health Care Provider Education in HIV/AIDS," "Evaluating Innovative Child Mental Health Systems," and "Demonstration Grants for Consumer & Family Networks."

- A draft version of the SAMHSA strategic plan, which outlines the agency's activities for the remainder of the decade.

VITAL STATS
Data: 800-424-2294 or
    301-443-0040
Voice: 301-443-7379
FedWorld gateway: 145
E-mail: nsc@aoa1.ssw.
    dhhs.gov

Science and Technology Information System (STIS)

DAS/IRM
National Science Foundation
4201 Wilson Blvd.
Arlington, VA 22230

The STIS BBS offers access to thousands of documents, including the *National Science Foundation Bulletin,* the *NSF Guide to Programs,* program announcements, press releases, statistical reports from the NSF's Division of Science Resources Studies, the NSF telephone book, reports of the National Science Board, NSF job vacancy announcements, and descriptions of research projects funded by the NSF.

The BBS does not have general information about scientific topics. Instead, it focuses on how the NSF supports scientific research. You will find information about how to apply for grants and descriptions of research funded by NSF, but no information about the results of the research. The box on the next page lists some sample document titles.

If you call direct or access the site using Telnet, once you reach the Main Menu you may want to start by choosing option 4, *Download STIS Manual.* The manual provides excellent help in using this complex board.

Next, you may want to choose option 5 at the Main Menu, *Download Index to Files for FTP.* The index is arranged by Internet FTP directory. Don't worry about that—just note the names of any documents that interest you.

After you have compiled a list of those names, at the Main Menu select option 1, *Search/Browse Documents (TOPIC).* That takes you into the board's full-text search and retrieval system. Choose to do a word search, and type in the name of the document you want. TOPIC will find the document and allow you to read it on-screen, download it, or send it to your e-mail address. With TOPIC, you also can ignore the index and search for documents by keywords.

If you expect to use this system much, you should download several documents:

- NSF9119, the STIS User's Guide (if you have not already downloaded this as option 4).

VITAL STATS

Data: 703-306-0212

Voice: 202-357-7555

FedWorld gateway: 61

Login (dial-in and Telnet only): **public**

Internet: telnet stis.nsf.gov
or gopher stis.nsf.gov
or http://stis.nsf.gov *or*
ftp stis.nsf.gov

E-mail: stis@nsf.gov

Note: If you connect through dial-in access, your communications software should be set to emulate a VT100 terminal. After connecting you must hit your Enter key.

- ACCESFAQ, which provides answers to frequently asked questions about accessing STIS and its files.

- DWNLDFAQ, which offers lots of information about downloading files, especially through the Internet.

- STISDIRM, which explains how to get summaries of new documents, full documents, or press releases automatically delivered to you by e-mail.

Selected National Science Foundation Documents

America's Academic Future

Antarctic Research Program Guide

Arctic Science, Engineering, and Education

Beyond National Standards and Goals: Excellence in Math and Science Education, K-16

Career Opportunities in Science and Technology

Federal Funds for Research and Development

Funding Opportunities for Astronomers

Human Resource Development for Minorities in Science and Engineering

In the National Interest: The Federal Government and Research-Intensive Universities

The National Science Foundation Global Change Research Program

NSF Blue Ribbon Panel on High Performance Computing

The NSF in the Decade of the Brain

Research Experiences for Undergraduates

Research on Digital Libraries

Research Priorities in Networking and Communications

Women Continue to Earn Increasing Percentage of Science and Engineering Baccalaureates

---

TABBy BBS

Transportation Computer Center
U.S. Department of Transportation
400 Seventh St., S.W.
Washington, DC 20590

The TABBy BBS allows vendors to read Requests for Quotes and to offer bids electronically. The Requests for Quotes generally seek bids for items such as software, printer ribbons, and computer hard drives costing from a few hundred to a few thousand dollars.

VITAL STATS
Data: 202-493-2359
Voice: 202-366-9996

VA Vendor Bulletin Board System

IRM Planning, Acquisitions and Security Service (711)
U.S. Department of Veterans Affairs
810 Vermont Ave., N.W., Room 744
Washington, DC 20420

The VA Vendor Bulletin Board System contains extensive information for companies wishing to sell goods or services—anything from pencils to X-ray machines—to the Department of Veterans Affairs (VA).
Here are some highlights:

- Numerous acquisition documents, including Requests for Proposals, Requests for Comments, and Requests for Quotations.

- Decisions from the VA Board of Contract Appeals.

- VA telephone directories.

- Procurement requests.

- VA advertisements from *Commerce Business Daily.*

- Various VA reference publications, including the Five-Year Information and Resources Management program plan and the Forecast of Nationwide Contracting Opportunities.

- A list of all VA medical centers nationwide.

VITAL STATS

Data: 800-735-5282 or 202-565-6971

Voice: 202-565-7088

Available: 8 a.m. to 8 p.m. EST

FCC Public Access Link (PAL)

Federal Communications Commission
Authorization and Evaluation Division
7435 Oakland Mills Road
Columbia, MD 21046

The FCC Public Access Link (PAL) is aimed at people who are trying to obtain FCC equipment authorizations for electrical equipment. These authorizations certify that the equipment's emissions do not interfere with radio frequency devices. The BBS also offers a small amount of general information about the FCC. Most of the information on the board is technical, and there is nothing of interest to general users.

Information on the board is separated into thirteen categories, some designated by numbers and some by letters:

VITAL STATS

Data: 301-725-1072

Voice: 301-725-1585, ext. 216

Time limit: Eight minutes per call (but you can call back as many times as you like)

1. **Access Equipment Authorization Database**   Information about the status of pending and granted applications. This database can be accessed only by people with proposed or validated FCC identification numbers.

2. **Definitions**   Definitions of the alphabetical and numeric codes used in the access equipment authorization database.

3. **Applying for an Equipment Authorization**   Information about preparing applications, fees, rules, forms, bulletins, and measurement procedures. This category also has a list of test firms approved by the FCC for performing compliance testing.

4. **Other Commission Activities and Procedures**   Information about obtaining FCC documents, forms, and rules and regulations. There is also a list of FCC field offices.

5. **Laboratory Operational Information**   Directions to the FCC Laboratory, a list of its hours, and a contact list.

6. **Public Notices**   Information about accessing FCC documents through the Internet and other online sources, directions about filing Freedom of Information Act requests through the Internet, and technical notices about radio frequency devices and related subjects.

7. **Bulletins/Measurement Procedures**   Technical documents about FCC regulations and procedures.

8. **Rulemakings**   Descriptions of current rulemaking proceedings concerning radio frequency devices.

9. **Help**   Assistance in using the BBS, including a list of information found in the various directories.

a. **Information Hotline**   News about new forms and bulletins, a fee guide, and new filing instructions.

b. **Processing Speed of Service**   Files explaining how long it takes the FCC Laboratory to process equipment authorizations.

c. **Test Sites**   A list of foreign and domestic firms that are authorized to test devices regulated by the FCC.

d. **Advisory Committee on Advanced Television Service Meetings** A schedule of meetings of the Advisory Committee on Advanced Television Service.

FCC World

Smithwick & Belendiuk, P.C.
1990 M St., N.W., Suite 510
Washington, DC 20036

FCC World is operated by a law firm that represents clients before the Federal Communications Commission, not by the FCC itself. Nonetheless, it offers more FCC documents than either of the BBSs operated by the FCC.
Here are some highlights:

- Notices about applications for new and renewed broadcast licenses.

- Notices about the granting and renewal of broadcast licenses.

- Broadcast license renewal decisions.

- Decisions in cable cases, including rate cases.

- Bills being considered by Congress that affect the FCC and companies it regulates.

- The FCC's equal employment opportunity report to Congress.

- The FCC *Daily Digest.*

- FCC meeting agendas.

- A few documents filed by telecommunications companies with the Securities and Exchange Commission.

- The section of the U.S. Code pertaining to telecommunications.

- FCC notices and decisions in cases involving common carriers.

- Notices and applications involving wireless communications.

VITAL STATS
Data: 202-887-5718
Voice: 202-785-2800
To access files: At the Main Menu type **l**

FCC-State Link

Industry Analysis Division
Federal Communications Commission
Mail Stop 1600 F
1919 M St., N.W.
Washington, DC 20554

FCC-State Link provides reports that telephone companies are required to file with the Federal Communications Commission. The reports include data on finances, quality of service, and infrastructure. The board is designed for use primarily by state public utility commissions, which regulate telephone companies on the state level. Most of the information is technical.

The FCC *Daily Digest* is also posted on the board. This document contains speeches by FCC officials, news releases, the titles of public notices, and brief descriptions of FCC actions in various cases. Normally, the *Daily Digest* is posted the day after it is published by the FCC.

VITAL STATS

Data: 202-418-0241

Voice: 202-418-0940

FedWorld gateway: 84

File list: ALLFILES.TXT (uncompressed) or ALLFILES.ZIP (compressed)

To access files: At the Main Menu type **f**

Available: Not available to the public Monday through Friday from 10:30 a.m. to 1:30 p.m. EST

ITC Chemicals BBS

U.S. International Trade Commission
Suite 513-I
500 E St., S.W.
Washington, DC 20436

The ITC Chemicals BBS provides quarterly reports on U.S. production of selected synthetic organic chemicals such as benzene, polypropylene, and acetone.

The reports, which are available in ASCII text or Lotus 1-2-3 format, can be accessed by typing **s** at the Main Menu. The BBS also has a chemicals dictionary database that you can access by typing **d** at the Main Menu. It lists chemical names, Chemical Abstract Service (CAS) registry numbers, and related chemical synonyms. This feature probably will not work for Macintosh users.

VITAL STATS
Data: 202-205-1948
Voice: 202-205-3352
To access files: At the Main Menu type **s**

National Marine Fisheries Service—NW Region

National Oceanic and Atmospheric Administration
7600 Sand Point Way N.E.
Seattle, WA 98115

Commercial fishermen in the Northwest are the primary audience for the National Marine Fisheries Service board. It has commercial fishing regulations affecting Northwest states, statistics on seafood exports to the European Economic Community, foreign trade information, and information about how to order reports on the market for fish in foreign countries.

VITAL STATS
Data: 206-526-6405
Voice: 206-526-6119

NCUA BBS

National Credit Union Administration
1775 Duke St.
Alexandria, VA 22314-3428

The NCUA BBS contains manuals, legal opinions, proposed regulations, and press releases from the National Credit Union Administration. The NCUA regulates and insures all federal credit unions and insures those state-chartered credit unions that apply for and qualify for insurance.

You can access a newsletter by typing **n** at the Main Menu. It lists upcoming meetings of the NCUA board, tells about important new files added to the BBS, and provides news about revisions of several NCUA manuals.

The files are divided into more than a dozen file areas. Here are some of the most interesting files:

VITAL STATS

Data: 703-518-6480

Voice: 703-518-6335

FedWorld gateway: 128

Manual: NCUABBS.TXT
(it's excellent)

To access files: At the Main Menu type **f**

Time limit: 2 hours per day

- The full text of a manual for credit union examiners.

- The full text of various rules and regulations. Sample titles include "Organizing a Federal Credit Union," "Mergers of Federally Insured CUs," and "Trustees and Custodians of Pension Plans."

- The full text of the Truth in Savings Act. However, like some other files on this board, it is compressed in a self-executing format that makes it unusable on most Macintosh computers.

- The full text of the Federal Credit Union Act.

- A bylaw document titled "Operations Following an Attack on the U.S."

- The full text of the "Supervisory Committee Manual."

- Opinion letters from the NCUA legal department dating back to January 1989.

- News about proposed legislation that would affect credit unions.

- A list of phone numbers at NCUA headquarters.

USBM-BBS

Bureau of Mines
U.S. Department of the Interior
Mail Stop 9800
810 7th St., N.W.
Washington, DC 20241-0002

Detailed data about mineral availability, demand, and production is available on the Bureau of Mines bulletin board.

The board offers a number of bulletins, which you can access by typing **b** at the Main Menu. Four bulletins, numbers 2, 6, 7, and 9, are particularly useful:

2. A user's guide for the board.

6. A list of commodity specialists at the Bureau of Mines, listed by mineral. Their telephone numbers are included.

7. A list of country specialists at the Bureau of Mines, listed by foreign country. Their telephone numbers are included.

9. A description of a free service that you can call to get current information about minerals delivered to your fax machine.

The files, which you can reach by typing **f** at the Main Menu, offer the following types of information:

- Data on mineral production, availability, and demand, listed by mineral. Data are available for dozens of minerals.

- Information about technology transfer that describes technical research regarding mining.

- A list of software programs and databases developed by the Bureau of Mines. Contact information is listed for each product.

- Monthly lists of Bureau of Mines publications and articles written by BOM personnel in non-BOM publications.

- Story tips for reporters.

VITAL STATS
Data: 202-501-0373
Voice: 202-501-0406
FedWorld gateway: 4
To access files: At the Main Menu type **f**

Centralized Electronic Filing Bulletin Board System

Internal Revenue Service
Stop 21
P.O. Box 12267
Covington, KY 41011

The Centralized Electronic Filing Bulletin Board System is aimed at developers of tax preparation software and tax preparation firms that file electronically. It has technical specifications and documents for these two audiences. The board contains no information for individuals who wish to file electronic tax returns.

VITAL STATS
Data: 606-292-0137
Voice: 606-292-5031
Time limit: 60 minutes per
    call

Information Systems Support BBS

Internal Revenue Service
1111 Constitution Ave., N.W.
Washington, DC 20224

The Information Systems Support BBS has hundreds of Internal Revenue Service tax forms and instructions. The documents are in Portable Document Format (PDF). You can view and print them with software that supports PDF, such as Adobe Acrobat Reader. Adobe Acrobat Reader software for Windows is available on the board, and Macintosh users can get a Mac version of the software from IRIS (see next entry).

In addition to tax forms, the board offers information about how to get recorded IRS tax information by telephone, a list of toll-free IRS telephone numbers, and descriptions of IRS publications, along with ordering information.

The board also has hundreds of shareware and freeware software programs related to OS/2, Windows, Unix, and databases.

VITAL STATS

Data: 202-219-9835

Voice: 202-501-4700, ext. 5173

FedWorld gateway: 5

To access files: At the Main Menu type **I**

IRIS (Internal Revenue Information Services)

National Technical Information Service
5285 Port Royal Road
Springfield, VA 22161

IRIS offers more than 500 tax forms, instructions, and publications from the Internal Revenue Service for individuals, businesses, and other organizations. You can download the tax forms, print them, fill them out, and send them to the IRS, but you cannot fill out the forms online and file electronically.

Most documents on the board, including the tax forms, are available in three formats: Portable Document Format (PDF), Printer Control Language (PCL), and PostScript Language (PS). The informational publications are also available in Standard Generalized Markup Language (SGML).

If this is all Greek to you, don't worry. You can download free Acrobat Reader software from the board that lets you read and print PDF files. The software is available for Windows and Macintosh computers.

VITAL STATS
Data: 703-321-8020
Voice: 703-487-4608
FedWorld gateway: 142
Login: **guest**

IRP-BBS

Internal Revenue Service
Information Reporting Program
Martinsburg Computing Center
P.O. Box 1359
Martinsburg, WV 25401

The IRP-BBS is aimed at businesses that must file information returns with the Internal Revenue Service. For example, if a bank pays you more than a certain amount of interest, it must file an information return telling the IRS about the payment.

The BBS has publications about how to file forms 1098, 1099, 5498, and W-2G electronically or on magnetic tape; how to report IRA contributions and distributions; vendors that provide products or services related to electronic filing of information returns; and similar information. It also has some publications from the Social Security Administration about how to file forms electronically and electronic copies of the *SSA/IRS Reporter*, a newsletter for employers. Businesses also can file IRS information returns through the BBS.

VITAL STATS

Data: 304-263-2749

Voice: 304-263-8700

Note: You may need to experiment with the terminal setting in your communications software. A setting of TTY works well.

IRS Statistics of Income Division Bulletin Board

IRS-SOI Division
Foreign Operations Section
Internal Revenue Service
P.O. Box 2608
Washington, DC 20013-2608

The IRS Statistics of Income Division Bulletin Board provides hundreds of files containing aggregate statistics from individual, corporate, and foundation tax returns. The board contains no tax information for specific persons or corporations. Unfortunately, nearly all of the files have been compressed in a self-extracting format that makes them unusable on most Macintosh computers.

Here are some examples of the information available:

- Individual income and tax data by state.

- Individual income returns by adjusted gross income.

- Highlights of corporate income tax returns by year.

- Highlights of tax returns for U.S. corporations controlled by foreign owners.

- Selected income and balance sheet items for tax-exempt organizations.

- Balance sheets and income statements for private foundations.

- Projections of the number of returns that will be filed with the IRS through 2001.

- A list of publications and data tapes produced by the Statistics of Income division.

- The full text of the *Commissioner's Annual Report.*

VITAL STATS

Data: 202-874-9574

Voice: 202-874-0277 or
202-874-0273

FedWorld gateway: 104

File list: FILELST.TXT
(uncompressed) or
FILELST.EXE (compressed in a self-extracting format that's unusable on most Macintosh computers)

To access files: At the Main Menu type **f**

Magnetic Media Bulletin Board System

Internal Revenue Service
Philadelphia Service Center
11601 Roosevelt Blvd.
Philadelphia, PA 19255

Businesses can use the Magnetic Media Bulletin Board System to upload electronic copies of IRS forms 940, 941, 941E, 1040NR, and 1041 to the Philadelphia Service Center. These forms include the Employer's Annual Federal Unemployment Tax Return, the Employer's Quarterly Federal Tax Return, and the Quarterly Return of Withheld Federal Income Tax and Medicare Tax, among others. Individuals cannot use the board to upload tax returns.

The board also contains information about how to file the forms electronically. To access this information, type **i** at the Main Menu.

VITAL STATS
Data: 215-516-7625
Voice: 800-829-6945

COMPUTERS

Ada Information Clearinghouse

c/o IIT Research Institute
P.O. Box 1866
Falls Church, VA 22041

The Ada Information Clearinghouse has anything and everything you ever wanted to know about Ada, a high-level programming language developed by the Defense Department that's used in military programming applications. The system is operated by a private company under a Defense Department contract.

Despite its wealth of resources, this system is extremely easy to use because with dial-in access you connect to a Gopher. The system offers Ada compilers, evaluation test suites, development tools, reports, bibliographies, education and training resources, utilities, source code, Ada standards, and much more.

VITAL STATS

Data: 703-681-2845

Voice: 800-232-4211 or
703-681-2466

Login: **guest**

Password: **Ada4sw-eng**

Internet: gopher sw-eng.
falls-church.va.us
or http://sw-eng.
falls-church.va.us

E-mail: adainfo@sw-eng.
falls-church.va.us

Ada Technical Support Bulletin Board System

Code N912.4
NCTAMS LANT
9456 Fourth Ave.
Suite 200
Norfolk, VA 23511-2199

Ada programmers and software engineers are the target audience for the Ada Technical Support Bulletin Board System. Among other features, the board offers:

- A files area that contains software for Ada programmers.

- An area where programmers can leave questions about the Ada language and get answers from the BBS staff.

- News items about Ada.

- A lengthy list of books about Ada.

- Ada product descriptions supplied by vendors.

VITAL STATS
Data: 804-444-7841
Voice: 804-444-4680
Manual: BBSGUIDE.TXT
To access files: At the Main
 Menu type **f**
Time limit: 2 hours per day

Air Force CALS Test Bed BBS

DET2HQ ESC/ENC
Suite 300
4027 Col. Glenn Highway
Dayton, OH 45431-1601

The Air Force CALS Test Bed BBS has information about CALS (Continuous Acquisition and Lifecycle Support), which is a government initiative to standardize digital text and graphics information. The board offers all of the CALS standards, files about the text and graphics standards, and test reports.

VITAL STATS
Data: 513-476-1273
Voice: 513-427-5869,
    ext. 351

Data Distribution System

Attn: CECPW-FM
Kingman Building, Room 2B10
Fort Belvoir, VA 22060-5516

The Data Distribution System supports users of two Army computer systems: the Housing Office Management System (HOMES) and the Integrated Facilities System Mini-micro (IFS-M). The board contains files and messages relating to these two systems. It also has a very small collection of DOS and Windows utilities.

VITAL STATS
Data: 703-355-3471
Voice: 703-355-0073
FedWorld gateway: 30
Internet: telnet 160.147.90.
240

NIST Computer Security Resource Clearinghouse

National Institute of Standards and Technology
U.S. Department of Commerce
Building 225
Gaithersburg, MD 20899

Virtually anyone who uses a computer will find interesting and valuable information at the NIST Computer Security Resource Clearinghouse. It contains hundreds of files about computer security—everything from detailed reviews of all the major anti-virus products for DOS and Macintosh computers to software to use in securing Unix systems.

If you use dial-in access, you are connected to the Clearinghouse's World Wide Web site rather than a traditional BBS interface. This allows you to link into other sites on the Web even if you don't have an Internet account.

Here are some highlights of what's available:

- Computer security alerts that describe new computer viruses. The alerts are usually posted long before the information appears in major computer publications.

- Detailed reviews of virtually every major anti-virus product for computers.

- A list of all the computer security publications produced by the National Institute of Standards and Technology.

- An NIST publication titled *Keeping Your Site Comfortably Secure: An Introduction to Internet Firewalls.*

- A calendar of computer security events.

- Links to other Internet sites around the world that offer computer security information.

- Current and historical reports about various types of computer viruses.

- Computer security policy documents, primarily from the Department of Commerce and the Office of Management and Budget.

- Federal guidelines from the Justice Department titled "Searching and Seizing Computers."

VITAL STATS

Data: 301-948-5717 or
    301-948-5140

Voice: 301-975-3359

FedWorld gateway: 10

Internet: gopher csrc.ncsl.
    nist.gov *or* http://csrc.
    ncsl.nist.gov *or* ftp
    csrc.ncsl.nist.gov

Login (FTP only): **anonymous**

Password (FTP only): your
    e-mail address

E-mail: webmaster@csrc.
    ncsl.nist.gov

- Digests from the PRIVACY Forum, an Internet mailing list about privacy in the information age.

- Digests from Risks-Forum, an Internet mailing list about risks to the public from computers and related systems.

- Digests from VIRUS-L, an Internet mailing list about computer viruses.

- Software to use in securing Unix systems.

- The text of the Computer Security Act of 1987.

CNSP/CNAP Bulletin Board

PRC Inc.
Suite 200
4065 Hancock
San Diego, CA 92110

The CNSP/CNAP Bulletin Board, which is operated for the Navy by a contractor, has thousands of shareware and freeware programs for DOS and Windows computers. There are no programs for Macintosh computers, and there are only a handful of files about Navy issues.

The board has a major flaw: its telephone lines are defective, which can cause lots of difficulties in connecting. If your first attempt at connecting fails, try a few more times.

There are two major file areas on this board. The first, which you can access by typing **f** at the Main Menu, contains hundreds of DOS and Windows programs separated into more than three dozen directories. A few of the directories contain a handful of Navy documents, but nothing very exciting.

The second file area offers the 12th and 14th editions of the PC-SIG CD-ROM, which contain thousands of freeware and shareware programs for DOS and Windows computers. The CD-ROMs are published by a private California company. To reach them, type **j** at the Main Menu, **10** at the "Conference # to join" prompt, and finally **f.**

The board also has conferences about Windows, operating systems, hardware, software, Navy issues, virus information, contracts, and a few other topics. These conferences serve as collection areas for messages on the topic. You an access them by typing **j** at the Main Menu.

VITAL STATS
Data: 619-556-0135 or
619-556-0136
Voice: 619-236-9083
File lists: PCBFILES.LST
and PC-SIG.ZIP

HSETC BBS

Naval Health Science Education and Training Command
Building 1, Room 1710, Code 33
8901 Wisconsin Ave.
Bethesda, MD 20889-5612

The HSETC BBS is difficult to use because of its poor design. It has numerous bulletins for people who work in the Naval Health Science Education and Training Command, along with a collection of utility programs for DOS computers. However, many of the programs are at least several years old.

VITAL STATS
Data: 301-295-3917
Voice: 301-295-2373
FedWorld gateway: 92

Judge Advocate General's Information Network (JAGNET)

JAGNET Information Center
U.S. Department of the Navy
200 Stovall St.
Alexandria, VA 22332-2400

Although JAGNET is primarily aimed at the U.S. Navy legal community, most of it is also open to the public. The board contains no files about activities of the Navy Judge Advocate General.

For the general user, the board's greatest strength is its collection of hundreds of shareware utilities and programs. These include a wide range of programs for word processing, communications, and graphics. There are even a few games. The board only includes programs for DOS computers.

File Directory 9 contains several files of general interest:

FED-EVID.ZIP The Federal Rules of Evidence in ASCII text.

FEDRCIVP.ZIP The Federal Rules of Civil Procedure.

NAVABB.ZIP A huge list of Navy acronyms and abbreviations.

NWP9A001.ZIP The first of three files providing the Annotated Supplement to the Law of Naval Operations.

SEXHNDBK.ZIP The full text of the *Commander's Handbook on the Prevention of Sexual Harassment.*

USCONST.ZIP The U.S. Constitution in ASCII text.

VITAL STATS

Data: 703-325-0748

Voice: 703-325-2924

FedWorld gateway: 25

File list: JAGNET.ZIP

To access files: At the Main Menu type **f**

DEFENSE

Navy Leadership Policy Bulletin Board (NLPBB)

Navy Office of Information
Code OI-5
Washington, DC 20350-1200

The Navy Public Affairs Library offers hundreds of files, including press releases, speeches, policies, and other documents regarding the Defense Department budget, women in the military, defense readiness, World War II, and other topics.

Here are some highlights of what's available:

- The Navy's *Handbook on Sexual Harassment.*

- Fact sheets about women in the Navy.

- Speeches and congressional testimony by Defense Department officials.

- Numerous documents about the proposed Navy and Defense Department budgets.

- Information about defense readiness.

- Numerous Navy policies, in addition to the full text of the *Navy Policy Book.*

- Lists of Navy ships.

- Information about how to find former shipmates.

- Articles from the Navy News Service.

- Articles from the Navy Wire Service Daily and the Navy Wire Service Weekly.

- Information about the Navy and Navy ships and submarines, aircraft, and weapons taken from the *Navy Fact File.*

- Dozens of files with excellent information about various aspects of World War II, including blimps, kamikazes, the Battle of the Atlantic, and the cracking of the Japanese naval code.

- Lists of flag officer promotions.

- Navy medical news.

- A directory of Navy public affairs officers.

VITAL STATS

Data: 800-582-2355, 800-582-6940, 703-695-6198, 703-695-6388, 703-697-2442, 703-697-2446

Voice: 703-695-5471

Time limit: 30 minutes per call

Internet: http://www.navy.mil *or* ftp ftp.ncts.navy.mil

Login (FTP only): **anonymous**

Password (FTP only): your e-mail address

Path (FTP only): *pub/navpalib*

E-mail: navpalib@opnav-emh.navy.mil

U.S. Arms Control and Disarmament Agency BBS

U.S. Arms Control and Disarmament Agency
320 21st St., N.W.
Washington, DC 20451

The U.S. Arms Control and Disarmament Agency BBS has hundreds of documents about arms control and nonproliferation issues. There are documents about nuclear weapons, chemical weapons, and biological weapons, among others.

The board has a chronology of key events in the control of chemical weapons from 1925 to 1989, information about U.S. export control laws relating to chemical weapons, the agreement between the United States and North Korea about the dismantling of North Korea's nuclear weapons program, numerous speeches by U.S. officials about treaties and arms control, and related documents.

VITAL STATS:
Data: 202-736-4436
Voice: 202-647-8677
FedWorld gateway: 120
To access files: At the Main
     Menu type **p**

VA ONLINE

Department of Veterans Affairs
810 Vermont Ave., N.W.
Washington, DC 20420

VA ONLINE offers extensive information about benefits available to active duty military personnel and veterans, in addition to numerous files for veterans who served in the Persian Gulf War. It is operated by the Department of Veterans Affairs, known more commonly as the VA.

One of the system's highlights is a searchable database that includes all of the names inscribed on the Vietnam Memorial in Washington, D.C. You can search the database by last name and by state. For each name, the database lists the date of birth, date of death, rank, branch, hometown, state of residence, and location of the name on the Vietnam Memorial.

Here are some other highlights of what's available:

- Numerous files about benefits available to active duty and retired military personnel, including insurance, education programs, home loans, survivors' benefits, burial benefits, disability compensation, disability pensions, and vocational rehabilitation programs.

- A publication titled *Federal Benefits for Veterans and Dependents.*

- Information about women veterans issues, including counseling and treatment for sexual trauma experienced while on active duty.

- Several files for veterans of the Persian Gulf War that discuss benefits available, health research, and Persian Gulf Syndrome.

- A monthly publication called the *Persian Gulf Review Newsletter.*

- A list of toll-free telephone numbers at the Department of Veterans Affairs.

- A list of addresses and telephone numbers for regional Department of Veterans Affairs offices around the country.

VITAL STATS

Data: 800-871-8387 or 301-427-3000

Voice: Telephone support is not provided

Available: 24 hours a day except from 6 a.m. to 7 a.m. EST Monday through Friday

Internet: telnet vaonline.va.gov *or* ftp vaonline.va.gov

Note: You must first register through the dial-in or Telnet connections before you can access the FTP site

- Extensive information about military cemeteries, including a directory of cemeteries and information about how to qualify for burial in a military cemetery.

- Statistical data about veterans from the National Center for Veteran Analysis and Statistics.

- Information from *The Journal of Rehabilitation Research and Development,* which is published by the Department of Veterans Affairs.

- Press releases from the VA.

- Speeches by VA officials.

EDUCATION

FEDIX and MOLIS

Federal Information Exchange
Suite 200
555 Quince Orchard Rd.
Gaithersburg, MD 20878

The FEDIX/MOLIS system, which is operated by a private firm under contract to a number of government agencies, offers information about federal programs aimed at assisting colleges and universities and their students.

If you use dial-in access, you connect to the FEDIX/MOLIS World Wide Web site instead of a traditional BBS interface. This makes the system quite easy to use (especially when compared with the old FEDIX/MOLIS BBS, which was awful). However, there is a bug: When you try to quit the system, you are returned to the initial login screen. To disconnect, you have to hang up your phone.

The system provides information about:

VITAL STATS

Data: 800-783-3349 or
    301-258-0953
Voice: 301-975-0103
FedWorld gateway: 52
Internet: http://www.fie.
    com *or* telnet fedix.fie.
    com
E-mail: comments@fedix.
    fie.com

- Education and research programs.

- Scholarships, fellowships, and grants.

- Used government research equipment available for sale.

- The availability of funding for specific research and education activities.

- Minority research and education programs.

- Procurement notices.

The system also provides extensive information about historically black colleges and universities and historically Hispanic colleges and universities, in addition to files about college and university programs, special services, and financial assistance for minorities and women.

LingNet

Defense Language Institute, Foreign Language Center
Attn: OPP-PP (LingNet)
Presidio of Monterey, CA 93944

LingNet offers an incredible collection of programs and files to help you learn foreign languages—everything from Chinese to Estonian to Russian to Vietnamese. The system also offers basic information about some foreign countries. It's run by the Foreign Language Center at the Defense Language Institute.

You must register online through the dial-in or Telnet systems to receive access to LingNet. Normally, you will receive full privileges within twenty-four hours. This registration must be completed before you can access the FTP site.

The freeware and shareware programs on the board are designed to run on DOS and Windows computers. However, the sysop reports that he will soon start adding programs for Macintosh computers.

Here are some highlights from among the hundreds of files:

- A computer program to help you learn Russian, a Russian dictionary, a Russian tutor program, a Russian word processor, and Russian fonts for Windows.

- A map of Moscow's subway system.

- A list of addresses and telephone numbers for bookstores in Russia.

- Lists of Russian BBSs and World Wide Web sites.

- Modules to use with the Intext word processor, which is available on the board. The modules are for Arabic, Farsi, Greek, Hebrew, Polish, Russian, Turkish, Urdu, Yugoslavian, and several European languages.

- A Windows programs to help you learn French, German, Spanish, or Italian.

- The Army Area Handbook for the Philippines.

- A program to help you learn advanced English.

VITAL STATS

Data: 408-242-6120

Voice: 408-242-5180

Username (dial-in only): **lingnet**

To access files: At the Main Menu type **f**

Internet: telnet lingnet.army.mil *or* ftp lingnet.army.mil

Login (FTP only): your name

Password (FTP only): your password from the dial-in or Telnet systems

E-mail: lloydr@pom-emh2.army.mil

- A Hebrew word processing program.

- Arabic reading comprehension exercises and an Arabic word processor.

- A world statistical atlas.

- A Japanese flashcard program, a Japanese language tutor, a Japanese word processor, and a Japanese/English dictionary.

- Information about the Japanese business culture and a file about Japanese for business and travel.

- A Chinese text utility, Chinese word processing programs, a Chinese character text editor, a program that teaches basic Chinese calligraphy, and a program to help you learn spoken Cantonese Chinese.

- The full text of the *CIA World Factbook*.

- A list of commercial vendors of language products that includes descriptions of their materials.

- A Croatian-English translator and dictionary.

- A DOS word processor for Thai.

- A Cyrillic word processing program and Cyrillic fonts.

- A list of sources for foreign language dictionaries.

- A list of codes used on diplomatic license plates in Washington, D.C.

- A French translator and word processor.

- A Spanish translator program.

- Fonts for twenty-three European languages, including Albanian, Croatian, Czech, Danish, Estonian, French, German, Italian, Polish, Slovak, and Turkish, among others.

- A list of Croatian and Slovenian BBSs.

- An interactive program to help you learn Spanish, Spanish flash cards, a Spanish tutorial, and a Spanish translation program.

- Vietnamese fonts and a Vietnamese word processing program.

- Schedules of Voice of America broadcasts, by frequency and language.

NIH EDNET

Office of Education
National Institutes of Health
Building 10, Room 1C129
Bethesda, MD 20892

NIH EDNET is primarily designed to allow students and teachers to communicate with scientists at the National Institutes of Health (NIH). The board also has a single file that lists health-related topics and corresponding telephone numbers at NIH.

Accessing the board requires a few steps, which vary depending on the access method you use:

1. **Dial-in**   After you connect, type **,vt100** (the comma is essential) and press your Enter key. You won't be prompted to do this. At the "Initials?" prompt, type **nak** and press Enter. At the "Account?" prompt, type **zzyz** and press Enter.

2. **Telnet**   At the "Enter Command" prompt, type **logon 3270** and press your Enter key. At the "Initials?" prompt, type **nak** and press Enter. At the "Account?" prompt, type **zzyz** and press Enter.

The board offers seven conferences that contain messages on specific topics:

Speakers   A list of topics that NIH employees can speak about at high schools. Teachers can use the conference to request speakers for their classrooms.

Resource   Messages describing educational materials and resources available to teachers and students.

Forum   A conference for students, teachers, scientists, educators, and others interested in biomedical sciences topics. Students and teachers can leave questions for NIH scientists.

VITAL STATS

Data: 800-358-2221 or 301-402-2221 (see login instructions in the description)

Voice: 301-402-1708

Internet: telnet tn3270.cu.nih.gov (see login instructions in the description)

Note: Dial-in users will have to experiment with the terminal setting in their communications software. A setting of VT100 works well. Also, your software must be set to even parity, 7 data bits, 1 stop bit, and half duplex (or local echo).

HHMIMCPS   A conference for participants in the HHMI/MCPS/NIH Student/Teacher Internship Program, which is open to students and teachers in the Montgomery County Public Schools in Maryland.

OE-News   Messages describing new educational and recruitment programs of interest to NIH employees.

Postdoc   Messages listing available positions for postdoctoral training.

ORWHnews   Messages about seminars, meetings, publications, and research and career development opportunities sponsored by the Office of Research on Women's Health.

OERI Bulletin Board System

Office of Educational Research Improvement
U.S. Department of Education
555 New Jersey Ave., N.W.
Washington, DC 20208-5725

Anything and everything you ever wanted to know about education is located somewhere on the OERI Bulletin Board System. It has two strengths: (1) hundreds of files of statistics about education and (2) hundreds of shareware and public domain education programs that teachers or parents can use with children. The board is operated by the Office of Educational Research Improvement, the primary research agency at the Department of Education.

The board is so popular (and has so few telephone lines) that it's extremely difficult to get a dial-in connection. If you have an Internet account, you can save yourself time and aggravation by accessing the Internet site instead of the BBS.

The board has several thousand files, which are divided into more than twenty directories. You can access the files by typing **I** at the Main Menu. Here are some highlights of what's available:

- A guide to Department of Education programs that describes funding available from federal education programs.

- Hundreds of ERIC Digests, which are brief reports on a variety of topics from the ERIC Clearinghouse on Reading and Communication Skills. Some titles include "Educating the Consumer About Advertising," "Computer Uses in Secondary Science Education," "School Role in Sexual Abuse Prevention," and "Teaching Students to View TV Critically." Each report includes a bibliography.

- A huge collection of statistics about public libraries nationwide.

- Electronic copies of brochures called "Help Your Child Learn to Write Well," "Helping Your Child Improve in Test-Taking," and "Helping Your Child Learn Science."

VITAL STATS

Data: 800-222-4922 or
   202-219-1511

Voice: 202-219-1526

To access files: At the Main
   Menu type **I**

Internet: gopher
   gopher.ed.gov *or*
   http://www.ed.gov *or*
   ftp ftp.ed.gov

Login (FTP only): **anonymous**

Password (FTP only): your
   e-mail address

- An electronic copy of *Educational Programs That Work,* a report that describes successful education programs around the country. A print version of the report costs $14.95, but you can download the electronic version for free.

- The *Digest of Education Statistics,* which has nearly 400 tables of education statistics. It provides data on school enrollment, dropouts, spending on schools, items most frequently cited by the public as major problems facing local public schools, pupil-teacher ratios and expenditures in public schools from 1960-1961 to 1990-1991, average teacher salaries for 1969-1970 to 1990-1991, administrative roadblocks reported by secondary school principals from 1965 to 1987, participation by high school seniors in extracurricular activities, trends in drug use by high school seniors from 1975 to 1989, revenues for public schools from 1919-1920 to 1988-1989, state spending on education from 1959-1960 to 1990-1991, selected statistics for historically black colleges and universities, trends in faculty salaries at colleges and universities, changes in scores on the Graduate Record Examination from 1964 to 1988, average undergraduate tuition and fees from 1964-1965 to 1989-1990, and international comparisons of education, among other subjects.

- The *OERI Bulletin,* which discusses information, publications, and data sets generated by the Office of Educational Research Improvement, as well as events sponsored by OERI.

- Projected education statistics on the national and state levels to the year 2002.

- Hundreds of shareware and public domain education programs for computers. While the largest number of programs work with IBM and compatible computers, the board also has smaller numbers of programs for Commodore, Atari, Tandy, and Apple computers. The programs include math and vocabulary games, programs that use PC speakers to teach children to count, a talking program that teaches children their ABCs, a geography test, a program that teaches anatomy, astronomy-related programs, library card catalog programs, a vocational program for culinary arts, chemistry drills, gradebook and attendance programs, a planetarium simulator, the periodic chart of the elements, American history quizzes, typing practice programs, an SAT verbal prep program, virus checkers, spelling programs, test writing programs, a Civil War timeline, the U.S. Constitution with amendments, and word processors for children.

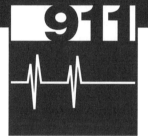

EMERGENCY RESPONSE AND FIRE SAFETY

Fire Research Laboratory Bulletin Board System

Building and Fire Research Laboratory
Building 224, Room A245
National Institute of Standards and Technology
Gaithersburg, MD 20899

The Fire Research Laboratory BBS specializes in technical information about fire research. Besides files, the board offers forums where users can exchange messages about fire-related issues.

Here are some highlights of what's available:

- Fire simulation programs developed or sponsored by the Building and Fire Research Laboratory. The programs, which only run on DOS computers, simulate the effects of fire in one room, simulate the activation of smoke detectors and sprinklers, model fire evacuations, model fire suppression, and provide related information.

- Lists of fire safety experts at the National Institute of Standards and Technology.

- Calendars of conferences.

- Information about fire research.

ITAL STATS

Data: 301-990-2272

Voice: 301-975-6862

To access files: At the Main Menu type **f**

Time limit: 30 minutes per call, 45 minutes per day

E-mail: birder@enh.nist.gov

Hazardous Materials Information Exchange (HMIX)

Federal Emergency
  Management Agency
Preparedness, Training, and
  Exercises Directorate
Preparedness Division
500 C St., S.W.
Washington, DC 20472

Department of Transportation
Research and Special Programs
  Administration
Office of Hazardous Materials
  Initiatives and Training
400 7th St., S.W.
Washington, DC 20590

HMIX provides information about numerous hazardous materials topics, including emergency management, training, resources, technical assistance, and regulations. Much of the material on the board is quite technical.

To access most of the files you must type **j** at the Main Menu for "Join a topic." Each of the more than two dozen topics has its own menu and file directory. Here are some highlights of what's available:

- Information about training in incident response, emergency preparedness, enforcement, and motor carrier safety offered by the Federal Emergency Management Agency, the Department of Transportation, the Department of Energy, the Occupational Safety and Health Administration, and the Environmental Protection Agency.

- A calendar of conferences.

- Lists of instructional literature, videos, software, and newsletters about fire protection and prevention, training, transportation, laws and regulations, emergency management and response, emergency medicine and decontamination, industrial hygiene and worker safety, and waste management.

- Information about toll-free technical assistance available from the federal and state governments, in addition to lists of federal, state, commercial, and private on-line databases and hazardous materials bulletin boards.

VITAL STATS

Data: 800-874-2884 (for state and local government officials only) or 708-252-3275 (for the public)

Voice: 800-752-6367 (800-367-9592 in Illinois)

FedWorld gateway: 143

Internet: telnet hmix.dis.anl.gov

Manual: GUIDE.TXT (ASCII text) or GUIDE.WP (WordPerfect). It's excellent.

File list: PCBFILES.LST

To access files: At the Main Menu type **j**

Time limit: 30 minutes per call

- Various laws and regulations from the Department of Transportation, the Environmental Protection Agency, the Occupational Safety and Health Administration, and other agencies.

- Lists of contacts at federal agencies, professional associations, trade associations, research centers, and environmental groups.

- A variety of materials about Department of Transportation programs, including the Motor Carrier Safety Program and hazardous materials program.

- Files for each Environmental Protection Agency region, including a regional calendar, news items, transportation and emergency response contacts, a list of Local Emergency Planning Committee contacts, and lists of training courses offered by private groups, state training offices, colleges and universities, and local agencies.

- Information about upcoming international meetings relating to transportation of dangerous goods.

- Information about the National Task Force on Hazardous Materials Emergency Preparedness.

- A list of resources on firefighting and emergency medical services (EMS), federal rules and regulations affecting firefighting and EMS, and related information.

OEPC BBS

Office of Environmental Policy and Compliance
U.S. Department of the Interior
Mail Stop 2340
1849 C Street, N.W.
Washington, DC 20240

The OEPC BBS specializes in environmental compliance information for industry. It is operated by the Interior Department's Office of Environmental Policy and Compliance.

Here are some highlights of what's available:

- Dozens of case studies of pollution prevention programs instituted by various companies.

- A report from the Environmental Protection Agency titled *Pollution Prevention Survey of the Organic Chemical Manufacturing Industry.*

- A document from the Defense Department titled *Environmentally Preferred Products Catalogue,* which lists more than 300 alternative chemicals and cleaners to use instead of substances which contain ozone-depleting substances and other hazardous materials.

- A file titled *Catalogue of Federal Agency Environmental Compliance Management Documents,* which summarizes documents from a wide variety of agencies. The file is a guide to existing information and guidance on environmental compliance and management topics.

VITAL STATS

Data: 202-208-7119 and
202-501-6946

Voice: 202-208-7555

FedWorld gateway: 80

File list: ALLFILES.ZIP

To access files: At the Main
Menu type **f**

Time limit: One hour per
day

State and Local Emergency Management Data Users Group (SALEMDUG) BBS

Argonne National Laboratory
Building 900
9700 S. Cass Ave.
Argonne, IL 60439

The SALEMDUG BBS is aimed at emergency management personnel at the national, state, and local levels. It is operated by Argonne National Laboratory for the Federal Emergency Management Agency (FEMA).

The board has more than two dozen conferences, which you can access by typing **j** at the Main Menu. They serve as collection points for messages about dam safety, emergency medical services, fire prevention and safety, law enforcement, search and rescue, and hazardous waste issues, among others.

Here are highlights from the six file directories:

1. **Emergency Management**   Information about radio and TV stations, civil preparedness agencies, hospitals, medical personnel, shelters, nuclear reactors, airports, dam safety, highway structures, wholesale businesses, and crisis relocation in south Florida; a series of reports about Hurricane Andrew; copies of *Disaster Research News;* an emergency management plan for Texas; copies of *EmergencyNet NEWS;* a shareware personnel, training, and equipment database organizer for fire departments; a special report about the Midwest flooding; a list of major high-rise fires in the twentieth century; two DOS programs for tracking hurricanes; a list of earthquakes in Oklahoma from 1897 through 1993; a list of state police frequencies around the country; a list of federal government frequencies; and FEMA situation reports on Hurricane Emily and Midwest flooding.

2. **Communications**   A list of citizens band frequencies, communications programs for DOS and Windows, and a utility program for checking modems.

3. **Utilities**   Dozens of utility programs, primarily for DOS computers. However, there also are a few Windows and Macintosh utilities.

4. **FEMA Publications**   Various FEMA fact sheets and publications, including "Emergency Preparedness Checklist," "Helping Children Cope with Disaster," "Checklist for People with Mobility Problems," "Your Family Disaster Supplies Kit," "Emergency Food and Water Supplies," and "Your Family Disaster Plan."

5. **General**   A wide range of programs, primarily for DOS and Windows. These range from a meal planning and grocery shopping program to a personal information manager.

6. **Recent uploads**   An automated telephone directory for the Federal Emergency Management Agency and various utility programs and games for DOS and Windows.

ENERGY

Bibliographic Retrieval System (BRS)

U.S. Nuclear Regulatory Commission
Public Document Room
Washington, DC 20555

The Bibliographic Retrieval System is a huge database that contains bibliographic references to reports about the licensing and inspection of nuclear power plants and other facilities regulated by the Nuclear Regulatory Commission (NRC).

As this book was being written, NRC librarians were adding thousands of full-text documents to the BRS. These documents, which were being transferred from another NRC database system called NUDOCS, include minutes from meetings of various NRC panels, inspection notices, generic letters, press releases, congressional correspondence, and related materials. The full-text documents do not include inspection reports for individual nuclear power plants, although the BRS does have bibliographic references for inspection reports. If you want to check up on events at your local nuclear power plant, you have two options:

1. Obtain bibliographic information for inspection reports from the BRS, and then travel to the Public Document Room for your local plant (the local PDR is usually housed at a public or university library) to look at the paper documents.

2. Check out the files at the Nuclear Regulatory Commission at FedWorld (p. 162), which has daily reports of unexpected events at nuclear power plants, preliminary notifications of problems, and reports about the status of operating nuclear plants.

While the NRC is best known for regulating nuclear power plants, it also oversees companies that process, transport, and handle nuclear materials and nuclear waste. For example, it regulates hospitals' use of nuclear materials in radiation treatments. Bibliographic references to documents about the licensing of these firms are also included in the BRS.

Because the BRS is a huge database, it is more difficult to use than a typical BBS. However, if you have any interest in the regulation of nuclear power plants and other facilities that use nuclear materials, it's well worth learning how to use the database.

To gain access to the BRS, you must call, fax, or send a letter to the NRC's Public Document Room. The NRC will send you a form to fill out, and after you return it you'll receive a password, an extensive manual, and other materials.

The NRC offers free BRS training in Washington, D.C., which it strongly encourages users to attend. The database also has an online tutorial for those who cannot travel to Washington.

Department of Energy Home Page

U.S. Department of Energy
Office of Scientific and Technical Information
175 Oak Ridge Turnpike
Oak Ridge, TN 37831

The Department of Energy Home Page provides links to dozens of Internet sites operated by DOE laboratories and field offices around the country.

If you access the site through a dial-in connection, you actually reach the Department of Energy's World Wide Web site. This allows you to link into all of the department's other Internet sites around the country using the Web interface even if you don't have an Internet connection.

Besides the links, the site offers access to the OpenNet database, which contains bibliographic references to more than 250,000 declassified documents about human radiation experiments, nuclear testing, radiation releases, fallout, and related topics. Each reference includes information about how to obtain the paper document.

The site also provides speeches by the secretary of energy, limited information about human radiation experiments, DOE press releases, and historical information about the department and its predecessor agencies.

VITAL STATS

Data: 615-241-3901

Voice: 615-576-1088

Login: (dial-in and Telnet only): **www**

Internet: http://www.doe. gov *or* telnet cupid. osti.gov

E-mail: webmaster@apollo. osti.gov

Note: After connecting with a dial-in connection, you may need to hit your Enter key a few times to reach a prompt

Energy Ideas Clearinghouse BBS

925 Plum Street, S.E.
Olympia, WA 98504-3171

The Energy Ideas Clearinghouse BBS has information about energy efficiency in the commercial and industrial sectors. Access to the board is limited to energy professionals and students in accredited energy-related college or university programs, although anyone can access the World Wide Web site. The BBS is managed by the Washington State Energy Office, with funding from the Bonneville Power Administration, the Western Area Power Administration, and the U.S. Department of Energy.

Here are some highlights of what's available:

- Nearly 1,000 files, which you can access by typing **s** at the Main Menu. There are documents about computer-aided drafting, energy accounting software, proceedings of the California Public Utility Commission, databases from the California Energy Commission, energy codes and related documents, files about hydropower, newsletters on energy and environment issues, files and newsletters about wind energy, and much more.

- More than seventy-five forums where users can exchange messages on specific topics. To access the forums, type **f** at the main menu. There are forums on computer-aided drafting, agriculture energy issues, energy codes, environmental energy issues, electric vehicles, low income home energy assistance programs, indoor air quality, energy-related software, sustainability, and natural gas issues, among other subjects.

- Databases that list training classes, resumés, and jobs.

VITAL STATS

Data: 800-762-3319 (in Washington, Oregon, Idaho, and Montana), 800-797-7584 (in other western states), 360-586-6854 (in other states)

Voice: 360-956-2237

Available: 24 hours a day except from 1 a.m. to 2 a.m. PST and Fridays from 4 p.m. to 6 p.m. PST

Internet: telnet eicbbs. wseo.wa.gov *or* http://www.eicbbs. wseo.wa.gov

E-mail: grewar@wseo.wa. gov

Energy Information Administration Electronic Publishing System (EPUB)

U.S. Department of Energy
1000 Independence Ave., S.W.
Washington, DC 20585

Virtually anything you want to know about energy supply, demand, and prices is available on EPUB. It offers everything from trend data on the number of offshore oil and gas wells to statistics on the cost of electricity nationwide.

The files contain statistics on subjects such as coal production and consumption, use of electric power, prices of winter fuels, natural gas production and consumption, petroleum production, the short-term energy outlook, energy consumption by source, energy imports by source, crude oil supply, drilling activity, electricity generation by utilities, the cost of imported crude oil, retail gasoline prices, world crude oil production, natural gas prices, the amount of electricity generated by nuclear power plants, and U.S. energy supply and demand.

Two files in File Area 8 provide useful lists of contacts:

- ME-FIRST lists contacts at the National Energy Information Center who can refer callers to experts or provide EIA publications, tapes, and computer disks.

- DATA lists dozens of contacts at the Energy Information Administration by topic. The contacts are experts on coal, electric power, electric utilities, nuclear power, uranium, renewable energy, natural gas, petroleum, energy consumption, energy economics, and international energy issues such as foreign investment and greenhouse gases.

VITAL STATS

Data: 202-586-2557

Voice: 202-586-8959

FedWorld gateway: 16

Time limit: 60 minutes per call

Internet: http://www.eia.doe.gov *or* gopher gopher.eia.doe.gov *or* ftp ftp.eia.doe.gov

Login (FTP only): **anonymous**

Password (FTP only): your e-mail address

E-mail: infoctr@eia.doe.gov

FERC Bulletin Board Network

Federal Energy Regulatory Commission
ED-23.2
Room 3026
941 N. Capitol St., N.E.
Washington, DC 20426

The FERC Bulletin Board Network provides access to four BBSs operated by the Federal Energy Regulatory Commission (FERC). The boards contain information about FERC's regulation of the natural gas, hydropower, electric utility, and gas pipeline industries. Unfortunately, many of the files on the boards have been compressed in a self-extracting format that makes them unusable on most Macintosh computers.

Here are highlights of what's available on each board:

Commission Issuance Posting System (CIPS)

The Commission Issuance Posting System (CIPS), which has general documents about FERC and specific documents about the regulation of public utilities, is the largest of the four boards. CIPS files are separated into seven directories: All CIPS Data, Electric Data, Gas Data, Hydropower Data, Oil Data, Rulemakings, and Miscellaneous Data. Each directory has numerous subdirectories. You can get a list of all the files in a specific subdirectory or conduct a search of all the subdirectories at once.

Here are some examples of what's available:

- FERC documents such as rules, initial decisions, opinions, notices, and orders.

- Electric rate filings by utilities.

- Applications by public utilities to sell themselves, purchase other utilities, or merge with other utilities.

- A daily list of all filings made at FERC that includes the date of the filing, the applicant name, the type of filing, the filer or originator, and the docket number. This list covers documents filed the previous day.

VITAL STATS

Data: 202-208-1397

Voice: 202-208-2474

FedWorld gateway: 19

Time limit: 60 minutes per call, 6 hours per day

Available: 24 hours per day except from 8 a.m. to 9 a.m. EST Monday through Friday

- A list of all documents issued on a particular day. Each entry includes the document title and number, the applicant name, and the date issued.

- A daily calendar of FERC events such as hearings and conferences.

- A quarterly report listing the status of all the court cases in which FERC is a party.

Electric Power Data (EPD)

Electric Power Data (EPD) has copies of several forms that companies file with FERC, including:

- Form No. 423, Monthly Report of Cost and Quality of Fuels for Electric Plants.

- Form No. 714, Annual Electric Control and Planning Area Report.

- Form No. 715, Annual Transmission Planning and Evaluation Report.

FERC Form 1 Forum

The FERC Form 1 Forum contains copies of a report that electric utilities file with FERC. The report is Form No. 1, Annual Report of Major Electric Utilities, Licensees, and Others.

Gas Pipeline Data (GPD)

Gas Pipeline Data (GPD) contains information about interstate natural gas pipelines that are regulated by FERC under the Natural Gas Act. It offers:

- Natural gas pipeline tariffs by company.

- Copies of reports that natural gas companies file with FERC titled Form No. 2, Annual Report for Major Natural Gas Companies, and Form No. 2A, Annual Report for Non-Major Natural Gas Companies.

- Copies of monthly reports titled Form No. 8, Underground Gas Storage Report.

- Copies of monthly reports titled Form No. 11, Natural Gas Pipeline Company Monthly Statement.

- Numerous environmental guidelines for the construction of natural gas pipelines, including "Office of Pipeline Regulation Guidelines for Reporting on Cultural Resources Investigations," "Wetland and Waterbody Construction and Mitigation Procedures," and "Upland Erosion Control, Revegetation, and Maintenance Plan."

Fossil Energy Telenews

Office of Fossil Energy Communications
U.S. Department of Energy
Mail Stop FE-5
1000 Independence Ave., S.W.
Washington, DC 20585

Fossil Energy Telenews offers information about research and development programs involving coal, petroleum, and natural gas. The BBS is operated by the Office of Fossil Energy in the Department of Energy.

The BBS has detailed Fossil Energy budget documents, Fossil Energy procurement notices published in *Commerce Business Daily,* press releases dating back to 1985, speeches, congressional testimony, calendars of upcoming speeches and special events, and lists of key Fossil Energy staff.

VITAL STATS
Data: 202-586-6496
Voice: 202-586-6503
FedWorld gateway: 45

Nuclear Regulatory Commission (NRC) at FedWorld

National Technical Information Service
5285 Port Royal Rd.
Springfield, VA 22161

The Nuclear Regulatory Commission (NRC) at FedWorld offers a wide range of information about nuclear power plants, including daily reports about problems at the facilities.

You can easily get thrown when you first connect to this system, since you actually connect to FedWorld and are greeted with FedWorld's opening menu (FedWorld's operators run this system for the NRC). Once you log in, however, you are switched to the NRC's system.

The system is extensive, and here are just some highlights of what's available:

VITAL STATS

Data: 800-303-9672 or
       703-321-3339

Voice: 703-487-4608

Time limit: 3 hours per day

Internet: telnet fedworld.
       gov *or* http://www.
       fedworld.gov

Note: If you access this BBS
       through the Internet,
       at the prompt that ap-
       pears after FedWorld's
       Main Menu type **/go
       nrc**

- Daily reports of unexpected events at nuclear power plants.

- Preliminary notifications of problems at nuclear power plants.

- Reports about the status of operating nuclear power plants.

- Generic communications from the NRC to the operators of nuclear power plants and other facilities it regulates. These documents include Information Notices, Bulletins, Generic Letters, and Administrative Letters. The system offers all of the generic communications issued by the NRC since 1971, a total of more than 2,000 documents. Sample titles include "Reactor Vessel Structural Integrity," "Circumferential Cracking of Steam Generator Tubes," "Significant Unexpected Erosion of Feedwater Lines," "Debris Plugging of Emergency Core Cooling Suction," and "Undetected Loss of Reactor Coolant."

- A list of new public documents released by the NRC.

- Transcripts of meetings of the Nuclear Regulatory Commission.

- The full text of the NRC's *Inspection Manual.*

- Information about proposed rules that the NRC is considering about topics such as decommissioning, changes in security requirements for nuclear power plants, and emergency planning and preparedness. Users can submit official comments about the proposed rules using the BBS.

- Gateways to other NRC BBSs and database systems.

- Petitions filed by members of the public with the NRC that raise potential health and safety issues involving nuclear power plants.

- Information about the NRC's enforcement program, including an electronic copy of the NRC's *Enforcement Manual.*

- NRC press releases.

- *Federal Register* notices concerning rulemaking and policy statements.

- A calendar of NRC meetings.

Nuclear Regulatory Commission Public Meetings Bulletin Board

U.S. Nuclear Regulatory Commission
Washington, DC 20555-0001

The Nuclear Regulatory Commission Public Meetings Bulletin Board provides a searchable database of upcoming meetings involving Nuclear Regulatory Commission staff. In many cases, these meetings are between NRC staff and the operators of nuclear power plants or other facilities regulated by the NRC. The database does not list meetings of the NRC's commissioners, NRC advisory boards, and similar groups.

You can search the database by meeting number, sponsoring office, meeting date, docket number, status, or keyword.

VITAL STATS
Data: 800-952-9676
Voice: 301-415-7092
FedWorld gateway: 60

Office of Statistics and Information (OSI) BBS

Minerals Management Service
Operations and Safety Management
U.S. Department of the Interior
Mail Stop 4610
381 Elden St.
Herndon, VA 22070-4817

The Office of Statistics and Information (OSI) BBS offers statistics about off-shore oil and gas exploration and development. The statistics are compiled by the Minerals Management Service, which leases oil and gas rights on the Outer Continental Shelf.

Typing **f** at the Main Menu gets you a list of the thirty-six file areas on the board, but only some of them contain files. To make matters worse, many of the files on the board are four or five years old.

Here are some highlights from among the up-to-date files:

- *Federal Offshore Statistics,* an annual report by the Minerals Management Service that lists a variety of statistics about offshore oil and gas leasing.

- The *Annual Report to Congress* prepared by the Office of Statistics and Information in the Minerals Management Service.

- The section of the Code of Federal Regulations pertaining to offshore operations of the Minerals Management Service.

- The Federal Offshore Oil and Gas Royalty Management Act.

- The Outer Continental Shelf Lands Act.

- The Submerged Lands Act.

VITAL STATS
Data: 703-787-1181
Voice: 703-787-1043
FedWorld gateway: 67
File list: MMSFILES.ZIP
To access files: At the Main
        Menu type **f**

Tech Specs Plus BBS

Technical Specifications Branch
Division of Operating Reactor Support
Office of Nuclear Reactor Regulation
U.S. Nuclear Regulatory Commission
Washington, DC 20555

The Tech Specs Plus BBS contains documents about the operation of nuclear power plants. Some of them can be very helpful in identifying generic problems affecting various types of nuclear plants. However, the board does not contain documents about individual plants.

The files are basically of three types:

- Documents that the Nuclear Regulatory Commission sends to operators of nuclear power plants that it lumps under the broad title "Generic Communications." Most of these documents alert operators to new NRC policies or to problems at other nuclear plants that the NRC believes could be widespread. The BBS has files of these documents dating back many years. However, Generic Communications issued since October 1, 1994, are now being loaded instead on Nuclear Regulatory Commission (NRC) at FedWorld (p. 162). Five specific titles are available on Tech Specs Plus:

1. Bulletins dating back to 1971.

2. Circulars from 1976 to 1981 (this document has been discontinued).

3. Generic Letters dating back to 1977.

4. Information Notices dating back to 1979.

5. Administrative Letters dating back to 1993.

- Technical specifications for operating nuclear power plants. The specifications detail which systems have to be operable, what tests must be performed, and what administrative procedures must be followed. People who have a rudimentary knowledge of nuclear power should be able to understand the specifications.

- The full text of the *NRC Inspection Manual.*

ENVIRONMENT

Gulfline BBS

Gulf of Mexico Program Office
Building 1103
Room 202
Stennis Space Center, MS 39529

The Gulfline BBS primarily covers environmental issues affecting the Gulf of Mexico and the five states that border it: Alabama, Florida, Louisiana, Mississippi, and Texas. It is a joint project of the U.S. Environmental Protection Agency (EPA) and the National Oceanic and Atmospheric Administration (NOAA).

The bulletins, which you can access by typing **b** at the Main Menu, describe the Gulf of Mexico Program, provide limited information about the BBS, and list environmental BBSs around the country.

The files area offers seventeen environmental programs developed by the EPA and Purdue University. The programs, which are designed for DOS computers, cover topics such as residential water conservation, surface water, wetlands, and prevention of agricultural pollution. To get a list of the available files, type **f** at the Main Menu, **p** at the File Menu, and then **l** for List.

More than twenty conferences allow users to exchange messages about specific issues. The board has public conferences about coastal and shoreline erosion, habitat degradation, living aquatic resources, marine debris, nutrient enrichment, public health, toxic substances and pesticides, and other issues. You can reach the conferences by typing **j** at the Main Menu.

The BBS also has four databases, or doors. You can access them by typing **d** at the Main Menu:

SEARCH   A database of environmental specialists, primarily in the five gulf states. It also includes listings for members of Congress from the gulf states and information about other environmental databases.

GULFINFO   Hundreds of files that include copies of the Gulf of Mexico Program Office's newsletter; public events calendars; the text of environmental bills introduced in Congress

VITAL STATS

Data: 800-235-4662 or
    601-688-2610

Voice: 601-688-1065

FedWorld gateway: 57

Available: 24 hours a day
    except from 3 a.m. to 4
    a.m. CST

Internet: http://gulfline.ssc.
    nasa.gov *or* telnet
    gulfline.ssc.nasa.gov
    or ftp gulfline.ssc.nasa.
    gov

Login (FTP only): **anonymous**

Password (FTP only): your
    e-mail address

and information about their progress; news articles about Gulf of Mexico environmental issues; press releases; and information about conferences and symposia about the Gulf of Mexico.

EPAPHONE   Telephone numbers and addresses of EPA employees nationwide. You can search the database by first and last name.

NOAPHONE   Telephone numbers and addresses of NOAA employees nationwide. You can search it by first and last name.

OAQPS Technology Transfer Network

Technical Support Division
Office of Air Quality Planning and Standards
U.S. Environmental Protection Agency
Mail Stop 14
Research Triangle Park, NC 27711

This BBS is a gateway to the Technology Transfer Network (TTN), a group of fourteen BBSs that provide information about controlling air pollution. Boards on the network contain the text of the Clean Air Act amendments of 1990, numerous summary files from the Toxic Release Inventory, the Environmental Protection Agency's *Fuel Economy Guide* for automobiles, and information about accessing EPA libraries and documents. The network is operated by the EPA's Office of Air Quality Planning and Standards.

After connecting, new users are presented with the Unregistered Users New Menu. It provides descriptions of the boards and a registration option. You must register to have full access to the network.

After you register, the Registered Users Top Menu appears. Type **t** to access the BBSs.

Here are descriptions of the fourteen boards available through the network:

1. **Aerometric Information Retrieval System (AIRS)** This board encourages the exchange of information among state and local agencies that use AIRS, the national database for ambient air quality, emissions, and compliance data. The BBS has newsletters; brochures and pamphlets about AIRS; information about upcoming meetings, conferences, and training sessions; telephone numbers for AIRS contacts; and AIRS-related software programs.

2. **Ambient Monitoring Technology Information Center (AMTIC)** This BBS specializes in information about ambient monitoring technology. It has copies of the *AMTIC News* and *IMPROVE* newsletters; sections of the Code of Federal Regulations about ambient monitoring; files about the effects of acidic pollution on auto finishes, recent observations in the Great Lakes Basin, the effect of acid rain on wood coatings, and the effect of benzene exposure; extensive informa-

tion about how to access EPA documents and libraries, including a list of all EPA libraries; and information about air pollution publications.

3. **Air Pollution Training Institute (APTI)**   Funded by the EPA, the APTI develops instructional materials relating to air pollution abatement. The board has information about courses offered by APTI.

4. **BLIS**   The BLIS BBS contains information from the Reasonably Achievable Control Technology (RACT)/Best Available Control Technology (BACT)/Lowest Achievable Emission Rate (LAER) Clearinghouse. The heart of the BBS is the BLIS database. It contains information about pollution limits and process modifications required under air pollution permits issued by state and local air pollution control programs around the country. You can search the database by state, region, pollutant, process, or a combination of options. The database is designed to help state and local officials determine what types of controls other air pollution agencies have applied to various sources. There is also a database of federal, state, and local air pollution regulations.

5. **Clean Air Act Amendments (CAAA)**   This BBS has extensive information about the Clean Air Act amendments of 1990. It has the text of the Clean Air Act amendments; policy and guidance documents; an index to the BBS that can be searched by topic; a Clean Air Act text search feature that allows searching by topic; files that define terms, explain acronyms, and provide summaries about topics such as dispersion modeling and ambient monitoring; congressional testimony about the Clean Air Act amendments; recently signed rules that have not yet been published in the *Federal Register;* and monthly updates of EPA's activities under the Clean Air Act amendments.

6. **Clearinghouse for Inventories and Emission Factors (CHIEF)**   CHIEF is designed to provide access to tools for estimating emissions of air pollutants and performing air emission inventories. It's operated by the EPA's Emission Inventory Branch. The board has contact lists, electronic copies of memos and letters, EPA emission inventory guidance reports, emission estimation software, and a newsletter about emission factors.

7. **Control Technology Center (CTC)**   The CTC provides technical support to state and local agencies and EPA's regional offices in implementing air pollution control programs. The BBS has a computer modeling system for surface impoundments, a computer model for estimating landfill air emis-

sions, electronic copies of the CTC newsletter, a list of ongoing CTC projects, and summaries of all documents available from the center.

8. **Emission Measurement Technical Information Center (EMTIC)**   This BBS provides technical guidance on stationary source emission testing issues. It's aimed at people who conduct or oversee emissions tests, and contains highly technical files and bulletins on emission testing, information about acid rain, and contact lists.

9. **New Source Review (NSR)**   This BBS provides information about New Source Review permitting. The board has the abstracted index of the "New Source Review Prevention of Deterioration and Nonattainment Area Guidance Notebook," which users can search by keywords; numerous EPA documents about NSR rulemaking and implementation; and news about upcoming meetings on NSR issues.

10. **Support Center for Regulatory Air Models (SCRAM)**   This board offers computer codes for regulatory air models. The board also has bulletins and news about model modifications.

11. **National Air Toxics Information Clearinghouse (NATICH)**   This BBS is aimed at helping federal, state, and local agencies control toxic air pollutants. It offers numerous summary files from the Toxic Release Inventory in spreadsheet format; electronic copies of the NATICH newsletter; lists of local, state, and EPA regional contacts; state and local regulatory program descriptions and contact lists; acceptable ambient guidelines; emissions inventory data; a NATICH publications list; and a list of publications from the Health Effects Research Laboratory.

12. **COMPLIance Information (COMPLI)**   The COMPLI BBS has three databases. They include the National Asbestos Registry System (NARS), which lists all asbestos contractors, inspections of the firms, and inspection results; the Determinations Index, which is a compilation of clarifications and determinations issued by the EPA concerning selected subparts of the *Federal Register;* and Woodstoves, which lists EPA-certified woodstoves and woodstove manufacturers.

13. **Office of Mobile Sources (OMS)**   This BBS is operated by the EPA's Office of Mobile Sources and its National Vehicle and Fuels Emissions Laboratory. It has the EPA's *Fuel Economy Guide* for automobiles, emissions rules for various types of vehicles, tips for better gas mileage, and

files about ozone pollution from automobiles, clean fuels, methanol as a fuel, electric vehicles, nonattainment cities, and milestones in automotive pollution control.

14. **Office of Radiation and Indoor Air (ORIA)**   This BBS has information about controlling exposure to radiation and indoor air pollution.

The system also provides access to the OAQPS TTN User Support Center, which has information about modems, downloading, communications software, and other telecommunications issues. The support center also has a public message area where users can post questions about using the Technology Transfer Network.

Online Library System (OLS)

National Library Network Program
U.S. Environmental Protection Agency
Mail Stop 291
26 W. Martin Luther King Dr.
Cincinnati, OH 45268

The Environmental Protection Agency's Online Library System (OLS) provides nine databases that offer bibliographic citations for books, reports, and journals held by EPA libraries around the country. The publications cover topics such as air quality, hazardous waste, laboratory methods, pollution prevention, toxic substances, water pollution, and the impact of pollution on health.

You can search the databases by title, author, corporate source, keywords, call number, year of publication, and report number. Three of the databases contain citations for holdings in EPA regional libraries in Boston, Chicago, and San Francisco. Here are descriptions of the other six databases:

National catalog Citations and summaries of documents on topics related to biology, chemistry, ecology, and other basic sciences. This database also contains citations for EPA reports distributed through the National Technical Information Service. Contains about 150,000 entries.

Hazardous waste Bibliographic information and abstracts for publications and databases about hazardous waste. Materials covered include books, EPA reports, policy and guidance directives from the Office of Solid Waste and Emergency Response (OSWER), periodicals, and commercial databases containing information about hazardous waste. Contains about 5,000 entries.

Access EPA Listings from *Access EPA*, a publication that has contact information for about 300 sources of environmental information.

Environmental financing information network Information about financing alternatives for state and local environmental programs and projects. The database contains abstracts and case studies that describe successful financing alternatives, in addition to information about contacts in government and nonprofit organizations that are familiar with public financing and environmental programs.

National Center for Environmental Publications and Information (NCEPI) A list of EPA publications that is updated biweekly and includes information about how to obtain the publications.

Chemical collection system Bibliographic information for items relating to chemicals. Contains about 140,000 entries.

Pesticide Information Network (PIN)

U.S. Environmental Protection Agency
Mail Stop H7507C
401 M St., S.W.
Washington, DC 20460

The Pesticide Information Network (PIN) provides information about pesticides that have restricted uses and pesticide monitoring projects around the country. Its databases allow detailed searches by numerous variables.

When you first connect, it looks like you have entered in the middle of a session. That's because the board offers lots of information before formally greeting you and asking you to log in. Just follow the prompts.

The Main Menu has six directories:

A. Instruction Manuals

B. Search the Chemical Index/View the Chemical Classes

C. Search the PMI File

D. Search the RUP File

E. Use the Mailroom

F. Send the System Operator a Message

New users should start in the instruction manual directory. It contains manuals for all three databases that you can read online or capture to your computer using your communications software's capture feature. The manuals are extremely useful, especially for users who lack extensive knowledge about chemicals.

The three databases contain the following information:

1. Chemical Index A cross-referenced list of the names, synonyms, and CAS (Chemical Abstract Service) numbers for all of the chemicals contained in the other two databases. The index also identifies the database(s) in which the chemical can be found. The Chemical Index is helpful if you are unsure about the correct chemical name to use or when you want to do a quick search to see if the databases have information about a specific chemical. The index allows you to search by chemical name or CAS number, and also has a list of chemical classes.

2. **PMI File** A compilation of pesticide monitoring projects being performed by federal, state, and local governments and private institutions. For each project, the database lists the chemicals, substrates, and location, in addition to the name, address, and telephone number of a person to contact for more information. You can search the database by chemical, CAS number, chemical class, chemical category, substrate, substrate breakdown, state, EPA region, country, sponsoring agency, revision date, body of water, or combinations of these categories. Searching this database is a complex process, so it's a good idea to read the manual before attempting a search.

3. **RUP File** A listing of all pesticide products that have been classified as Restricted Use Pesticides (RUP) under 40 CFR Part 152, Subpart I. For each pesticide, the file contains the EPA chemical code number, active ingredient name, EPA registration number and product name, Product Manager number, criteria for classification, formulations and uses restricted, and the EPA actions that led to the classification. The file is updated monthly. You can access the file in three ways:

   - Download the entire file, a process that takes about forty minutes. To do this, turn on your communications software's capture feature and choose option **B.**

   - Download the list of Product Managers. This list contains the name, address, and telephone number of the manager who is assigned to each product. To download the list, turn on your communications software's capture feature and choose option **C.**

   - Search the file to develop a unique list. Doing a search is complicated, so it's a good idea to read the manual first.

Pesticide Special Review and Reregistration Information System

U.S. Environmental Protection Agency
Special Review and Reregistration Division
Office of Pesticide Programs
401 M St., S.W.
Washington, DC 20460

The Pesticide Special Review and Reregistration Information System contains information about pesticides that the Environmental Protection Agency is examining again for possible threats to health or the environment. The pesticides being reexamined were initially registered before November 1, 1984, when standards for government approval were less stringent than they are today.

The bulletins, which you can access by typing **b** at the Main Menu, describe the EPA's pesticide reregistration review process, provide contact information for EPA regional offices, list telephone numbers for employees in the Special Review and Reregistration Division, list pesticide active ingredients that are subject to reregistration, describe how to order hard copies of documents, and provide information about the National Pesticide Telecommunications Network.

Here are some highlights from among the files:

- Reregistration decisions in cases involving individual pesticides and active ingredients.

- Fact sheets about individual pesticides and active ingredients that contain brief descriptions of uses, human health and environmental assessments, tolerance reassessments, and labeling changes required in conjunction with reregistration. These are also known as Red sheets.

- An annual report titled *Status of Pesticides in Reregistration and Special Review,* also known as the Rainbow Report, which lists pesticides that are undergoing or that have completed EPA's Special Review Process or the reregistration process.

- The annual report from EPA's Office of Pesticide Programs.

VITAL STATS

Data: 703-308-7224

Voice: 703-308-8000

FedWorld gateway: 11

File list: ALLFILES.TXT

Internet: gopher earth1. epa.gov

Path (Gopher only): *EPA Offices and Regions/Office of Prevention, Pesticides and Toxic Substances/ Pesticides*

- A huge database containing the names of inert ingredients found in pesticides.

- A lengthy document that defines in nontechnical language many terms and acronyms that appear in regulatory documents, reports, correspondence, testimony, and other documents produced by EPA's Office of Pesticide Programs.

- New rules affecting pesticides.

Remote Access Chemical Hazards Electronic Library (RACHEL)

Environmental Research Foundation
P.O. Box 5036
Annapolis, MD 21403

Among other features, RACHEL offers documents from the U.S. Coast Guard and the U.S. Environmental Protection Agency about toxic chemicals. The BBS is operated by the Environmental Research Foundation, a private organization.

The federal government documents are located in the RACHEL database, which you can access by typing **r** at the Main Menu. You can search the database by document number, keywords, publication date, and other variables.

Two types of federal government documents are available:

- U.S. Coast Guard fact sheets on chemicals. There are more than 1,000 documents from the Coast Guard's Chemical Hazard Response Information System (CHRIS). Each document has extensive information about a toxic chemical.

- Information about polluters sued by the U.S. Environmental Protection Agency from 1972 to 1990. These documents are from the EPA's Civil Enforcement Docket. Each document lists the name and address of the company that was sued, the outcome of the case, any penalties assessed, the law involved, the violation charged, the date filed and concluded in federal court, the judicial district, and the court docket number, among other information.

The BBS also has extensive nonfederal information about toxic chemicals, including abstracts from newspapers and magazines, New Jersey Department of Health fact sheets on chemicals, reference information about the environment, copies of *Rachel's Hazardous Waste News*, and information about landfills, incinerators, and waste-handling companies.

VITAL STATS

Data: 410-263-8903

Voice: 410-263-1584
(answered only from
3 p.m. to 6 p.m. EST)

Manual: RACHEL.DOC

Research and Development Electronic Bulletin Board

U.S. Environmental Protection Agency
Office of Research and Development
Mail Stop G75
26 W. Martin Luther King Drive
Cincinnati, OH 45268

The Research and Development Electronic Bulletin Board provides a bibliographic database of more than 18,000 publications prepared by EPA's Office of Research and Development (ORD) and its contractors. The database has abstracts of all ORD publications from 1976 to the present. They cover a wide range of environmental issues. For example, a search of the topic word "PCB" turned up more than 100 hits.

To access the database, type **open 1** at the Main Menu. You can search the database by title and abstract words, authors, laboratories, sponsoring agencies, performing organizations, EPA report number, NTIS order number, contract or grant number, and report year. Documents identified through the database can be ordered online.

The board also has more than twenty bulletins, which you can access by typing **b** at the Main Menu. They provide information about using the BBS, list upcoming Office of Research and Development meetings, and list other EPA BBSs.

A variety of files are available by typing **f** at the Main Menu. Here are some highlights:

VITAL STATS
Data: 513-569-7610 or
    513-569-7700
Voice: 513-569-7272
Manual: BBSMAN.TXT
To access files: At the Main
    Menu type **f**

- A software package called EPANET that can be used to model hydraulic and water quality behavior within water distribution systems.

- Information about research grant solicitations.

- The RREL Treatability Database.

- SWAMI 2.0, a software program that uses process analysis for identifying waste minimization opportunities for industries.

- The Surface Water Treatment Rule from the Code of Federal Regulations.

- The Total Coliform Rule from the Code of Federal Regulations.

- A database containing the coordinated list of chemicals.

- A wetlands database.

RTK NET

OMB Watch and The Unison Institute
1742 Connecticut Ave., N.W.
Washington, DC 20009

RTK NET provides access to more than a dozen federal databases containing information about toxic chemicals, home mortgages, and other subjects. This is a tremendous service, since obtaining some of these databases from the federal government can cost hundreds or thousands of dollars. RTK NET is a joint project of OMB Watch and The Unison Institute, two public interest organizations in Washington, D.C.

You must register online to receive full access to the databases. Within a week or two of registering, you will receive a password that allows you to access everything.

RTK NET provides extensive documentation about how to use each of the databases. The databases are quite sophisticated, but if you run into problems you can call the voice number for assistance.

Here's what's available:

- BRS-RCRA Biennial Reporting System: This database contains reports filed by companies that generate, ship off site, or receive hazardous waste. You can search the database by facility, geographic area, industry, type of waste generated, and type of waste received, among other variables.

- 1990 U.S. Census (by ZIP code): This database contains data from the 1990 Census of Population and Housing. You can search the database only by ZIP code.

- CERCLIS: This database has information about all the potential Superfund sites, as well as proposed and final sites that have been included on the National Priority List. It contains records for about 38,000 sites. For each site, the database lists its name, address, National Priority List status, and latitude and longitude, among other information. You can search the database by site or by geographic area.

- CUS-IUR Chemical Production Database: The Chemical Update System database contains information about production levels of hazardous chemicals. The database contains 25,000 records, which list the facility name, facility address, chemical name, Chemical Abstract Service number, and production volume, among other information.

- DOCKET: DOCKET contains records of all civil cases filed by the Department of Justice on behalf of the Environmental Protection Agency. For each case, the database offers the name of the case, the case number, the facility name, the facility address, the defendant's name, the environmental law violated, the penalty imposed, the waste material or chemical involved in the violation, and other information. The database does not have records for criminal cases (which are more serious than civil cases) or of EPA administrative actions (which are less serious than civil cases).

- ERNS: The Emergency Response Notification System database contains records of all phone calls made to the National Response Center (NRC). The NRC is supposed to be notified when various types of spills or releases of toxic substances occur. The database also has records of sightings by the Coast Guard of spills at sea. You can search the database by discharge, geographic area, material, and other variables. Data are available for 1987 to 1992.

- FINDS: The Facility Index System database (FINDS) lists the names, addresses, and identification numbers of all facilities regulated by the Environmental Protection Agency. FINDS also provides "pointers" to other sources of information about the facility, such as other EPA databases. You can search the database by facility, geographic area, industry, and other variables. FINDS data are updated on RTK NET about every six months.

- HMDA: The Home Mortgage Disclosure Act database offers data about home purchase and home improvement loans made by banks, savings associations, credit unions, and other mortgage lenders. Regulators use the data to ensure that the institutions are properly serving their communities and are not engaging in discriminatory lending practices. You can search the database by bank name, market area, geographic area, and other variables.

- NPL: The National Priority List database lists all of the contaminated waste sites on the Superfund National Priorities List. The database contains records for about 1,200 sites. Each listing includes the site name, site address, date the site was listed, a score that measures the site's relative threat, and a text description of the site when it was placed on the National Priority List. Many of the descriptions are out of date because they were written when the site was first listed.

- PCS: The Water Permit Compliance System database contains surface water permits issued under the Clean Water Act. The database offers basic facility and permit data, information about each pipe in a facility that can release effluent, and data about the limits on effluent from each pipe allowed under the permit.

- ROADMAPS: ROADMAPS is a database created by the Environmental Protection Agency that contains reference information for regulatory and health studies of toxic chemicals listed in the Toxic Release Inventory. You can search the data to assess the threats posed by a chemical. The database contains information about health and environmental effects, carcinogenicity and other properties, and federal regulations.

- RODS: The Records of Decision System database contains records about Environmental Protection Agency decisions made about certain Superfund sites. These records provide extensive textual descriptions of sites. You can search the database by site, geographic area, and other variables.

- TRIS: The Toxic Release Inventory System is a database containing information about releases and transfers of toxic chemicals from manufacturing facilities. The database is compiled from reports that facilities file with the Environmental Protection Agency.

- Water Use Database: This U.S. Geological Survey database records how much water is used for various purposes on a county-by-county basis.

- TRI Off-Site Destination Database: This database was created by RTK NET staff using data from the 1991 Toxic Release Inventory. The database shows where hazardous waste was shipped.

U.S. EPA Region 10 BBS

U.S Environmental Protection Agency
Region 10
1200 Sixth Ave.
Seattle, WA 98101

The U.S. EPA Region 10 BBS has a wide range of environmental information for Alaska, Idaho, Oregon, and Washington. It also offers nearly two dozen conferences on various topics.

You can join the conferences by typing **j** at the Main Menu. They serve as collection areas for messages on specific topics. Some of the topics covered include environmental education, toxics, pesticides, tribal affairs, wetlands, air toxics, chemical emergency planning, Alaska rural sanitation, and Alaskan seafood processors.

Here are some highlights from the files area, which you can access by typing **f** at the Main Menu:

- Information about sites contaminated with hazardous chemicals, including Superfund sites, in Alaska, Idaho, Oregon, and Washington. The file A_README.TXT explains how to use this information.

- A list of other environmental BBSs.

- Sludge reviews for Oregon and Washington.

- A telephone directory for EPA's Region 10 offices.

- Instructions about how to design a small field lab.

- A list of solid waste funding sources for Region 10.

- Several sections of the Clean Air Act.

VITAL STATS

Data: 800-781-2241 (good only in Alaska, Idaho, Oregon, and Washington) or 206-553-2241

Voice: 206-553-1026

Manual: EPA_BBS.TXT

To access files: At the Main Menu type **f**

Internet: telnet 134.67.80.41

Alternative Treatment Technology Information Center (ATTIC)

Office of Research and Development
U.S. Environmental Protection Agency
2890 Woodbridge Ave. (MS-106)
Edison, NJ 08837-3679

The Alternative Treatment Technology Information Center (ATTIC) offers extensive information about technologies available for treating hazardous waste. It has searchable databases, databases that you can download to your own computer, technical bulletins, and numerous full-text reports. The BBS also has a calendar of events, which you can access by typing **8** at the Main Menu.

ATTIC offers three online databases. To reach a database, type its number at the Main Menu:

1. Treatment Technology Database   Contains more than 2,500 abstracts and citations of articles and technical reports on biological, chemical, physical, solidification/stabilization, and thermal treatment technologies. The database can be searched by keywords, free text, ATTIC control number, region or state, title, site name, and site history. Entries provide information on the treatment process, contaminants, cost, and performance.

2. RREL Treatability Database   Contains information about the removal and destruction of chemicals in water, soil, debris, sludge, and sediment. It includes data on more than two dozen alternative technologies.

3. UST Abstract Database   Contains case history files that provide information about hazardous material spills, remedial and removal actions for Superfund sites, and corrective actions for underground storage tank problems.

ATTIC also has five databases that you can download to your own computer. These databases run only on IBM and compatible computers. To access them, type **5** at the Main Menu:

• Bioremediation in the Field Search System, which contains information about more than 150 waste sites where bioremediation is being used.

- RREL Treatability Database, which offers information about the removal or destruction of chemicals in water, wastewater, soil, debris, sludge, and sediment.

- Vendor Information System for Innovative Treatment Technologies (VISITT), which contains information about innovative treatment technologies for hazardous waste that have been developed by private companies.

- P2P, which can be used to measure progress in pollution prevention resulting from product redesign, reformulation, or replacement. It compares the pollution generated by the original product with that from the modified product.

- RODS, which helps track site cleanups under the Superfund program. For each site, RODS has information about the technology being used, the site history, community participation, enforcement activities, site characteristics, and other issues.

ATTIC also offers dozens of technical bulletins, which you can access by typing **6** at the Main Menu. The bulletins provide descriptions and contact information for databases, hotlines, and BBSs about environmental issues; information about Superfund-related projects and research; and lists of seminars and conferences.

Finally, ATTIC has dozens of full-text documents, including more than thirty that describe results from demonstration projects and several that describe emerging technologies being used at various facilities. It also offers some major reports, including:

- *Superfund Innovative Technology Evaluation Program Technology Profiles,* which describes technologies being developed for cleaning up Superfund sites.

- *Remediation Technologies Screening Matrix and Reference Guide,* which describes various treatment technologies.

- *Innovative Treatment Technologies: Annual Status Report,* which describes the status of new technologies being used in the Superfund program and at non-Superfund sites under the jurisdictions of the departments of Defense and Energy.

- *EPA Handbook: Approaches for the Remediation of Federal Facility Sites Contaminated With Explosive or Radioactive Wastes,* which provides an overview of technical issues involved in cleaning up soil and groundwater contaminated with explosive and radioactive waste at federal sites.

- *21st Annual RREL Research Symposium Abstract Proceedings,* which presents research findings from ongoing and recently completed projects funded by the EPA's Risk Reduction Engineering Laboratory.

- *Contaminants and Remedial Options at Solvent-Contaminated Sites.*

- *Contaminants and Remedial Options at Wood Preserving Sites.*

- *Contaminants and Remedial Options at Pesticide Sites.*

- *The Superfund Innovative Technology Evaluation Program Annual Report to Congress.*

- The *MSW Factbook,* a huge reference manual about municipal solid waste.

Cleanup Information Bulletin Board (CLU-IN)

Office of Solid Waste and Emergency Response
Technology Innovation Office
U.S. Environmental Protection Agency
Mail Code 5102W
401 M St., S.W.
Washington, DC 20460

The Cleanup Information Bulletin Board (CLU-IN) specializes in information about cleaning up hazardous waste. It's aimed at people involved in site cleanups under the Superfund program and the Resource Conservation and Recovery Act—anyone from state officials to consulting engineers to citizens.

First-time callers can access only a registration questionnaire. After you fill out the questionnaire, you normally receive full access to the board within one working day.

Information on the board is presented in bulletins, files, databases, and special interest groups (SIGs). The board has dozens of bulletins, which you can access by typing **bu** at the Main Menu. The bulletins explain how to use the board, provide calendars of meetings and conferences, describe other environmental BBSs, and summarize *Commerce Business Daily* procurement and contract award notices that pertain to hazardous waste, solid waste, underground storage tank remediation, and other environmental topics.

You can access the files by typing **f** at the Main Menu. Here are some highlights of what's available:

VITAL STATS

Data: 301-589-8366

Voice: 301-589-8368

FedWorld gateway: 7

Manual: MANUAL.CLU (the manual is excellent)

File list: PCBFILES.LST

To access files: At the Main Menu type **f**

- Numerous Environmental Protection Agency reports, including *In Situ Remediation Technology Status Report: Electrokinetics, Guide to Documenting Cost and Performance for Remediation Projects, In Situ Remediation Technology Status Report: Thermal Enhancements, Selected Alternative and Innovative Treatment Technologies for Corrective Action and Site Remediation (A Bibliography of EPA Information Resources), Abstracts of Remediation Case Studies, Innovative Treatment Technologies: Annual Status Report,* and *Catalogue of Hazardous and Solid Waste Publications.*

- *Bridging the Valley of Death: Financing Technology for a Sustainable Future,* a report prepared by the Small Business Administration for the EPA that looks at the impact of environmental preservation on the economy and at financial barriers to technology development.

- Documents from the Federal Remediation Technologies Roundtable, including *Accessing Federal Data Bases for Contaminated Site Cleanup* and *Federal Publications on Alternative and Innovative Treatment.*

- *Federal Register* notices about hazardous waste, separated by week.

- Portions of the Code of Federal Regulations pertaining to hazardous waste.

- *Commerce Business Daily* procurement and contract award notices that pertain to hazardous waste, solid waste, underground storage tank remediation, and other environmental topics, divided by quarter.

- The *National Biennial RCRA Hazardous Waste Report,* a huge document divided into many files that contains all kinds of data about hazardous waste such as quantities generated, shipments and receipts, and interstate imports and exports. The report also has a list of the largest generators of hazardous waste, overviews of generation and management practices in individual states, and a list of facilities that treat, store, and dispose of hazardous waste.

- An EPA manual for inspections under the Resource Conservation and Recovery Act.

- A list of Superfund sites that contains listings by state, region, and site name.

- The RREL Treatability Database, which contains information about the removal or destruction of chemicals in water, wastewater, soil, debris, sludge, and sediment.

- The Bioremediation in the Field Search System (BFSS) database, which provides information about more than 150 bioremediation sites nationwide.

- The Hazardous Waste Superfund database.

- The Pesticide Treatability Database.

- A database containing the coordinated list of chemicals.

The board also has three databases, which you can access by typing **op** at the Main Menu:

1. COURSES: Descriptions of training courses.

2. RCRAPUBS: Abstracts of documents from the *Catalogue of Hazardous and Solid Waste Publications.*

3. CASESTUD: Case studies of applications of remediation technologies.

Finally, the board has several special interest groups (SIGs), which have messages and files. The public SIGs include:

- Groundwater Technologies: Information about using innovative technologies to clean up groundwater contamination.
- UST/LUST: Information about underground storage tanks.

Cleanup Standards Outreach (CSO) BBS

Radiation Studies Division
U.S. Environmental Protection Agency
Mail Code 6603J
401 M St., S.W.
Washington, DC 20460

The Cleanup Standards Outreach (CSO) BBS seeks public comments about proposed rules for cleaning up sites that are contaminated with radioactivity. The new regulations will apply to Superfund sites, facilities operated by the departments of Energy and Defense, and sites operating under licenses issued by the Nuclear Regulatory Commission.

The board's files include an explanation of the rulemaking, background information about radiation cleanup, the draft Environmental Protection Agency radiation site cleanup regulation, comments about the draft regulation, meeting summaries, and news about upcoming meetings related to the rulemaking.

VITAL STATS

Data: 800-700-7837 or
    703-790-0825

Voice: 703-893-6600

FedWorld gateway: 134

To access files: At the Main
    Menu type **f**

Time limit: 60 minutes per
    day

Nuclear Regulatory Commission Decommissioning Rulemaking Bulletin Board

U.S. Nuclear Regulatory Commission
Washington, DC 20555

The purpose of the Nuclear Regulatory Commission Decommissioning Rulemaking Bulletin Board is to help the NRC develop rules for decontaminating nuclear facilities that are removed from service. Most of these facilities are nuclear power plants.

Previously, decisions about the extent to which radioactive contamination had to be cleaned up before a site could be closed were made on a case-by-case basis. The purpose of the rulemaking is to develop consistent rules about the required level of decontamination.

Files on the board provide the following information:

- A draft of the decommissioning rules.

- Comments from various parties about the decommissioning rules.

- Background documents about the decommissioning rulemaking.

- Case studies about decommissioning reactors.

- A list of decommissioned and shutdown reactors.

- *Federal Register* notices about NRC policy changes regarding radioactive waste.

- A list of hotline numbers for people who participated in radiation experiments in past decades.

- A list of telephone numbers for selected NRC offices.

VITAL STATS
Data: 800-880-6091
Voice: 301-415-6026
FedWorld gateway: 133
To access files: At the Main
Menu type **f**
Time limit: 2 hours per day

MODELS

Applied Modeling Research Branch (AMRB) BBS

Chief, Applied Modeling Research Branch (MD-80)
Atmospheric Characterization and Modeling Division
U.S. Environmental Protection Agency
Research Triangle Park, NC 27711

The Applied Modeling Research Branch BBS contains computer models of air dispersion. The models, which run on IBM and compatible computers, can be used in support of the Clean Air Act.

VITAL STATS
Data: 919-541-1325
Voice: 919-541-1376

CEAM BBS

Center for Exposure Assessment Modeling
National Exposure Research Laboratory
U.S. Environmental Protection Agency
960 College Station Rd.
Athens, GA 30605-2700

About a dozen environmental models for DOS computers are available on the CEAM BBS, in addition to files that support the software models. Only certain models are available through the Internet.

The models are designed to help federal, state, and local environmental officials make risk-based decisions concerning the protection of air, water, and soil.

The models simulate urban and rural nonpoint sources, tidal hydrodynamics, geochemical equilibrium, aquatic food chain bioaccumulation, and conventional and toxic pollution of streams, lakes and estuaries. All of the models are in the public domain, so they are free.

VITAL STATS

Data: 706-546-3402

Voice: 706-546-3549

File list: CEAMFILE.LST

To access files: At the Main
Menu type **f**

Available: 24 hours a day
except Fridays from 8
a.m. to 8:30 a.m. EST

Internet: ftp earth1.epa.gov

Login (FTP only): **anonymous**

Password (FTP only): your
e-mail address

Path (FTP only): *pub/athens*

E-mail: ceam@athens.ath.
epa.gov

CSMoS-BBS

Subsurface Remediation Information Center
U.S. Environmental Protection Agency
Robert S. Kerr Environmental Research Laboratory
P.O. Box 1198
Ada, OK 74820

The CSMoS-BBS provides computer models of the flow of groundwater and contaminants such as pesticides through soil. You can download the models and use them on your own computer. The models, which are in the public domain, are designed for DOS computers.

VITAL STATS
Data: 405-436-8506
Voice: 405-436-8655

National Ecology Research Center (NERC) Bulletin Board

National Ecology Research Center, NBS
4512 McMurry Ave.
Fort Collins, CO 80525-3400

The National Ecology Research Center (NERC) Bulletin Board contains software for modeling environmental habitats. The software, which is available only for IBM and compatible computers, is quite technical.

The software is designed for environmental officials in the federal and state governments. It allows them to determine the effects of various management practices on a large project, to establish in-stream flows for rivers, and to model other environmental conditions.

The board also has special interest groups where users can exchange messages about the software and a small collection of utility programs.

VITAL STATS

Data: 303-226-9365

Voice: 303-226-9335

To access files: At the Main Menu type **f**

WATER

Drinking Water Information Exchange (DWIE)

P.O. Box 6064
Morgantown, WV 26506-6064

The Drinking Water Information Exchange (DWIE) is primarily aimed at people who operate public water systems. It has files about actions by Congress, the release of various contaminant studies, how to operate water systems, funding for water systems, and how to use water efficiently. The system is operated by the National Drinking Water Clearinghouse at West Virginia University, with funding from the U.S. Environmental Protection Agency.

VITAL STATS
Data: 800-932-7459 or
    304-293-7108
Voice: 800-624-8301
FedWorld gateway: 81
To access files: At the Main
    Menu type **f**

Nonpoint Source Program Electronic Bulletin Board

U.S. Environmental Protection Agency
Mail Stop WH553
401 M St., S.W.
Washington, DC 20460

The primary focus of the Nonpoint Source Program Electronic Bulletin Board is water pollution, although the board also includes information on other environmental issues. The BBS presents information in files, special interest groups (SIGs), and doors to online databases.

Even if you are not interested in water pollution, log on at least long enough to download the user's manual. Besides providing information specific to the Nonpoint BBS, it also offers details about navigating around BBSs in general. It includes an excellent online tour of the BBS that you can first read and then perform online. If you are new to BBSs, this manual is indispensable.

While the board has dozens of bulletins, they are of limited use because most are several years old. You can reach the bulletins by typing **bu** at the Main Menu.

Many of the files also are old, so you need to check their creation dates to make sure they're really useful. Here are some highlights from among the files, which you can reach by typing **f** at the Main Menu:

- A list of environment-related BBSs and hotlines.

- The Earth Charter from the environmental summit in Rio de Janeiro.

- A conference calendar.

- An EPA report titled *Cleaner Water Through Conservation.*

- Instructions for constructing a tabletop model of an aquifer.

- A document titled *A State and Local Government Guide to Environmental Program Funding Alternatives.*

- A publication titled *Around the Home: Pollution Prevention and Environmental Activities.*

VITAL STATS

Data: 301-589-0205

Voice: 301-589-5318

FedWorld gateway: 79

Manual: MAN-ASCI.ZIP (ASCII text) or MAN-WP51.ZIP (WordPerfect 5.1)

To access files: At the Main Menu type **f**

- A publication titled *Common Groundwork: A Practical Guide to Preserving Rural and Urban Land.*

- A file about how to have a beautiful (and environmentally responsible) lawn.

- An extensive file for consumers about lead poisoning (available in English and Spanish versions).

- A catalog of free environmental software packages available from the Environmental Protection Agency and Purdue University.

- Numerous large documents containing examples of solutions to water quality problems caused by nonpoint source pollution.

- A huge document titled *Reinventing NEPA* that discusses the National Environmental Policy Act.

- A document titled *Protecting America's Wetlands: A Fair, Flexible, and Effective Approach,* produced by the White House Office on Environmental Policy.

- Numerous issues of the *NPS News-Notes Newsletter.*

- Copies of a newsletter from the EPA headquarters library about water-related materials.

- A newsletter titled *The Water Monitor: Surface Water Assessment Report.*

The board also has special interest groups (SIGs) devoted to various issues. SIGs frequently have bulletins or files, and each one has its own e-mail system. To join a SIG, at the Main Menu type **j** and then choose the SIG you want. There are seven SIGs:

1. **Agricultural issues**   This is a forum for discussing issues related to agricultural nonpoint source pollution. The SIG contains more than forty bulletins that list agriculture-related newsletters, key personnel at the National Agricultural Library, recommended publications about agriculture and the environment, and contain news items about pesticides. It also has files that list periodicals about alternative farming, describe educational and training opportunities in sustainable agriculture, provide facts about Atrazine, and offer numerous case studies about projects in agricultural conservation.

2. **Waterbody system**   This forum supports EPA's Waterbody system. Its files include a list of Waterbody system contacts at the EPA and states and a

manual for the WBS computer program, which must be requested separately.

3. **Nonpoint source research**   This is a forum about EPA activities and products of interest to professionals in nonpoint source pollution prevention. The SIG's bulletins describe technical assistance available from EPA's Office of Research and Development (ORD), list recent ORD publications, describe agricultural research, and describe global climate research.

4. **Watershed restoration network**   This forum for exchanging information about watershed restoration has more than two dozen bulletins. Sample titles include "A watershed approach to fisheries restoration on the Klamath River," "Guidelines for collection of cuttings to maintain genetic diversity," and "California Native Grass Association founded." The SIG also has a door to EPA's Watershed Registry, where users can provide or read information about specific watershed projects.

5. **Total Maximum Daily Load (TMDL)**   This is a forum for people engaged in water resources management on a watershed/basin scale. Its files provide numerous case studies of Total Maximum Daily Load projects.

6. **Volunteer monitoring**   This forum covers monitoring of waterways by volunteers. Its bulletins list upcoming conferences and meetings about volunteer monitoring, provide news about volunteer monitoring, and provide information about state volunteer monitoring programs, including program names, addresses, and coordinators. The files include documents about citizen action, a fact sheet about getting started in volunteer monitoring, documents that describe volunteer monitoring programs nationwide, and copies of newsletters about volunteer monitoring. The SIG also has a door to an online database that provides references to documents that can help volunteer monitors. Subjects include citizen action programs, environmental education, monitoring methods, and pollution control approaches. Each record provides a citation and abstract and, where available, a contact and cost information.

7. **Coastal nonpoint pollution**   This SIG covers issues related to Section 6217 of the Coastal Zone Act Reauthorization Amendments of 1990. It is intended to help states develop and implement their Coastal Nonpoint Pollution Control Programs. The SIG's files include chapters from EPA's Management Measures Guidance, a directory of agricultural extension program leaders, a list of EPA nonpoint source coordinators, and a list of state extension water quality coordinators.

The BBS also has two doors to databases. To access them, at the Main Menu type **open** and then choose the database you want:

NPS News-Notes Database   The full text of articles from the *NPS News-Notes Newsletter,* produced by EPA's Office of Wetlands, Oceans, and Watersheds. You can search the database by article number, title, and keywords.

Educational Materials Database   Information about projects, videos, pamphlets, posters, and other items produced by state and local governments as outreach materials for their nonpoint source programs. The database contains information about outreach activities, public education programs, educational materials, communication techniques, and public involvement projects. You can search it by title and description.

Technology Transfer BBS

U.S. Environmental Protection Agency
Region IV
4WM-MF
345 Courtland St., N.E.
Atlanta, GA 30365

Files and conferences on the Technology Transfer BBS focus on the design, operation, maintenance, and regulation of wastewater treatment plants, although there is also information about drinking water, storm water, and water quality.

The bulletins, which you can access by typing **b** at the Main Menu, explain how to use the board, provide details about the conferences, explain how to decompress files and display graphics files available on the BBS, list new technology transfer publications, and provide news about rules and regulations.

The ten conferences are available only to users who request access from the sysop. To do so, at the Main Menu type **c** and then write a message asking for access. To get descriptions of the conferences, read the bulletin called CONFER. The conferences serve as message collection points on such topics as sewage sludge, wastewater reclamation, and drinking water quality.

Most of the files, which you can access by typing **f** at the Main Menu, are quite old. They include a list of wastewater publications available from the Environmental Protection Agency, a layman's guide to technical terms, information about environmental regulations for very small communities, sludge regulations, and related information.

VITAL STATS

Data: 404-347-1767
Voice: 404-347-3633
Manual: BBSGUIDE.ZIP
(it's excellent)

Universities Water Information Network (UWIN)

UWIN
4543 Faner Hall
Southern Illinois University
Carbondale, IL 62901

The Universities Water Information Network (UWIN), which is aimed at water professionals, is a joint project of the U.S. Geological Survey and the Universities Council on Water Resources. UWIN is a sister system to WaterTalk (p. 206).

If you access UWIN through a dial-in connection, you're connected to the UWIN Gopher. This makes the system extremely easy to use. Following are highlights of what it offers:

VITAL STATS

Data: 618-453-3324 or 618-453-3090

Voice: 618-453-6453

Login (dial-in and Telnet only): **guest**

Password (dial-in and Telnet only): **uwin**

Internet: http://www.uwin.siu.edu *or* gopher gopher.uwin.siu.edu *or* telnet gopher.uwin.siu.edu

E-mail: admin@uwin.siu.edu

- The Selected Water Resources Abstracts database, which contains more than 265,000 abstracts and citations to literature about water resources. Some of the subjects covered include municipal water supplies, pollution and water management, aquaculture, biotechnology, public utilities and policy, industrial water usage and treatment, agriculture and irrigation, finance and economics, and climatology, among many others. The database, which contains abstracts from 1967 to October 1993, can be searched using keywords. You must search each year separately.

- A searchable directory of water resources experts around the country. For each expert, the directory lists the person's name, title, university or firm, address, telephone number, fax number, e-mail address, areas of expertise, and language proficiencies.

- A calendar of water events, including conferences, meetings, and calls for papers and proposals.

- Extensive information from the National Institutes for Water Resources (NIWR), the professional organization of the fifty-four Water Resources Institutes. The directory lists the institutes, describes expertise available in various states, and lists NIWR publications.

Wastewater Treatment Information Exchange (WTIE)

National Small Flows Clearinghouse
P.O. Box 6064
Morgantown, WV 26506

The Wastewater Treatment Information Exchange (WTIE), which is part of the National Small Flows Clearinghouse, contains hundreds of files about wastewater management and prevention issues.

There are more than forty bulletins, which you can access by typing **b** at the Main Menu. They provide news about grants, list upcoming events, explain the board's features, and describe publications.

The files, which you can access by typing **f** at the Main Menu, are divided by year. They offer descriptions of publications produced by the National Small Flows Clearinghouse, news about state and federal regulations, articles about wastewater issues, and news about workshops for small communities.

VITAL STATS

Data: 800-544-1936 or 304-293-5969

Voice: 800-624-8301 or 304-293-4191

FedWorld gateway: 37

To access files: At the Main Menu type **f**

WaterTalk

UWIN
4543 Faner Hall
Southern Illinois University
Carbondale, IL 62901

WaterTalk has a series of forums where users can exchange messages about water-related topics, including hydrology, international water resources issues, water quality, water resources policy, and similar issues. It is operated by the Universities Council on Water Resources and the U.S. Geological Survey.

If you have Internet access, you should access this board using the World Wide Web. It is much easier to use than the interface for dial-in and Telnet connections, which is poorly designed.

WaterTalk is a sister system to the Universities Water Information Network (p. 204).

VITAL STATS

Data: 618-453-3324 or 618-453-3090

Voice: 618-453-6453

Login (dial-in and Telnet only): **bbs**

Password (dial-in and Telnet only): **uwin**

Internet: http://bbs.uwin.siu.edu *or* gopher gopher.uwin.siu.edu *or* telnet gopher.uwin.siu.edu

Path (Gopher only): *WaterTalk/Access WaterTalk*

E-mail: admin@uwin.siu.edu

ETHNIC GROUPS AND MINORITIES

INDIANnet

Americans for Indian Opportunity
22571 Smoky Ridge Road
Rapid City, SD 57702

American Indians and Native Alaskans are the primary audience for INDIAN-net. The BBS is sponsored by Americans for Indian Opportunity, a nonprofit advocacy organization that receives funding from the Bureau of Indian Affairs, the Administration on Native Americans, the Environmental Protection Agency, and the Department of Agriculture.

The board is set up differently from most others, but it's relatively easy to use. The board's biggest flaw is that most of the file lists do not provide file descriptions. This makes it virtually impossible to determine what's in a file without downloading it and taking a look.

Here are some highlights of what's available:

VITAL STATS

Data: 605-394-6858

Voice: 605-348-7293

Internet: telnet indiannet. sdserv.org

- News about various federal government actions affecting Native Americans, including information about the Indian Dams Safety Act, Environmental Protection Agency rules affecting tribal air quality, and the Indian Health Service loan repayment program.

- Data about various Indian tribes extracted from the 1990 U.S. Census.

- More than a dozen publications from the Small Business Administration, including *Minority Businesses, How to Write a Business Plan, Raising Money for Small Businesses, Women Business Ownership,* and *Starting a Home Business.*

- Background information about the Administration for Native Americans, a federal program that seeks to promote social and economic self-sufficiency among Native Americans.

- Hundreds of shareware and freeware programs for Macintosh computers. These files are not being updated.

Minority Impact BBS

National Minority Energy Information Clearinghouse
Office of Minority Economic Impact
U.S. Dept. of Energy
Room 5B110
1000 Independence Ave., S.W.
Washington, DC 20585

The Minority Impact BBS contains information about opportunities for minorities through the Department of Energy (DOE). The information is presented in bulletins, which you can access by typing **b** at the Main Menu.

The bulletins have information about DOE's Office of Minority Impact, programs for minorities at DOE's national laboratories and its energy program offices, DOE's programs for historically black colleges and universities, and the Socioeconomic Research and Analysis Program in DOE's Office of Minority Impact.

The BBS also has an electronic version of the DOE's Forecast of Contracting and Subcontracting Opportunities. To access the document, type **f** at the Main Menu.

VITAL STATS

Data: 800-543-2325 or
202-586-1561

Voice: 202-586-7898

FedWorld gateway: 62

National Archaeological Database (NADB) Online System

Center for Advanced Spatial Technologies
12 Ozark Hall
University of Arkansas
Fayetteville, AR 72701

The National Archaeological Database (NADB) Online System offers two searchable archaeological databases. It's operated by the University of Arkansas in cooperation with the National Park Service, Army Corps of Engineers, and Department of Defense.

The first database, called NADB-Reports, contains bibliographic references to more than 100,000 archaeological reports produced in the United States. You can search the database by state, county, cultural group, material, keyword, date, author, and title, and you can download the results in American Antiquity citation format.

The second database, called NADB-NAGPRA, offers documents related to implementation of the Native American Graves Protection and Repatriation Act. Many of the documents in the full-text database are notices of completion of inventory and of the intent to repatriate Native American graves. You can search the database or browse through its documents.

VITAL STATS

Data: 501-575-2021

Voice: 501-575-6159

Login: **nadb**

Internet: telnet cast.uark.edu *or* http://cast.uark.edu

E-mail: boss@cast.uark.edu

GOVERNMENT

Ethics Bulletin Board System

Office of Information Resources Management
U.S. Office of Government Ethics
1201 New York Ave., N.W., Suite 500
Washington, DC 20005-3917

The Ethics Bulletin Board System contains ethics laws, regulations, policies, and opinions affecting the executive branch of the federal government.

Information is presented in bulletins that can be read online and files that can be downloaded. The bulletins and files contain nearly identical information, so you may want to go directly to the files.

Downloading files is a bit of a pain. To download a file, you must be in the file area where it's located. If you want to download files from several areas, you must enter each of them. The files are separated into six areas:

VITAL STATS

Data: 202-523-1186

Voice: 202-523-5757

FedWorld gateway: 91

To access files: At the Main Menu type **f**

Available: 24 hours a day except from 7 a.m. to 8 a.m. EST

Regulations   Copies of regulations issued by the Office of Government Ethics (OGE) and the section of the Code of Federal Regulations pertaining to the OGE.

Opinions   Formal advisory opinions, informal letter opinions, and policy memoranda issued by the Office of Government Ethics. They discuss how to interpret and comply with conflict of interest, post-employment, standards of conduct, and financial disclosure requirements in the executive branch. The opinions date from 1979.

DAEOgrams   DAEOgrams are memoranda from the OGE to executive branch ethics officials. They provide guidance on interpreting and complying with ethics rules and information about ethics workshops and education materials.

Education/training   An ethics game called "Dangerous Dilemmas."

Public affairs   Copies of proposed and final ethics rules published in the *Federal Register* and an OGE staff directory.

Miscellaneous   A list of ethics officials at federal agencies, a manual titled *Public Financial Disclosure: A Reviewer's Reference,* and a list of ethics reports that agencies must file, complete with due dates.

GAO Watchdog

U.S. General Accounting Office
P.O. Box 1736
Washington, DC 20013

Members of the public can use GAO Watchdog to report federal government misconduct and wrongdoing to the General Accounting Office, the investigative arm of Congress.

Callers are asked to use their real names, which are kept confidential upon request. People who are uncomfortable using their real names can use aliases. If you use an alias, be sure to remember it so that you can exchange messages with GAO investigators.

The bulletins provide an introduction to the board, offer hints about reporting problems relating to federal money or programs, and list the telephone numbers of federal hotlines where callers can report fraud, waste, and abuse.

Callers can leave a report either by using the e-mail system or by uploading a document. Callers cannot access any files on the board, and can only exchange messages with GAO investigators.

VITAL STATS
Data: 202-371-2455
Voice: 202-512-7476
FedWorld gateway: 41

CASUCOM

Cooperative Administrative Support Program
18th & F Sts., N.W.
Room 7007
Washington, DC 20405

The Cooperative Administrative Support (CASU) program enables federal agencies to share services in an effort to save money and improve efficiency. It is conducted under the auspices of the President's Council on Management Improvement. The CASUCOM BBS serves agencies involved in the program.

The files, which you can access by typing **I** at the Main Menu, provide information about the CASU program, CASU policy documents, profiles of sites that are using the program, and profiles of participating agencies.

The files area also contains a large collection of documents about telecommuting, including bibliographies, evaluation materials, legislation, policies of various federal agencies, and reports.

The board also has more than a dozen forums, which serve as collection points for messages on a specific topic. There are forums about mail management, marketing the CASU program, recycling, equipment and software for telecommuting, and the benefits of telecommuting, among other subjects.

VITAL STATS

Data: 202-501-7707

Voice: 202-273-4660

FedWorld gateway: 73

To access files: Type **I** at the Main Menu

Enterprise Integration News BBS

Defense Information Systems Agency
2100 Washington Blvd.
Arlington, VA 22204

The Enterprise Integration News BBS is primarily aimed at employees and contractors of the Defense Information Systems Agency. It has information about topics such as business process re-engineering, information systems, enterprise integration, and data administration, among others.

VITAL STATS
Data: 800-727-3618 or
703-521-7289
Voice: 703-681-2429
FedWorld gateway: 78

GAO Office of Policy's BBS

U.S. General Accounting Office
Office of Policy
441 G St., N.W., Room 6800
Washington, DC 20548

The GAO Office of Policy's BBS offers more than 4,000 files from the U.S. General Accounting Office, which is the investigative arm of Congress. The board has the full text of selected GAO reports, policy manuals, and information about auditing.

Here are some highlights of what's available:

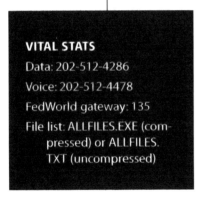

VITAL STATS

Data: 202-512-4286

Voice: 202-512-4478

FedWorld gateway: 135

File list: ALLFILES.EXE (compressed) or ALLFILES. TXT (uncompressed)

- The full text of selected GAO reports about technology challenges facing the information superhighway, pay comparisons between the federal government and the private sector, the North American Free Trade Agreement, workforce reductions, Medicaid, long-term care, child care, charter schools, Norplant, the condition of America's schools, block grants, medical education, electric vehicles, cholesterol measurement, and other topics.

- Summaries of GAO reports issued from 1992 to the present.

- GAO policy manuals about analyzing and presenting data, preparing testimony, commenting on legislative bills, preparing financial statement audit reports, conducting investigations, obtaining and analyzing data, and related topics.

- Lists of GAO recommendations that have not been implemented.

- A huge report titled *An Automated Audit Guide for Assessing Acquisition Risk.*

- Another huge report titled *Government Auditing Standards,* which is also known as the Yellow Book.

- An electronic version of GAO's telephone book.

GSA Electronic Management Information (GEMI) BBS

U.S. General Services Administration
Room 3111
18th and F Sts., N.W.
Washington, DC 20405

The GEMI BBS contains information about other General Services Administration (GSA) boards, sub-boards on topics such as computer accommodation for people with disabilities, information for contractors, and the National Performance Review report.

The following list describes areas that you can access from the Main Menu. To reach an area, type the appropriate letter:

D. Directory   This area contains descriptions of every GSA BBS. You can read the list online and save it using your communications program's capture feature. There is no version to download. From this area you also can connect to other GSA BBSs located in the Washington, D.C., area.

A. PAL   The Public Affairs Library has information about contracting opportunities with GSA, a publication titled *Doing Business With GSA*, press releases, and a publication titled *Your Right to Federal Records*.

VITAL STATS
Data: 202-219-0132 or
  202-219-0140
Voice: 202-501-3481
FedWorld gateway: 100

C. COCA   This sub-board is operated by GSA's Clearinghouse on Computer Accommodation. The Files Menu, which you can reach by typing **I** at the COCA Menu, offers files about federal government electronic information, a list of vendors and producers of access products, and COCA reports. The sub-board also has a forum, a news section that primarily describes new files, and its own e-mail system.

P. PASS (Planning, Quality Assurance, Systems Security Programs)
This sub-board presents extensive information about GSA's Information Resources Management plan, including a copy of the five-year plan. Other files contain directives, IRM reviews and reports, lists of contacts, and system security guidelines.

F. Files   This area contains a few general files, including the full text of the National Performance Review report.

L. Local GEMI functions   This area has an e-mail system, but otherwise all of the functions duplicate those in other areas of the board.

IRMa BBS

Office of Information Resource Management
U.S. Department of Transportation
400 Seventh St., S.W.
Washington, DC 20590

The IRMa BBS was being redesigned when this book was being written, and it offered only a few files. Eventually, it is supposed to provide details about information resource management activities at the Department of Transportation.

VITAL STATS
Data: 202-366-3373
Voice: Telephone support
        is not provided

ACF BBS

Administration for Children and Families
Aerospace Building
370 L'Enfant Promenade, S.W.
Washington, DC 20447

The ACF BBS has information about programs operated by the Administration for Children and Families. It's aimed primarily at ACF employees, state agencies, and organizations that receive ACF grants. Here are some highlights of what's available:

- More than two dozen brief fact sheets about ACF programs, including Aid to Families with Dependent Children, refugee resettlement, child support enforcement, Head Start, foster care and adoption assistance, and runaway and homeless youth.

- A searchable database containing thousands of files from the Child Welfare Bureau, Administration on Developmental Disabilities, Office of Family Assistance, Office of Child Support Enforcement, and the Office of Public Affairs. The database also contains general ACF files, laws, regulations, and sections of the Code of Federal Regulations that pertain to the agency.

- Sub-boards that provide information from the Office of Child Support Enforcement, Administration on Developmental Disabilities, Family and Youth Services Bureau, Children's Bureau, and the Office of Community Services.

- Staff directories for the ACF and the Department of Health and Human Services.

- ACF press releases.

VITAL STATS
Data: 800-627-8886 or
    202-401-5800
Voice: 202-401-5682
FedWorld gateway: 108

OCA BBS Document Exchange

U.S. Postal Rate Commission
Office of the Consumer Advocate
1333 H St., N.W.
Washington, DC 20268-0001

The OCA BBS Document Exchange contains documents filed in rate cases being considered by the Postal Rate Commission. Most of the documents are filed by major customers and competitors of the U.S. Postal Service. The BBS contains documents filed only electronically; it has no documents filed in paper form.

While most of the files are comments in rate cases, the files area also offers:

- The Postal Rate Commission's Rules of Practice and Procedure.

- The Domestic Mail Classification Schedule.

- A report by the Joint Task Force on Postal Ratemaking.

- Orders, opinions, and proposed rules from the Postal Rate Commission.

TELECONX

Cooperative Administrative Support Program
Office of Workplace Initiatives (CW)
U.S. General Services Administration
18th and F Sts., N.W., Room 7007
Washington, DC 20405

TELECONX has government reports about telecommuting, telecommuting policies from various federal agencies, several message forums about telecommuting issues, and related information.

The BBS has an obnoxious feature that forces you to answer an eighteen-question telecommuting poll before you can access anything else. The poll asks how many days a week you telecommute, what computer operating software you use, whether your agency has a telecommuting policy, and the average amount of time you spend using a computer each day, among other questions. Many of the questions are irrelevant—especially if you aren't a federal employee—but there's no way to avoid the poll or to answer "not applicable."

VITAL STATS

Data: 202-501-7741

Voice: 202-273-4660

FedWorld gateway: 56

To access files: At the Main
    Menu type **I**

E-mail: casu@gsa.gov

HUD News and Events Bulletin Board

U.S. Department of Housing and Urban Development
Room 10136
451 7th St., S.W.
Washington, DC 20410

The HUD News and Events Bulletin Board contains information from the public affairs office at the Department of Housing and Urban Development (HUD).

Here are some highlights of what's available:

- Fact sheets about major HUD programs.

- HUD responses to proposals to abolish the agency.

- Information about reinvention at HUD.

- Details about how to buy a home with FHA mortgage insurance.

- Annual surveys of mortgage lending activity.

- HUD's budget proposal.

- HUD news releases.

- Speeches, statements, and congressional testimony by HUD officials.

- The public schedule of the HUD secretary.

- Biographies of senior HUD personnel.

- Contact information for HUD field offices.

- Fair market rent data.

- Files from the Interagency Council on the Homeless.

VITAL STATS

Data: 202-708-3460 or
      202-708-3563
Voice: 202-708-0685, ext.
      113
FedWorld gateway: 85
To access files: At the Main
      Menu type **f**

Client Information Center BBS

U.S. General Services Administration
18th and F Sts., N.W.
Washington, DC 20405

The Client Information Center BBS is aimed at General Services Administration employees who manage federal government buildings. While the board is still operating, it appears to be inactive.

The files provide the policy handbook for the Office of Real Property Management and Safety, recycling policies and procedures, and information about cleaning and repairing federal buildings.

VITAL STATS
Data: 202-208-1747 or
202-501-2038
Voice: 202-501-4455

Federal Real Estate Sales Bulletin Board

U.S. General Services Administration
Room 4242
18th and F Sts., N.W.
Washington, DC 20405

The Federal Real Estate Sales Bulletin Board offers information about real estate for sale by federal government agencies. The board has general information about federal agencies that sell real estate, listings of specific properties for sale by the General Services Administration, and lists of military base closings nationwide.

To access information on the BBS, type the first letter of the area's name as it appears on the Main Menu:

[I]ntroduction for public users   Provides an overview of the BBS and instructions for using its Query Area.

[C]ontacts   Lists federal agencies that sell excess, seized, forfeited, or repossessed real estate. The agencies sell individual houses, multifamily units, office buildings, industrial plants, and vacant land. The area describes the types of property that each agency sells and provides instructions about where to call or write for further information.

[Q]uery   Allows users to examine listings of properties for sale by the General Services Administration. The board normally lists about fifty properties. You can search the listings by state, GSA region, first three digits of the ZIP code, agency selling the property, type of property, sale date, and sale type.

[B]ase closures   Lists military base closures by state and contacts for each of the military branches.

[G]SA   Lists addresses and telephone numbers for GSA Federal Property Resource Service offices nationwide.

FMS Inside Line

Cash Management Directorate
Financial Management Service
U.S. Department of the Treasury
401 14th St., S.W., 5th Floor, LCB
Washington, DC 20227

FMS Inside Line, which is operated by the Treasury Department's Financial Management Service, is an eclectic BBS. While its primary focus is management of federal inventories, assets, and finances, the board also has numerous files for BBS operators, Shakespeare's sonnets, and historic documents such as the Declaration of Independence.

Here are some highlights of what's available:

- The complete text of the *Treasury Financial Manual,* which provides instructions about fiscal management for federal agencies and departments.

- Selected circulars from the Office of Management and Budget about information policy, financial management systems, federal credit programs, internal controls, management of advisory committees, and other subjects.

- The full text of Treasury Department Circular 570, which lists insurance companies that can insure or reinsure federal bonds. For each company listed, the following information is provided: company name, business address, telephone number, the financial limit on how many bonds it can underwrite, the states in which it has surety licenses, and the state where it's incorporated.

- The full text of the Electronic Communications Privacy Act of 1986, the Computer Security Act of 1987, the Cash Management Improvement Act of 1990, the Chief Financial Officer Act of 1990, and a few other public laws.

- Extensive information about the distribution of federal funds to states and territories. One table lists each state's ranking, the total funds received, and the funds received per capita.

- Data about the federal deficit from 1970 to 1994.

- A list of financial officers at federal agencies and departments.

VITAL STATS
Data: 202-874-6817 or
202-874-6953 or
202-874-7034
Voice: 202-874-6995
FedWorld gateway: 50

- Numerous files containing population projections to the year 2050.

- Historic documents such as the Mayflower Compact, the Virginia Declaration of Independence, the Articles of Confederation, the Treaty of Paris, the Annapolis Convention, the Northwest Ordinance, the Constitution, the Neutrality Proclamation, the Monroe Doctrine, and the Emancipation Proclamation, among others.

- Historic speeches such as Washington's Farewell Address, the Gettysburg Address, and inaugural speeches by every president from George Washington to George Bush.

- The complete text of Shakespeare's sonnets.

- Various writings of Thomas Paine and Henry David Thoreau.

- Text files for people who are considering starting a BBS.

- Numerous programs and utilities for BBS operators.

Sales Bulletin Board System

U.S. General Services Administration
33rd Floor
525 Market St.
San Francisco, CA 94105

The Sales Bulletin Board System has information about surplus federal government property available for sale in Alaska, Arizona, California, Hawaii, Idaho, Oregon, Utah, and Washington State.

The BBS is arranged differently from most other federal BBSs, and it's quite cumbersome. After logging in you'll see the Private Mail Sub-board, which is of no use unless you send or receive private mail. Hit your Return key to pass it by.

Next, you'll be told that you can access two sub-boards, Personal Mail and GSA Sales. To reach GSA Sales, type **95** at the prompt. When you get another menu, type **f** to get a list of the files. The files provide auction catalogs and basic information about sealed bid sales.

VITAL STATS

Data: 415-744-8970

Voice: 415-744-5415

Account code: **gsasales**

Password: **sales**

Note: You must set your communications software to emulate a VT100 terminal

HEALTH AND MEDICINE

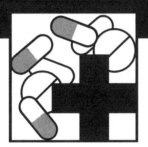

ABLE INFORM BBS

NARIC & ABLEDATA
Suite 935
8455 Colesville Road
Silver Spring, MD 20910-3319

ABLE INFORM has hundreds of files and five databases related to disabilities, assistive technology, and rehabilitation. The BBS is operated by a private contractor with funding from the National Institute on Disability and Rehabilitation Research (NIDRR), which is part of the Department of Education.

Information on the board is divided into bulletins, files, and databases. The bulletins, which you can access by typing **b** at the Main Menu, describe how to use the BBS, list publications from the NIDRR, describe how to access disability information on the Internet, and list conferences and job opportunities.

You can reach the files by typing **f** at the Main Menu. To help find your way through the hundreds of files, be sure to download the list of all files on the board. ABLE INFORM's list is far better than most because it provides detailed descriptions of each file. Here are some highlights of what's available:

- Information about other BBSs with disability information.

- Fact sheets about accessible housing, computer access, office equipment for people with visual disabilities, wheelchairs for children, van lifts, car seats, bath lifts, reclining bath seats, powered scooters, ramps, stair lifts, patient lifts, wheelchairs, seat cushions, standing aids, modular seating components, assistive devices for arthritis, and other devices.

- Pre-run searches of the ABLEDATA database, which contains information about assistive technology and rehabilitation equipment. Searches are available about wheelchairs, emergency alert systems, exercise equipment, grab bars, modified keyboards, adjustable beds, exercise equipment, and other devices.

- The *Directory of National Information Sources on Disabilities,* a 555-page book published by the NIDRR.

VITAL STATS

Data: 301-589-3563

Voice: 800-227-0216 or
301-588-9284

FedWorld gateway: 115

File list: A_INFORM.LST
(uncompressed) or
A_INFORM.ZIP (compressed)

To access files: At the Main
Menu type **f**

Time limit: 60 minutes per
day

Internet: http://www.naric.
com/naric/home.html

E-mail: naric@capaccess.
org

- Resource guides about spinal cord injury, traumatic brain injury, and stroke.

- Pre-run searches of the REHABDATA database, which contains bibliographic records with abstracts of more than 40,000 documents in the NARIC library. Searches are available about funding issues in rehabilitation, costs and cost benefit analysis in rehabilitation, legislation affecting disabled persons, management issues in rehabilitation, service issues, multiculturalism, and social service issues in rehabilitation.

- Extensive information about the Americans with Disabilities Act, including the full text of the act, a bibliography of ADA resources, information about the ADA from the Department of Justice, ADA guidelines from the Architectural Barriers and Compliance Board, final ADA rules from the Department of Transportation, the *ADA Technical Assistance Manual* from the Equal Employment Opportunity Commission, a list of statutory deadlines for the ADA, analyses of various sections of the ADA, and *The Americans with Disabilities Act: A NARIC Resource Guide,* which lists organizations, documents, periodicals, online resources, software, and videos pertaining to Titles 1-4 of the act.

- Reports about the needs of people with disabilities prepared by the Rehabilitation Engineering Center at the Electronic Industries Foundation.

- A number of thesaurus files to use in searching ABLEDATA.

ABLE INFORM also has five databases, which you can access by typing **dbs** at the Main Menu. The board has an excellent file that explains how to search the databases, and you should download it before starting a search. The uncompressed version is called DBS-V2.TXT, and the compressed version is called DBS-V2.ZIP. The databases include:

- REHABDATA: Bibliographic records with abstracts of more than 40,000 items in the National Rehabilitation Information Center library. The materials include research reports, books, journal articles, and audiovisual items. Photocopies of materials identified through the database are available for five cents per page.

- ABLEDATA: Detailed descriptions of about 20,000 assistive technology products, ranging from white canes to voice output programs. Price and company information is provided for each product. In addition, the database has information on noncommercial prototypes, customized and one-of-a-kind products, and do-it-yourself designs.

- NIDRR Program Directory: More than 300 records that describe research, demonstration, and dissemination projects funded by the NIDRR.

- NARIC KnowledgeBase: A referral directory that lists information sources of both local and national scope. It contains about 3,000 records.

- NARIC Guide to Periodicals: A directory of newsletters, magazines, and journals about disability and rehabilitation. It contains about 400 records.

Americans with Disabilities Electronic BBS

Public Access Section
Civil Rights Division
U.S. Department of Justice
Washington, DC 20035-6738

You will find a wealth of information about the rights of people with disabilities on the Americans with Disabilities Electronic BBS. Nearly all of the files concern the Americans with Disabilities Act (ADA).

You can access the files by typing **I** at the Main Menu. Here are some highlights:

- The full text of the ADA.

- ADA regulations developed by federal agencies.

- ADA enforcement status reports from the Justice Department.

- Booklets about the rights of employees and the responsibilities of employers under the ADA.

- Information about specific Justice Department enforcement actions under the ADA.

- Citations to private lawsuits filed under the ADA.

- A technical assistance manual for employers who must comply with the ADA.

- Standards for accessible design of new construction and alterations.

- Information about technical assistance grants awarded by the Justice Department under the ADA.

VITAL STATS
Data: 202-514-6193
Voice: 202-307-1084 or
    202-307-0663 (TDD)
FedWorld gateway: 9
To access files: At the Main
    Menu type **I**

Dial-JAN BBS

West Virginia Research and Training Center
5088 Washington St. W., Suite 200
Cross Lanes, WV 25313

DIAL-JAN contains information about job accommodations for people with disabilities. It has files about the Americans with Disabilities Act, the Rehabilitation Act of 1973, and the Randolph-Sheppard Act. The board also has discussion groups about adaptive technology and disability law.

The BBS is a sister board of Project Enable (next page), which is much more extensive but does not have a toll-free number. Although Dial-JAN is not operated by a federal agency, it is funded primarily by the President's Committee on Employment of People with Disabilities.

The files are located in three directories:

1. Rehabilitation Act of 1973: The full text of the law and of the 1992 reauthorization.

2. Randolph-Sheppard Act: The full text of the law, regulations, and related files.

3. Americans with Disabilities Act: Nearly 100 files about the act, many of which have been copied from the Americans with Disabilities Electronic BBS operated by the Department of Justice (p. 233). The files provide the full text of the ADA, deadlines for compliance, questions and answers about the law, a list of federal agencies and other organizations that can provide assistance in complying, a summary of federal tax credits and deductions that can help businesses complying with the ADA, a description of the law's legislative history, information about related federal disability laws, booklets published by the Equal Employment Opportunity Commission called *The ADA: Your Employment Rights as an Individual with a Disability* and *The ADA: Your Responsibilities as an Employer,* ADA regulations, the ADA Accessibility Guidelines, and news articles about the ADA.

VITAL STATS

Data: 800-342-5526

Voice: 800-624-8284 or
    304-759-0716

FedWorld gateway: 65

To access files: At the Main
    Menu type **f**

Time limit: 45 minutes per
    call

Project Enable

West Virginia Research and Training Center
Suite 200
5088 Washington St., W.
Cross Lanes, WV 25313

Project Enable has more than 1,000 files on disability topics, searchable data-bases of disability information, and more than 100 conferences. Many of the conferences, which primarily cover topics related to disability, rehabilitation, employment, and education, are "echoes" from international networks. Project Enable is operated by the West Virginia University Rehabilitation Research and Training Center, with funding from the U.S. Department of Education.

The bulletins provide information about Project Enable and how to use the BBS. You can reach them by typing **b** at the Main Menu.

The files, which you can access by typing **f** at the Main Menu, are divided into more than three dozen directories. Here are some highlights:

- Software and text files related to visual impairments and blindness, hearing impairments, mobility impairments, education for people with disabilities, and legal issues related to disabilities.

- Regulations under the Family and Medical Leave Act.

- Dozens of files about the Americans with Disabilities Act. Most of them have been uploaded from the Americans with Disabilities BBS operated by the U.S. Department of Justice (p. 233).

- Information about the Rehabilitation Act of 1973 and its 1992 reauthorization, the Randolph-Sheppard Act, and the Individuals with Disabilities Education Act.

- The Health Security Act of 1993 and related documents.

- A list of Internet mailing lists about disabilities.

- General guides to using the Internet.

- A guide to online disability information.

- A manual about using modems.

VITAL STATS

Data: 304-759-0727

Voice/TDD: 800-624-8284 or 304-759-0716

Manual: P-ENABLE.ZIP (compressed) or P-ENABLE.TXT (uncom-pressed)

File list: PCBFILES.ZIP

To access files: At the Main Menu type **f**

Internet: telnet enable. wvnet.cedu

E-mail: enable@rtc2.icdi. wvu.edu

- Communications programs, decompression utilities, and off-line mail readers for a variety of computers.

- A large collection of Windows 3.1 fonts that are freeware or shareware.

- Guide dog access laws for each state, Canadian province, and some other areas.

- Information about chronic fatigue syndrome, including a bibliography of articles and a list of BBSs that carry information about CFS.

- Dozens of different newsletters about disabilities.

- Graphics and images related to disabilities.

Most of the databases, which you can access by typing **open** at the Main Menu, allow you to search large documents using keywords. For example, you can search the Americans with Disabilities Act, the Rehabilitation Act of 1973 and related regulations, and the Randolph-Sheppard Act and related regulations. Another database allows you to check your eligibility for food stamps, Aid to Families with Dependent Children, Medicaid, and other federal programs.

The board also has more than 100 conferences, many of which are echoes from international networks such as FidoNet and QuickLink. Most of the conferences are public, although a few are not. You can request access to a private conference by sending a message to its moderator. You can access the conferences by typing **j** at the Main Menu.

There are conferences about sports for people with disabilities, artists with disabilities, occupational disabilities, disability rights, Alzheimer's disease, arthritis, blindness and other visual impairments, cancer, chronic fatigue syndrome, diabetes, environmental illness, nutrition, rare conditions and diseases, stress management, dealing and coping with terminally ill relatives, working from home, K-12 education (broken down by subject), desktop publishing, home schooling, Native American issues, computer viruses, and writing, among many other subjects.

RSA BBS

Rehabilitation Services Administration
U.S. Department of Education
330 C St., S.W., Room 3033
Washington, DC 20201

The RSA BBS, which is operated by the Rehabilitation Services Administration, serves people with disabilities and agencies that provide them with services. It focuses on programs funded under the Rehabilitation Act and the Randolph-Sheppard Act, including vocational rehabilitation, independent living, supported employment, and client assistance. Most of the files are quite technical.

You can access the files by typing **I** at the Main Menu. They offer grant information, arbitration decisions under the Randolph-Sheppard Act, a calendar of events, information memos from the RSA, chapters from the RSA manual, numerous RSA policy directives, and related materials.

VITAL STATS

Data: 202-205-5574

Voice: 202-205-8444

FedWorld gateway: 125

To access files: At the Main Menu type **I**

Aeromedical Forum

Federal Aviation Administration
Office of Aviation Medicine
800 Independence Ave., S.W.
Washington, DC 20591

The Aeromedical Forum is aimed at FAA aviation medicine employees. Although it is open to the public, only FAA employees can access the conferences about aviation medicine.

New users can examine parts of the board and download some files. The available files primarily consist of utility programs for DOS computers, but most are at least several years old. FAA employees who wish to access the aviation medicine conferences must fill out a questionnaire. To do so, type **a** at the Main Menu.

VITAL STATS
Data: 202-366-7920
Voice: 202-267-3535

Bureau of Health Professions (BHPr) BBS

Room 8809
5600 Fishers Lane
Rockville, MD 20857

The Bureau of Health Professions (BHPr) BBS provides information about students and professionals in the health field, along with a few health-related statistics. It also has a huge report that lists transplant survival rates by medical facility.

Information on the board is divided into bulletins and files. The bulletins, which you can access by typing **b** at the Main Menu, describe Bureau of Health Professions programs, list BHPr telephone numbers, list national professional meetings and international conferences, and provide information about reports and publications.

You can reach the files by typing **f** at the Main Menu. Here are some examples of what's available:

- A list of community health centers, migrant health centers, public housing primary care programs, rural health clinics, and other sites that serve the medically underserved. The file is compressed in a format that makes it unusable on most Macintosh computers.

- A list of 200 ways to put your talent to work in the health field.

- A report that lists survival rates for transplants of the heart, lung, kidney, liver, and pancreas at medical facilities around the country.

- A list of organ transplant centers.

- Several lengthy files about how to finance a medical education, including "Finance Your Health Professions Education" and "Financial Planning and Debt Management for Health Professions Students."

- Statistics on the number of families living below the poverty level for 1973-1990.

- AIDS death rates for 1987-1989.

- Maternal mortality rates for 1970-1989.

- Statistics about patient visits to doctors and dentists.

- Statistics about the enrollment of minorities and women in health education programs.

- A huge book filled with statistics about health professionals. The files are compressed in a format that makes them unusable on most Macintosh computers.

- A book about public health.

- Information about compliance by states with the Radiation Health and Safety Act of 1981.

- A book with extensive information about health occupations.

- A 1991 list of geriatric education centers.

CDC WONDER/PC

Centers for Disease Control and Prevention
1600 Clifton Road, NE, MS F-51
Atlanta, GA 30333

CDC WONDER/PC allows users to access and analyze data maintained by the Centers for Disease Control (CDC) on subjects such as mortality, cancer incidence, hospital discharges, AIDS, behavioral risk factors, diabetes, and other topics. The system also provides access to reports and guidelines prepared by the CDC and a directory of CDC experts you can contact.

You must register before using the system. To do so, you should call the voice number to request a registration form and then fill it out. You also must pay a one-time fee of $49.95, which gets you the special software required for CDC WONDER/PC and a manual. There are no other charges for accessing the system, and it even has a toll-free data number so you don't pay for long-distance telephone calls. Unfortunately, the software is available only for DOS computers.

The CDC WONDER/PC software allows you to access CDC datasets; analyze them and create charts, maps, and tables using them; send electronic mail; and transmit data files. Although the system is aimed at public health professionals, anyone from journalists to academic researchers should find it enormously useful.

VITAL STATS

Data: Number provided after you register

Voice: 404-332-4569

Note: You must register before using this system. To request a registration form, call the voice number.

CDRH Electronic Docket

Center for Devices and Radiological Health
U.S. Food and Drug Administration
12200 Wilkins Ave., Room 202
Rockville, MD 20852

Documents on the CDRH Electronic Docket advise the medical device industry about how to create products that will meet with approval from the Food and Drug Administration. The board also has announcements about related advisory committee meetings. The board is operated by the Division of Small Manufacturers Assistance in the FDA's Center for Devices and Radiological Health (CDRH).

The CDRH regulates a wide range of medical devices—everything from patient examination gloves to breast implants to heart valves to X-ray machines. The CDRH is charged with ensuring the devices are safe and effective.

The board offers medical device regulations, evaluation guidance, compliance policy guides, safety alerts, a medical gloves manual, radiological health guides, letters to industry by the director of the CDRH, congressional testimony, press releases, newsletters published by the CDRH, and minutes of meetings by various committees.

VITAL STATS

Data: 800-252-1366 or
301-594-2741

Voice: 301-443-6597

FedWorld gateway: 18

E-mail: gsc@fdadr.cdrh.
fda.gov

Note: You must set your communications software to emulate a VT100 terminal

Comprehensive Epidemiologic Data Resource (CEDR)

Mailstop 50F
Lawrence Berkeley Laboratory
University of California
One Cyclotron Road
Berkeley, CA 94720

The Comprehensive Epidemiologic Data Resource (CEDR) is an online catalog of epidemiologic data collected by the Department of Energy (DOE) during studies of people exposed to radiation. Most of the data sets come from studies of workers at DOE nuclear weapons manufacturing facilities.

If you use dial-in access, you are connected to CEDR's World Wide Web site. However, as this book was being written, the site's operators were designing a BBS interface that may be online by the time you read this.

Logging into the site through dial-in access requires a few steps:

1. After you connect, you'll get a prompt that says "ENTER - DIRECTORY(D), NETWORK(N), OUTSIDE(O), OR TERMINAL TYPE CHANGE(T)." Type **d** and hit your Return key.

2. The next prompt will say, "ENTER DESTINATION NUMBER." Type **cedr** and hit your Return key.

3. The next prompt will say "cedr login:" (if you don't get this prompt, press your Return key once or twice and it should appear). Type **www** and hit your Return key.

VITAL STATS

Data: 510-486-7996 (9600 baud and above) or 510-486-7900 (2400 baud)

Voice: 510-486-5742

Internet: http://cedr.lbl.gov or gopher cedr.lbl.gov

E-mail: cedr@cedr.lbl.gov

Note: See the detailed login instructions

For each data set, the catalog offers a detailed description and information about any studies where it has been used. The data sets, which DOE collected over the past thirty years, vary widely in the time span covered and in the number, type, and format of variables included.

Although the data sets are available to the public, they are not accessible at this site. Instead, people interested in using them must complete an access request and sign a form promising to keep the names of individuals confidential. Once the paperwork is approved, the user receives instructions about how to access the data sets using the Internet.

FDA Electronic Bulletin Board

Press Office
U.S. Food and Drug Administration
5600 Fishers Lane
Rockville, MD 20857

A wide range of information about the Food and Drug Administration's regulation of food, drugs, medical devices, animal feed and drugs, cosmetics, and the blood supply is available on the FDA Electronic Bulletin Board.

The FDA establishes standards, inspects domestic manufacturing facilities, inspects imports, and orders recalls of hazardous products. In recent years, it has done everything from developing food labeling regulations to approving new AIDS drugs to approving a fat substitute for use in foods.

After you connect to the system, you reach a World Wide Web interface. This makes the system extremely easy to use. It's a huge improvement over the old BBS.

Documents on the system are divided into more than a dozen topic areas. You can explore areas of interest, or if you prefer you can search all of the documents on the system at once using keywords. You can reach the sophisticated search engine by choosing "Search" at the opening menu.

Here are descriptions of the topic areas:

AIDS Various information about AIDS, divided into six sub-topics: press releases, policy, articles, fraud, speeches, and meetings.

ANSWERS Answers to current questions arising as a result of news stories. Sample titles include "FDA Approves Treatment for Impotence," "The Safety of Blood and Blood Products," "BST Update: First Year Experience Reports," and "Availability of Fertility Drugs." Files are available dating back to 1987.

APPROVALS The complete text of the *Drug and Device Product Approvals List,* which is published monthly. The list describes human drugs, veterinary drugs, and medical devices that have been approved for sale. Files are available dating back to December 1989.

VITAL STATS

Data: 800-222-0185 or
   301-227-6857

Voice: 301-443-4908

FedWorld gateway: 17

Login: **bbs**

Password: **bbs**

Internet: http://www.fda.
   gov/bbs/bbs_topics.
   html *or* telnet www.
   fda.gov

Note: After you connect, at
   the Parklawn Com-
   puter Center Menu
   choose item 1, FDA
   Bulletin Board Service

CDRH   Two bulletins published by the Centers for Devices and Radiological Health. The *Medical Device Bulletin* and the *Radiological Health Bulletin* are each issued monthly, and contain information about recent CDRH developments and meetings. Files are available dating back to 1990.

CONGRESS   The full text of selected prepared statements delivered by FDA officials at congressional oversight hearings. Statements are added to the board the same day as the hearing. Files are available dating back to 1990.

CONSUMER   Selected issues of *FDA Consumer*, the FDA's official monthly magazine, and a catalog of consumer publications and audiovisual materials developed by FDA.

ENFORCE   The weekly *FDA Enforcement Report*, which lists FDA-regulated products that are being recalled. Each listing includes the product, the manufacturer, who recalled it, the quantity recalled, where the product was distributed, and the reason for the recall. Also listed are seizure orders, injunctions, and prosecutions. Files are available dating back to 1990.

FDA_DATEREG   Summaries of all FDA *Federal Register* announcements arranged by publication date. Typically, these announcements are about new rules or upcoming meetings. Each contains a short summary of the article and the name of a contact person. In the case of announcements about public meetings, the file also lists where and when they will be held.

FDA_INDEX   Indexes of press releases and answers to news media questions issued by the FDA press office from January 1984 to date.

IMPORT_ALERT   Import Detention Summaries, which are reports about imported items that have been detained because they violate a law. Each detention summary lists the product, quantity, shipper, country of origin, port of entry, date, and reason for detention. This area also has a booklet titled *Current Good Manufacturing Practice in Manufacturing, Packing, or Holding Human Food.*

MEETINGS   Lists of upcoming meetings of various FDA panels, committees, and boards. Each listing includes the date, time, and place for the meeting, a contact person, and a description of the topics to be discussed.

NEWS   Press releases about FDA actions, including any recalls. Sample titles include "Infant Formula Alert," "FDA Licenses Chickenpox Vaccine," and "Reinventing Drug and Medical Device Regulations." This area also has the most recent edition of the *FDA Consumer* magazine.

SPEECH   The full text of prepared speeches delivered by the FDA commissioner and deputy commissioner at various meetings. Selected speeches are available dating back to 1990.

VETNEWS   CVM Updates, which are news items issued by the FDA's Center for Veterinary Medicine.

FDA Prime Connection

Food and Drug Administration
HFS-625
200 C St., S.W.
Washington, DC 20204-0001

The FDA Prime Connection offers a wealth of information about food safety. It focuses primarily on retail food protection, milk safety, and shellfish sanitation, and is aimed at federal, state, and local regulatory officials. Most of the files are produced by the Office of Compliance at the Food and Drug Administration's Center for Food Safety and Applied Nutrition.

Access to the board is restricted. If you want to use the board, you must first call, fax, or write to obtain a password, the data number, and access instructions.

The board has hundreds of files. Here are some highlights:

- Information about recent outbreaks of foodborne illnesses around the country.

- *Foodborne Pathogenic Microorganisms and Natural Toxins,* a book that has chapters about salmonella, viruses, shellfish toxins, mushroom toxins, and other microorganisms and toxins.

- Information about foods, medicines, and other products regulated by the FDA that are being recalled. Each listing includes the product, the manufacturer, where the product was distributed, how much of the product was distributed, and the reason for the recall.

- An FDA database containing information about pesticides used on foods and FDA's methods to determine the residues of these pesticides. This file is compressed in a self-extracting format that makes it unusable on most Macintosh computers.

- The full text of the Food and Drug Administration's food labeling regulations. These files are compressed in a self-extracting format that makes them unusable on most Macintosh computers.

- Information about exemptions from the food labeling regulations, including exemption requests from small businesses divided by state, city, and firm.

VITAL STATS

Data: Number provided after you register

Voice: 202-205-8140

Fax: 202-205-5560

Note: New users must call, fax, or write to obtain a password, the data number, and access instructions

- The full text of various food codes and regulations.
- A list of firms that ship milk between states.
- Numerous files about milk safety.
- A list of firms that ship seafood between states.
- A list that includes the market name, scientific name, common name, and regional name for various fish.
- A glossary of molluscan shellfish.
- Amendments to the federal Food, Drug, and Cosmetic Act.

Grateful Med BBS

MEDLARS Management
National Library of Medicine
National Institutes of Health
Building 38A, 8600 Rockville Pike
Bethesda, MD 20894

The Grateful Med BBS supports users of Grateful Med, a software program that provides a menu-driven interface for MEDLARS. MEDLARS is a fee-based collection of more than twenty databases at the National Library of Medicine.

The Grateful Med software is easier to use than the normal MEDLARS interface. In addition, it can help save on connect charges because you compose all searches off-line.

This BBS has a very strange opening message: "Grateful Med users are better served via the Service Desk." If this is true, why is the National Library of Medicine still running this BBS?

The bulletins, which you can access by typing **b** at the Main Menu, provide information about the Grateful Med software and describe how to order it. The software costs $29.95 and is available for DOS and Macintosh computers.

The files, which you can access by typing **f** at the Main Menu, offer a demo version of the DOS version of Grateful Med, an application for a MEDLARS account, case studies of Grateful Med searches, and support files for the DOS version of Grateful Med.

VITAL STATS
Data: 800-525-5756
Voice: 800-638-8480

HSTAT (Health Services/Technology Assessment Text)

National Information Center on Health Services Research and Health Care
  Technology
National Library of Medicine
8600 Rockville Pike
Bethesda, MD 20894

HSTAT (Health Services/Technology Assessment Text) provides numerous health-related documents, including Clinical Practice Guidelines from the Agency for Health Care Policy and Research and Consensus Development Statements from the National Institutes of Health.

If you have Internet access, it's much easier to access the site with Gopher than with a dial-in or Telnet connection.

Here are some highlights of what's available:

- Clinical Practice Guidelines from the Agency for Health Care Policy and Research on topics such as acute pain management, urinary incontinence in adults, cataracts, depression, sickle cell disease, HIV, cancer pain, heart failure, and post-stroke rehabilitation. The extensive guidelines provide advice to both physicians and patients.

- Copies of the *Morbidity and Mortality Weekly Report* from the Centers for Disease Control.

- The *U.S. Task Force Guide to Clinical Preventive Services*, which has chapters about screening and immunization for a number of diseases and disorders.

- NIH Consensus Development Statements, which provide information about dozens of health issues such as hip replacement, optimal calcium intake, ovarian cancer, early identification of hearing impairment in children, impotence, diagnosis and treatment of depression in late life, and treatment of panic disorder, among others.

- NIH Technology Assessments, which provide information about various biomedical technologies.

VITAL STATS

Data: 800-952-4426

Voice: 800-272-4787 (select 1,6,3,2) or 301-496-0176

Login (dial-in and Telnet only): **hstat**

Login (FTP only): **anonymous**

Password (FTP only): your e-mail address

Internet: gopher gopher.nlm.nih.gov *or* telnet text.nlm.nih.gov *or* ftp nlmpubs.nlm.nih.gov

Path (Gopher only): *HSTAT - Health Services/Technology Assessment Text*

Path (FTP only): *hstat*

MEDLARS AIDS Databases

National Library of Medicine
8600 Rockville Pike
Bethesda, MD 20894

The MEDLARS AIDS Databases are four AIDS-related databases operated by the National Library of Medicine. The databases are part of MEDLARS, a fee-based system operated by the library. However, accessing the AIDS databases is free.

You must register to use this system. To do so, call the voice number listed in the box and request an "AIDS code." You'll be sent an application form, and after you fill it out and return it, the library will send you access instructions.

Searching the AIDS databases is not intuitive, even for experienced searchers. To get around this problem, the National Library of Medicine created a software program called Grateful Med that provides an easier interface to the databases. NLM librarians strongly suggest that users of the AIDS databases order this program, and I concur. The program costs $29.95, and is available for DOS and Macintosh computers. To order it, call the National Technical Information Service at 800-423-9255. The order number for the DOS version is PB92-105444, and the number for the Macintosh version is PB93-502433.

Here are brief descriptions of the four databases:

VITAL STATS

Data: Toll-free number provided after you register

Voice: 800-638-8480

Internet: Telnet address provided after you register

E-mail: mms@nlm.nih.gov

Note: You must register before using this system

AIDSLINE   Provides more than 90,000 bibliographic references to journal articles, books, and audiovisual materials about HIV/AIDS published since 1980. More than half of the entries include abstracts provided by the author. AIDSLINE also contains abstracts from the International Conference on AIDS. The database is updated weekly, and about 1,000 new citations are added every month.

AIDSTRIALS   Contains information about clinical trials of drugs being tested for the treatment of HIV/AIDS. The database has information about trials that are still seeking patients and those that are closed. For each trial, the database describes the trial's purpose, eligibility criteria, contact persons, drugs being tested, and trial locations. Information about clinical trials sponsored by the National Institutes of Health is provided by the National Institute of Allergy and Infectious Diseases, while details about privately sponsored efficacy trials are provided by the Food and Drug Administration.

AIDSDRUGS   Offers information about the drugs being tested in trials included in AIDSTRIALS. The database contains descriptive information for each drug, such as pharmacologic action and contraindications.

DIRLINE   Provides a directory of more than 17,000 organizations and resources that offer biomedical information. The directory includes information about more than 2,000 HIV/AIDS-related resources such as organizations, federal agencies, self-help groups, and databases.

NIDR Online

Management Information Systems & Analysis Section
National Institute of Dental Research
National Institutes of Health
Room 707 Westwood Building
Bethesda, MD 20892

NIDR Online allows users to order free publications from the National Institute of Dental Research (NIDR), search databases that list dental schools and dental libraries, and learn about grants and contracts that are available or that have been awarded.

There are three ways to access this BBS:

1. **Through dial-in access**   You must set your communications software to 7 data bits, even parity, 1 stop bit, and half duplex. If your communications program does not have a half-duplex setting, turn on local echo instead. In addition, you may need to experiment with your terminal setting to see what works. A VT100 setting works well. After you connect, type **,gen1** (the comma is essential) and press your Enter key. You won't be prompted to do this. At the "Initials?" prompt, type **kil** and press Enter. At the "Account?" prompt, type **hdt1** (that's hdt and the number 1) and press Enter.

2. **Through FedWorld**   You must switch to a half-duplex communications setting when you move from FedWorld. If your communications program doesn't have a half-duplex setting, turn on local echo instead. A message will tell you when to make the change. If you don't change the setting, what you type will be invisible on the screen.

3. **Through the Internet**   After you connect, type **,gen1** (the comma is essential) and press your Enter key. You won't be prompted to do this. At the "Initials?" prompt, type **kil** and press Enter. At the "Account?" prompt, type **hdt1** (that's hdt and the number 1) and press Enter.

You can read all the documents on the BBS online and capture them by using your communications program's capture feature. There are no files to download.

VITAL STATS

Data: 800-358-2221 or
301-402-2221

Voice: 301-594-5590

FedWorld gateway: 69

Internet: telnet wylbur.cu.nih.gov

Note: Dial-in users will have to experiment with the terminal setting in their communications software. A setting of VT100 works well. Also, your communications software must be set to even parity, 7 data bits, 1 stop bit, and half duplex (or local echo).

The Main Menu lists six sub-menus, most of which lead to additional sub-menus:

1. **Science Information and Transfer**   This sub-menu offers a description of the National Institute of Dental Research, news releases from the NIDR, a bulletin board for dental librarians, a list of upcoming conferences sponsored by the NIDR and other organizations, a detailed list of films about dental health, a list of NIDR publications aimed at the general public and health professionals, and a link to NIH EDNET, a bulletin board operated by the NIH Office of Education. For a full description, see p. 141.

2. **Grants and Contracts**   This sub-menu has information about grants and contracts either available from or awarded by the NIDR. Documents provide NIH grant policies and guidelines, list grant availability, and list grants awarded. By selecting option 10, you access a database of active grants. You can search the database by project number; investigator name; institution; city, state, or country; and title words. For each grant, the database lists the project number, investigator name, amount awarded, institution, project title, and dates the grant starts and ends.

3. **Directories**   Three searchable databases are available:

   - NIDR telephone directory, which you can search by last name or organizational component.

   - Dental school directory, which lists dental schools in the United States and Canada. You can search it by state, dean's name, or institution name. Each listing includes the dean's name, address, and telephone number.

   - Dental library directory, which lists dental libraries in the United States and Canada. You can search it by state, librarian name, or institution name. Each listing includes the library director's name, address, and telephone number.

4. **Message to NIDR**   This option allows you to send an electronic message to NIDR.

5. **Clinician Research Scientist Awardees**   This searchable database lists scientists in the Clinician Research Scientists program. The database lists the scientist's name, year of degree, institution that granted the degree, grant number and institution, start and end dates, clinical interest, science track, project title, and mentor.

6. **Online Services for Oral Health Information**   Details about how to access other online sources of oral health information.

NIH Information Center

National Institutes of Health
Building 31, Room 2B09
Bethesda, MD 20902

You can find a vast quantity of information about diseases and the National Institutes of Health on the NIH Information Center BBS.

After you connect, the board presents a list of toll-free NIH information lines about various diseases. It then presents the Bulletin Menu, which you also can access by typing **b** at the Main Menu. The bulletins provide a glossary of communications terms, an overview of NIH, and information about how to access other sources of health information.

You can access the files by typing **f** at the Main Menu. Here are some highlights of what's available:

- Hundreds of NIH publications about subjects such as adult brain tumors, Hodgkin's disease, Agent Orange, artificial sweeteners, breathing disorders during sleep, breast cancer, providing care for people with AIDS, cataracts, cervical cancer, chemotherapy, cholesterol in children, chronic pain, depression, diabetes, eating disorders, food additives, chronic fatigue syndrome, fever blisters and canker sores, hemorrhoids, alcoholism, skin cancer, headaches, heart transplants, radiation, kidney stones, lactose intolerance, learning disabilities, lyme disease, menopause, nutrition, the health benefits of pets, smoking, seasonal affective disorder, mental health, tooth decay, vaginal infections, vasectomy safety, AIDS prevention, and stress.

- An index of diseases being investigated at NIH, along with contact numbers.

- Publication lists from institutes at NIH (see box, p. 257).

- Press releases from NIH.

- Dozens of official NIH news stories. Sample titles include "Alcohol and Creativity: No Connection," "Blood Transfusions May Raise Cancer Risk in Older Women," and "Information on Risks Associated with Cholesterol."

- Calendars of NIH events and biomedical meetings.

- Maps of Washington's Metrorail system in GIF and PCX formats.

VITAL STATS

Data: 800-644-2271 or
    301-480-5144

Voice: 301-496-6610

FedWorld gateway: 127

To access files: At the Main
    Menu type **f**

E-mail: dennist@helix.
    nih.gov

- Maps of roads and parking lots at NIH and of regional roads surrounding NIH.

- NIH organizational charts.

- A history of NIH.

- Background information about many of the NIH institutes.

- Clinical Alerts for doctors reporting research findings at NIH.

- The full text of the 1993 Surgeon General's report on HIV infection and AIDS.

- Information about the National Library of Medicine and an NLM publications list.

- A list of cancer information sources.

- A list of AIDS-related bulletin boards.

- A list of federal health information centers and clearinghouses.

- A huge list of health information resources in the federal government.

- A handbook from the Department of Agriculture about the nutritive content of foods.

- Guidelines for research involving recombinant DNA molecules.

- A list of organizations that offer services to cancer patients.

- A list of toll-free telephone numbers for health information.

- Articles written by NIH scientists that have appeared in the *Journal of the American Medical Association.*

- A directory of alternative healthcare associations.

- A bibliography of publications about health problems experienced by Gulf War veterans.

- NIH Consensus Statements, which evaluate the safety and efficacy of various biomedical technologies. Some sample titles include "Defined Diets and Childhood Hyperactivity," "Health Implications of Obesity," "Geriatric Assessment Models for Clinical Decisionmaking," "Urinary Incontinence in Adults," "Noise and Hearing Loss," "Treatment of Early-Stage Breast Cancer," "Optimal Calcium Intake," and "Diagnosis and Treatment of Depression in Late Life."

Participating NIH Institutes

National Institute on Aging
National Institute on Alcohol Abuse and Alcoholism
National Institute of Allergy and Infectious Diseases
National Institute of Arthritis and Musculoskeletal and Skin Diseases
National Cancer Institute
National Institute of Child Health and Human Development
National Institute on Deafness and Other Communications Disorders
National Institute of Dental Research
National Institute of Diabetes and Digestive and Kidney Diseases
National Institute on Drug Abuse
National Institute of Environmental Health Sciences
National Eye Institute
National Institute of General Medical Sciences
National Heart, Lung, and Blood Institute
National Center for Human Genome Research
National Institute of Mental Health
National Institute of Neurological Disorders and Stroke
National Institute for Nursing Research

Nutrient Data Bank Bulletin Board

U.S. Department of Agriculture
Agricultural Research Service
Beltsville Human Nutrition Research Center
Nutrient Data Laboratory
4700 River Rd., Unit 89
Riverdale, MD 20737

The Nutrient Data Bank Bulletin Board provides limited information about the nutritional content of food. Primarily, the files contain technical information used during national surveys of eating patterns.

Unfortunately, all of the files are compressed in a self-extracting format that makes them unusable on most Macintosh computers. Following are some of the most interesting files available for downloading:

FNICELEC.EXE   A list of electronic sources of food and nutrition information.

PYRAMDDB.EXE   Nutrition education materials that use the food guide pyramid.

DAPZ.EXE   A freeware program that allows you to analyze what you eat over a three-day period. The program analyzes the food for twenty-eight nutrients and food components, including calories, protein, total fat, saturated fatty acids, monounsaturated fatty acids, polyunsaturated fatty acids, carbohydrates, dietary fiber, cholesterol, vitamin A, carotenes, vitamin E, vitamin C, alcohol, thiamin, riboflavin, preformed niacin, vitamin B6, vitamin B12, folacin, calcium, phosphorus, magnesium, iron, potassium, sodium, copper, and zinc. It produces bar graphs showing the percentage of calories from protein, carbohydrate, fat, saturated fatty acids, and alcohol, in addition to other data. If ordered from the National Technical Information Service, the program costs $60. Downloading it from the BBS is free. The program is available only for DOS computers.

SUGAR.EXE   Information about the amounts of monosaccharides, disaccharides, other sugars, and total sugar in more than 500 foods.

HG72.EXE   Nutrient data expressed in common household units for more than 900 foods.

OASH BBS

National AIDS Program Office
Department of Health and Human Services
Hubert Humphrey Bldg.
Room 729-H
200 Independence Ave., S.W.
Washington, DC 20201

A wide range of information about AIDS, including reports from the National Commission on AIDS, bibliographies of materials about AIDS, and the *Surgeon General's Report to the American People on HIV Infection and AIDS,* can be found on the OASH BBS. The board also has a limited number of files on other health subjects, including copies of the *Morbidity and Mortality Weekly Report* from the Centers for Disease Control.

The board has one drawback: Some of its files are compressed in a self-extracting format that makes them unusable on most Macintosh computers.

Here are some highlights of what's available:

VITAL STATS
Data: 202-690-5423
Voice: 202-401-8646
FedWorld gateway: 51
Time limits: 90 minutes per call, 3 hours per day

- Daily summaries of articles about AIDS from newspapers, wire services, and magazines. Each listing includes a summary, headline, date published, page number, and author.

- More than a dozen training bulletins on basic AIDS issues prepared for the National AIDS Hotline staff. These have the latest information on such subjects as the use of spermicides and condoms, transfusions and AIDS infection, HIV transmission in health care settings, and AIDS transmission during dental procedures.

- Weekly editions of the *Morbidity and Mortality Weekly Report,* which is published by the Centers for Disease Control.

- A document titled *USPHS/IDSA Guidelines for the Prevention of Opportunistic Infections in Persons Infected with HIV: A Summary.*

- A document titled *U.S. Public Health Service Recommendations for HIV Counseling and Voluntary Testing for Pregnant Women.*

- A report titled *Public Health Threat: Cryptosporidiosis in the Nation's Water Supply.*

- Numerous fact sheets about AIDS, including "Facts about Adolescents and HIV/AIDS," "Facts about HIV/AIDS and Preventing HIV Infection," "Facts about Drug Use and HIV/AIDS," "Facts about HIV/AIDS and Race/Ethnicity," "Facts about HIV and its Transmission," "Facts about the Scope of the HIV/AIDS Epidemic," and "Facts about Women and HIV/AIDS," among others.

- The Centers for Disease Control's *HIV/AIDS Prevention Newsletter*.

- Bibliographies of scientific articles, audiovisual materials, and reports about AIDS, which are compiled by the National Library of Medicine. The bibliographies are updated monthly.

- A report titled *The Public Health Impact of Needle Exchange Programs in the United States and Abroad*.

- The 1993 *Surgeon General's Report to the American People on HIV Infection and AIDS*.

- A list of AIDS-related BBSs.

- The Public Health Service's Strategic Plan to Combat HIV/AIDS.

- Resource guides prepared by the Centers for Disease Control's National AIDS Clearinghouse. Some sample titles include "A Guide to Selected AIDS-Related Internet Resources," "A Guide to Selected AIDS-Related Electronic Bulletin Board Systems," "A Guide to Locating Information about HIV/AIDS," "A Guide to Locating Information about Condom Efficacy and Use," "A Guide to HIV/AIDS and College Students," "A Guide to Selected Resources for Women Living with HIV and AIDS," and "A Guide to Locating Basic Resources for Persons Living with HIV and AIDS."

- Detailed information about sexually transmitted diseases.

- HIV/AIDS surveillance reports published by the Centers for Disease Control.

- A newsletter published by the National Library of Medicine titled *NLM AIDSLINE*.

- Huge databases of AIDS drugs and AIDS trials, which are updated monthly.

- Public Health Service press releases about AIDS.

- Reports from the National Commission on AIDS, including *Preventing HIV Transmission in Health Care Settings*, *The Challenge of HIV/AIDS in Com-*

munities of Color, Living with AIDS, Failure of U.S. Health Care System to Deal with HIV Epidemic, and *AIDS in Rural America.*

- *Federal Register* notices relating to the national vaccine program.

- *Federal Register* notices relating to women's health.

- The *ORI Newsletter,* which is published by the Office of Research Integrity at the Public Health Service. The quarterly newsletter has articles about lawsuits, cases, and federal actions involving scientific integrity. It also lists publications and upcoming meetings about scientific misconduct.

- The annual report from the Office of Research Integrity.

- A huge report from a conference about plagiarism and the theft of ideas sponsored by the Office of Research Integrity and the American Academy for the Advancement of Science.

- The executive summary from the 1994 Surgeon General's report titled *Preventing Tobacco Use Among Young People.*

- The budget request from the Public Health Service.

- A searchable calendar of HIV/AIDS events. To access it, type **5** at the Main Menu.

PHS Drug Pricing EDRS

Bureau of Primary Health Care
Tenth Floor
4350 East-West Highway
Bethesda, MD 20814

The PHS Drug Pricing EDRS is aimed at drug manufacturers and health care providers who participate in a program to provide discounted out-patient drugs to indigent patients.

The board has a database called the EDRS Database Query System that drug manufacturers can use to determine which providers qualify for the discounted drugs. It also has lists of manufacturers that are eligible to participate in the program and *Federal Register* notices about eligibility requirements.

VITAL STATS
Data: 301-594-4992
Voice: 301-594-4353
FedWorld gateway: 122

PREVline (Prevention Online)

The National Clearinghouse for Alcohol and Drug Information
P.O. Box 2345
Rockville, MD 20847-2345

PREVline offers hundreds of files about alcohol, tobacco, and other drugs from the National Clearinghouse for Alcohol and Drug Information. They include publications about prevention, government reports, speeches, bibliographies, and resource guides.

One caution about the files: Many have outdated information, such as research data from the mid-1980s or bibliographies that stop with publications produced in the early 1990s. Despite that, however, there is still lots of valuable information here.

To access the files, type **f** at the Main Menu. Then type **s** to download a catalog of all the files with short descriptions, **l** to download the catalog with long descriptions, or **k** to conduct a keyword search of all the files.

The files offer:

- Bibliographies about adult children of alcoholics, advertising and alcohol, Alcoholics Anonymous, alcohol and drug use on college campuses, children of alcoholics, cocaine and pregnancy, the physiological effects of alcohol, and fetal alcohol syndrome.

- Data on advertising expenditures for alcohol, alcohol-related fatal traffic accidents, arrests for alcohol-related offenses, alcohol involvement in plane crashes, drug use by high school students, trends in drug-related deaths, alcohol consumption per capita, alcohol problems among the elderly, global tobacco use and advertising, and tobacco use by women, minorities, and youths.

- Basic descriptions of drugs such as cocaine and marijuana.

- A list of the street names of drugs.

- Sample drug policies from various organizations.

- Numerous files with success stories from corporate Employee Assistance Programs.

VITAL STATS:

Data: 301-770-0850

Voice: 800-729-6686 or 301-468-2600

FedWorld gateway: 137

To access files: At the Main Menu type **f**

Internet: telnet ncadi.health.org *or* ftp ftp.health.org

Login (FTP only): **anonymous**

Password (FTP only): your e-mail address

Path (FTP only): *pub/files*

E-mail: info@prevline. health.org

- Resource guides that focus on alcohol-related violence, tobacco, people with disabilities, teenage pregnancy, children of alcoholics, community action, the workplace, rural communities, lesbians and gay men, impaired driving, inhalants, and pregnant women.

- Separate resource guides for elementary and secondary school teachers about alcohol, tobacco, and other drugs.

- The *1995 National Drug Control Strategy*, which was issued by the Office of National Drug Control Policy in the Executive Office of the President.

- Summaries of dram shop laws for every state.

- A report titled *Growing Up Tobacco-Free: Preventing Nicotine Addiction in Children and Youth*, which was prepared by the Institute of Medicine at the National Academy of Sciences.

- Electronic copies of a bimonthly publication called *Prevention Pipeline*, which is produced by the Center for Substance Abuse Prevention.

- Portions of the North American Free Trade Agreement that pertain to alcohol and tobacco.

Besides the files, the BBS offers:

- A catalog of print publications, videotapes, and other materials available from the National Clearinghouse for Alcohol and Drug Information. To download it, type **c** at the Main Menu.

- A searchable database called the Citizen's Guide to Alcohol, Tobacco, Other Drugs, and HIV/AIDS Resources. It lists more than 1,800 resources, including state alcohol agencies, federal agencies and clearinghouses, national organizations, and foundations. To access the database, type **y** at the Main Menu.

Quick Facts BBS

CSR, Inc.
Suite 200
1400 Eye St., N.W.
Washington, DC 20005

Virtually any statistic you could possibly want about alcohol and alcohol abuse can be found on the Quick Facts BBS. It is operated by a private contractor for the National Institute on Alcohol Abuse and Alcoholism (NIAAA).

Here are some highlights of what's available:

- Estimated and projected numbers of alcohol abusers and alcoholics.

- Two dozen NIAAA "Alcohol Alert" publications about alcohol and aging, alcohol withdrawal syndrome, children of alcoholics, alcohol and women, fetal alcohol syndrome, alcohol and AIDS, the genetics of alcoholism, alcohol and cancer, and related subjects.

- Statistics on alcohol consumption for individual states, the United States, and foreign countries.

- Statistics on state tax revenues from alcohol.

- Alcohol advertising expenses for 1975-1993.

- Statistics on hospital admissions for alcohol-related problems.

- A wide range of statistics on alcohol-related deaths from cirrhosis and traffic accidents.

- More than two dozen files containing demographic information about drinking. The files contain information on drinking patterns by whites, blacks, Mexican Americans, Cuban Americans, Puerto Ricans, high school seniors, and other people.

VITAL STATS
Data: 202-289-4112
Voice: 202-842-7600
FedWorld gateway: 118
To access files: At the Main Menu type **f**

JOBS AND EMPLOYMENT

Automated Vacancy Announcement Distribution System (AVADS) BBS

U.S. Geological Survey
206 National Center
Reston, VA 22092

The Automated Vacancy Announcement Distribution System (AVADS) BBS lists job vacancies at the U.S. Department of the Interior. Vacancies are listed for eleven Interior divisions: Bureau of Indian Affairs, Bureau of Land Management, Bureau of Mines, Bureau of Reclamation, Fish and Wildlife Service, Minerals Management Service, National Biological Survey, National Park Service, Office of the Secretary, Office of Surface Mining, and the U.S. Geological Survey.

Searching the vacancy lists is a bit tricky. New users should type **h** at the Main Menu to access several brief files that explain how to use the BBS.

The job descriptions are very detailed. They include opening and closing dates for the vacancy, a telephone number for further information, a mailing address, information about how to apply, and descriptions of the skills needed and the job duties.

VITAL STATS

Data: 703-648-6000
Voice: 703-648-7239
FedWorld gateway: 132

Automated Vacancy Announcement System (AVAS)

National Institutes of Health
B31/B3C1S
9000 Rockville Pike
Bethesda, MD 20892

The Automated Vacancy Announcement System (AVAS) provides weekly lists of job openings at the National Institutes of Health. You can download the lists in various formats or search them for particular positions. The system is operated by the NIH Division of Personnel Management.

Accessing the system requires a few steps, which are identical whether you use dial-in or Telnet access:

1. After you connect, type **,gen2** (the comma is essential) and press your Enter key. You won't be prompted to do this.

2. At the "Initials?" prompt, type **av4** and press your Enter key.

3. At the "Account?" prompt, type **agy1** (that's agy and the number 1) and press Enter.

VITAL STATS

Data: 800-358-2221 or 301-402-2221 (see login instructions in the description)

Voice: 301-496-2403

Internet: telnet wylbur.cu.nih.gov (see login instructions in the description)

Note: Dial-in users will have to experiment with the terminal setting in their communications software. A setting of VT100 works well. Also, your software must be set to even parity, 7 data bits, 1 stop bit, and half duplex (or local echo).

BUPERS Access

Bureau of Naval Personnel Command
PERS 471C
Federal Building 2
Washington, DC 20370

BUPERS Access is available only to federal government employees and active, reserve, and retired military personnel. It primarily serves as a way for Navy personnel to learn where they will be assigned next. Navy personnel also can send electronic messages in an effort to negotiate their next duty station.

The BBS also has some news and computer programs of interest to Navy personnel.

VITAL STATS
Data: 703-695-6900
Voice: 703-614-8083
FedWorld gateway: 83

Census Personnel Board

Personnel Division
Bureau of the Census
U.S. Department of Commerce
Room 1412, FB3
Washington, DC 20233

The Census Personnel Board provides information about job openings at the Bureau of the Census. Most of the openings are for clerk-typists, statisticians, geographers, mathematical statisticians, and administrative managers.

Besides the job listings, the board has descriptions of various jobs at the Census Bureau, information about the federal government pay scale, and a shareware interview simulator program.

VITAL STATS
Data: 301-457-1310
Voice: 301-457-3371

Detroit Service Center BBS

U.S. Office of Personnel Management
Federal Job Information Center
477 Michigan Ave., Room 565
Detroit, MI 48226

The Detroit Service Center BBS has federal job listings from Office of Personnel Management offices around the country. The lists are updated weekly.

Information on the board is separated into bulletins and files. The bulletins, which you can access by typing **b** at the Main Menu, describe how to use the BBS, list addresses for Federal Job Information Centers in the Chicago Region, and describe the Career America Smart and the Presidential Management Intern programs.

The files area has federal job lists issued by OPM offices in Albuquerque, Anchorage, Atlanta, Boston, Chicago, Dayton, Denver, Detroit, Honolulu, Huntsville, Kansas City, Los Angeles, Norfolk, Philadelphia, Raleigh, Sacramento, San Antonio, San Francisco, San Juan, Seattle, St. Louis, Syracuse, Twin Cities (Minneapolis and St. Paul), and Washington, D.C.

The files area also has a list of vacancies in the Senior Executive Service, a list of federal jobs commonly filled by recent college graduates, Merit Promotion listings, a description of federal employee benefits, general information about federal career opportunities, and a description of special programs for veterans, students, and the disabled.

VITAL STATS

Data: 313-226-4423

Voice: 313-226-6950 (leave a message on the automated system)

File list: FILELIST.ASC

To access files: At the Main Menu type **f**

Time limit: 5 hours per day

Note: This BBS also can be accessed through the OPM Mainstreet gateway

Federal Job Opportunity Board (FJOB)

U.S. Office of Personnel Management
Staffing Service Center
4685 Log Cabin Drive
Macon, GA 31298

The Federal Job Opportunity Board (FJOB) is the best BBS-based source of up-to-the-minute information about federal government job openings across the United States and overseas. The lists of federal jobs are updated daily, Tuesday through Saturday, at 5:30 a.m. If you find a job of interest, you can leave a message on the BBS requesting that the application materials be mailed to you.

You can download the job files, which are divided by region and state, or you can search all of the job files online. You can search the job files by series number or job title, and you can narrow the search by specifying a state to search or a grade level.

Besides the job files, the board offers:

- The optional application form for federal employment, form OF-612.

- A brochure titled *How to Apply for a Federal Job.*

- Details about Internet sites that provide federal job information.

- A computer program that allows you to search the job files offline on your computer. The program works only on DOS computers.

- Resumé programs.

- A list of state job service centers.

- A list of Federal Job Information Centers.

- Information about student work programs.

- A preparation manual for the U.S. Border Patrol Language-Learning Ability Test.

- Conferences about recruiting, Reduction in Force (RIF) procedures, personnel issues, and veterans policy issues.

VITAL STATS

Data: 912-757-3100

Voice: 912-757-3090

Available: 24 hours a day except Monday from 2 a.m. to 4 a.m. EST and Tuesday through Saturday from 4:30 a.m. to 6 a.m. EST

Internet: telnet fjob.mail.opm.gov *or* ftp fjob.mail.opm.gov

Login (FTP only): **anonymous**

Password (FTP only): your e-mail address

Note: This BBS also can be accessed through the OPM Mainstreet gateway

OPM Mainstreet

U.S. Office of Personnel Management
AG/OIRM/OSB
Theodore Roosevelt Building
1900 E St., N.W., Room 6H30
Washington, DC 20415-0001

OPM Mainstreet, which is operated by the Office of Personnel Management (OPM), provides extensive information about federal government job openings and employment policies.

Following are descriptions of the major areas available on the board:

Jobs-Jobs-Jobs You can access this area by typing **7** at the Main Menu. It has lists of federal job openings in the United States and overseas, lists of vacancies in the Senior Executive Service, a free link to another BBS called the Federal Job Opportunity Board that is OPM's primary source for lists of federal job openings, access to Internet mailing lists that list job openings, and a list of federal personnel offices with addresses.

File Areas for Download To access the files, type **2** at the Main Menu. Here are some highlights of what's available:

- Lists of job fairs and career days, federal personnel offices, Office of Personnel Management offices, and personnel offices in the Washington, D.C., area.

- Information about federal policy on hiring people with disabilities.

- Electronic copies of various forms used by federal personnel offices.

- Shareware anti-virus programs for DOS and Windows computers.

- Information about employment opportunities for veterans.

- Shareware communications and decompression programs for DOS and Macintosh computers.

- Information about federal government locality pay.

- Files that explain how to use OPM Mainstreet.

Forums You can access the forums by typing **1** at the Main Menu. All of the forums have their own e-mail systems, and most also have files. The board offers forums on quality management, personnel records and systems, OPM procurement, training, retirement and insurance services, downsizing, work and family, compensation and leave policy, employee and labor relations, and other issues.

OPM Mainstreet Information and Utilities You can access this area by typing **5** at the Main Menu. It contains information about how to use the BBS.

Internet Access To enter this area, type **i** at the Main Menu. It offers an e-mail gateway to the Internet; access to several dozen Internet newsgroups about job openings, reinventing government, and computer hardware and software; and guides to using the Internet (although most of them are a bit outdated).

Connect to Other BBSs This is a gateway to other Office of Personnel Management BBSs in Detroit, Washington, D.C., and Macon, Georgia. There is no charge for accessing these systems, and OPM pays for the long-distance call. To reach the gateway, type **c** at the Main Menu.

Boards of Wage and Service Contract Appeals BBS

Wage Appeals Board
U.S. Department of Labor
200 Constitution Ave., N.W., Room N1651
Washington, DC 20210

The Boards of Wage and Service Contract Appeals BBS contains hundreds of administrative decisions in disputes involving wages paid to employees of federal government contractors and subcontractors.

To access the files, type **f** at the Main Menu. Here are some highlights of what's available:

- Numerous files detailing the legislative history of the Davis-Bacon Act. The law, which was originally passed in 1931, requires the payment of prevailing wages and fringe benefits to laborers and mechanics employed by contractors and subcontractors working on federal construction projects.

- The text of decisions by the Wage Appeals Board, which helps enforce the Davis-Bacon Act.

- The text of decisions by the Service Contract Appeals Board from 1987 to the present. The board helps enforce the McNamara-O'Hara Service Contract Act, a law passed in 1965 that set wage rates and other labor standards for employees of contractors and subcontractors that provide services to the federal government. The decisions are arranged chronologically and list the company involved. Most involve relatively small companies, although there are a few decisions affecting large firms such as McDonald's.

VITAL STATS

Data: 800-735-7396 or
202-219-5286
Voice: 202-219-9039
FedWorld gateway: 90

Labor News

Office of Public Affairs
U.S. Department of Labor
Room N-6511
Washington, DC 20210

Labor News provides a wide range of economic data, lists of federal job openings, the text of selected OSHA regulations, information about the employment rights of the disabled, descriptions of recent mining accidents, the text of the Family and Medical Leave Act, and hundreds of other files.

Here are some highlights of what's available:

- A report titled *The New OSHA: Reinventing Worker Safety and Health.*

- *Federal Register* notices, which are updated daily.

- Background information about the Bureau of Labor Statistics, which produces a wide range of economic statistics.

VITAL STATS
Data: 202-219-4784
Voice: 202-219-8831
FedWorld gateway: 26
Manual: MANUAL.ASC
(it's superb)

- Fact sheets produced by the Employment Standards Administration that discuss the Migrant and Seasonal Agricultural Worker Protection Act, the Employee Polygraph Protection Act of 1988, black lung benefits, workers' compensation for federal workers, federal child labor laws, and minimum wage and overtime pay, among other subjects.

- Extensive information from the Mine Safety and Health Administration, including reports about injury trends and lists of mining disasters in the United States.

- Numerous documents from the Occupational Safety and Health Administration about subjects such as safety with video display terminals, access to exposure and medical records, employee rights and responsibilities, farm safety, and OSHA help for new businesses.

- Information about the Labor Department's Office of Inspector General and how to report fraud, waste, and abuse.

- A list of major labor laws.

- A brief history of the Labor Department.

- Hundreds of files about how to comply with labor laws.

- The producer price index, the consumer price index, import and export price indexes, and related economic statistics.

- A list of acronyms used by the Labor Department.

- Lists of federal government job openings in the United States and overseas.

- The text of selected Occupational and Health Administration regulations.

- Pamphlets titled *The Americans with Disabilities Act: Your Responsibilities as an Employer* and *The Americans with Disabilities Act: Your Employment Rights as an Individual with a Disability.*

- The full text of the Family and Medical Leave Act and regulations under it.

- A publication titled *Small Business Handbook: Laws, Regulations, and Technical Assistance Services.*

- Fact sheets prepared by the Pension and Welfare Benefits Administration with titles such as "How to Become Eligible for Pension Benefits," "Your 'Right to Know' Under the Pension Reform Law," "Filing Claims for Pension and Welfare Benefits," and "Survivor Benefits."

- Press releases from various Labor Department agencies, including details about enforcement actions taken by the department.

- Files from the Veterans' Employment and Training Service that describe the service's programs and list addresses and phone numbers for the service's regional offices.

PayPerNet

U.S. Office of Personnel Management
Office of Compensation Policy
1900 E St., N.W., Room 7420
Washington, DC 20415

PayPerNet has hundreds of extremely technical files about federal government employment and wages. It provides information about pay and performance management programs, special rates authorized under Title V, standards in position classification, federal pay administration, Total Quality Management (TQM), significant court cases involving labor relations, job opportunities and developments in the Senior Executive Service, pay issues related to the Federal Employees Pay Comparability Act of 1990, and federal personnel records processing and management, among other issues.

You can access the bulletins by typing **b** at the Main Menu. Several provide useful information:

BULLETIN 2   A user's guide.

BULLETIN 5   Tips on downloading files.

BULLETIN 6   Information about BBSs operated by the Office of Personnel Management around the country.

You can read these bulletins online. If you prefer to download them, copies are available in the Utility Conference, which you can reach by typing **f** at the Main Menu and **2** at the Utility Conference Directory Menu.

Files on this BBS are organized differently from most other federal BBSs. Nearly all of the files are organized under eleven conferences. To join a conference, type **j** at the Main Menu. You will then be presented with a list of the conferences, and you can type the number of the one you want. To download files, you must be in the conference where they're located. If you want to download files from several conferences, you have to keep switching conferences, which quickly becomes a nuisance. Each conference also has its own e-mail function.

Following are brief descriptions of the conferences:

1. **SRTIS**   Information about the Title V Special Rates program.

2. **UTILTY**   Shareware utility programs for DOS computers.

VITAL STATS

Data: 202-606-2675

Voice: 202-606-2092

FedWorld gateway: 71

Manual: BULLETIN 2

File list: PCBFILES.LST (ASCII text) or PCBFILES.ZIP (compressed). Both are in the Utility Conference.

To access files: At the Main Menu type **j** and then choose a conference to join

Time limit: 60 minutes per call

3. **QUALNET**   Total Quality Management issues.

4. **CLASSIF**   New developments in position classification.

5. **PAYAD**   Information about pay issues and the Family and Medical Leave Act of 1993.

6. **PERFMANA**   Information about performance management.

7. **LABORREL**   Information about labor relations.

8. **SES**   Information about Senior Executive Service job opportunities and development programs.

9. **FEPCA**   Information about pay issues and initiatives relating to the Federal Employee Pay Comparability Act of 1990.

10. **PERSRCDS**   Guidance for federal personnel offices.

11. **WAGESYS**   Information about the federal wage system.

LABOR STATISTICS

ASC-LMI

South Carolina Employment Security Commission
1550 Gadsden St.
Columbia, SC 29202

ASC-LMI offers lists of job openings, labor market information, and census data for South Carolina. It is operated by the South Carolina Employment Security Commission, with substantial funding from the U.S. Labor Department.
Here are some highlights of what's available:

- Lists of current job openings, including federal job openings, in South Carolina. They are updated every Monday.

- South Carolina population statistics from the 1990 Census.

- Population projections by county to 2005.

- A profile of South Carolina that provides information about the climate, population, education, recreation and tourism, cost of living, employment, wages, and other information sources.

- Labor force data.

- Nonfarm employment data for South Carolina from 1970 to 1993, listed by industry.

- A wide range of historical economic indicators for the state.

- The Consumer Price Index and the Producer Price Index.

VITAL STATS
Data: 803-737-2832
Voice: 803-737-2831

D.E.S. Data Center

Iowa Department of Employment Services
1000 E. Grand Ave.
Des Moines, IA 50313

The D.E.S. Data Center offers a searchable database of job openings in Iowa and around the nation, in addition to labor market and demographic data for Iowa. It's operated by the Iowa Department of Employment Services, which receives substantial funding from the U.S. Department of Labor.

You can search the database for job openings in Iowa, around the nation, or with the federal government. The federal government listings are broken down by region: Atlanta, Chicago, Dallas, Philadelphia, San Francisco, and Washington, D.C. The federal job listings are updated each Wednesday. You can access the jobs database by typing **d** at the Main Menu. The information in the database is also available as files that you can download.

Here are some other highlights of what's available:

VITAL STATS

Data: 515-281-3472 or
    800-572-3942 (in Iowa
    only)
Voice: 515-281-7307 or
    800-562-4692 (in Iowa
    only)

- Statistical briefs for each county in Iowa.

- Data about the labor force, employment, unemployment, and the unemployment rate in Iowa.

- Current employment statistics for Iowa.

- A list of the ten largest employers in Iowa and in each Iowa county.

- Iowa data from the 1990 Census regarding population age, commuting patterns, educational attainment, household income, and poverty level by county and school district.

- Data about changes in Iowa's population from 1980 to 1990 by county.

- Employment tables by county.

- Consumer Price Index data.

- Wage and salary data.

- Current data about the U.S. employment situation from the Bureau of Labor Statistics.

- National employment projections by occupation.

Department of Industry, Labor and Human Resources (DILHR) ON-LINE

Wisconsin Department of Industry, Labor and Human Relations
201 E. Washington Ave.
Madison, WI 53707

The Department of Industry, Labor and Human Resources (DILHR) ON-LINE offers a wide range of labor data for Wisconsin. It's operated by the Wisconsin Department of Industry, Labor and Human Resources, with funding from the U.S. Department of Labor.

Here are some highlights of what's available:

- Data on plant closings and mass layoffs.

- Employment data.

- Wisconsin unemployment statistics dating back to January 1980.

- A list of labor market publications and data available from the Wisconsin Department of Industry, Labor and Human Relations.

- Projections for 2005 of the Wisconsin population, labor force, industries, and occupations.

- Leading economic indicators by month dating back to January 1990.

VITAL STATS

Data: 608-264-6813
Voice: 608-267-4438

IDES LMI Bulletin Board

EI&A - IDES
Illinois Department of Employment Security
401 S. State St.
Chicago, IL 60605

The IDES LMI Bulletin Board has labor market information for Illinois. It's operated by the Illinois Department of Employment Security, which receives major funding from the U.S. Department of Labor.

Here are some highlights of what's available:

- Labor force data for Illinois and the United States, some of it reaching back to 1979.

- Employment and unemployment statistics.

- Data about unemployment insurance claims.

- Employment projections for Illinois for 2005.

- Information about commuting patterns in Illinois, based on data from the 1990 Census.

- A glossary of terms used in labor market reports.

- A directory of labor market economists at the Illinois Department of Employment Security.

- A list of other sources of labor market information.

VITAL STATS
Data: 312-793-5493
Voice: 312-793-9223

LMEA

Labor Market and Economic Analysis Branch
Washington State Employment Security Department
P.O. Box 9046
Olympia, WA 98507-9046

LMEA offers information about the labor market in Washington State. It has unemployment data, average weekly wage data, profiles of the labor market and economic conditions by county, reports about average weekly wages, state and county employment figures, and related information. It's operated by the Washington State Employment Security Department, with funding from the U.S. Department of Labor.

VITAL STATS
Data: 360-438-3177
Voice: 360-438-3163

LMI NET

Bureau of Labor Market Information
Florida Department of Labor and Employment Security
2012 Capitol Circle, S.E.
Tallahassee, FL 32301

LMI NET offers employment and unemployment data for Florida, wage survey data, lists of the top-ranked occupations in Florida, and population projections for selected Florida counties through 2005. It also has the *BLS Daily Report* from the federal Bureau of Labor Statistics. The BBS is operated by the Florida Department of Labor and Employment Security, which receives much of its funding from the U.S. Department of Labor.

The sysop reports that he hopes to soon start posting information about Florida job openings.

VITAL STATS

Data: 904-487-4187
Voice: 904-488-1048
Internet: telnet 199.44.49.
178

LMI On-Line

Labor Market Information Division
California Employment Development Department
MIC57
P.O. Box 826880
Sacramento, CA 94280-0001

LMI On-Line offers extensive labor market information for California, in addition to lots of help for job seekers. It's operated by the California Employment Development Department, with funding from the U.S. Department of Labor. Some of the files are compressed in a self-extracting format that makes them unusable on most Macintosh computers.

Here are some highlights of what's available:

- Detailed occupational guides for dozens of jobs that describe the job, the working conditions, employment outlook, hours, wages and fringe benefits, entrance requirements and training, advancement opportunities, how to find a position, and further sources of information.

- Information about licensing requirements for various occupations.

- Occupational trends and outlooks for California and individual counties.

- A database of California organizations that administer local job programs.

- Data on current employment by county.

- Statistics regarding agricultural employment and earnings in California and in individual counties.

- Employment projections by occupation.

- A database that lists Metropolitan Statistical Areas in California and the counties included in them.

- Income and population data from the 1990 Census.

- A list of publications available from the Employment Development Department's Labor Market Information Division.

VITAL STATS
Data: 916-262-2227
Voice: 916-262-2213
File list: ALLFILES.EXE (this is compressed in a self-extracting format that makes it unusable on most Macintosh computers)

LMI ON-LINE

Michigan Employment Security Commission
300 East Michigan Ave., Room 103
Lansing, MI 48913

LMI ON-LINE has lots of information for Michigan job seekers. It's operated by the Michigan Employment Security Commission, with substantial funding from the U.S. Department of Labor and the Bureau of Labor Statistics.

The board has only one serious downside: Most if not all of the files are compressed in a self-extracting format that makes them unusable on most Macintosh computers. Mac users can read at least some of the files online and save them using the capture feature in their communications software.

Here are some highlights of what's available:

VITAL STATS

Data: 800-551-5627 or
     313-876-6696

Voice: 517-334-6653

- Lists of job openings in Michigan.

- Lists of federal job openings in Michigan, which you can search by occupation and geographic area. The job listings, which are provided by the U.S. Office of Personnel Management, are updated weekly. The sysop reports that he hopes to soon start posting federal job openings for the entire country.

- A file that briefly describes nearly 200 occupations and provides information about the type of education needed, the salary, and the outlook.

- Several files about conducting a job search, including "Guide to Writing Resumés," "How to Complete a Job Application," "Interviews That Get the Job," "Finding a Job With Skills You Already Have," "Getting Experience: Job Tips for Teens," and "How to Keep the Job Now That You Are Hired."

- Numerous files with employment statistics and wage information.

- Occupational outlooks for Michigan for 2000 that list wages, annual openings, and educational requirements for various occupations.

- News releases from the Michigan Employment Security Commission.

Minnesota Department of Economic Security Research & Statistics Labor Market Information Bulletin Board System (MN DES R&S LMI BBS)

Research and Statistics Office
Minnesota Department of Economic Security
390 N. Robert
St. Paul, MN 55101

The Minnesota Department of Economic Security Research & Statistics Labor Market Information Bulletin Board System (MN DES R&S LMI BBS) has a heck of a name that pretty well describes what it offers. It's operated by the Minnesota Department of Economic Security, with funding from the U.S. Department of Labor.

Here are some highlights of what's available:

- A list of job openings in Minnesota, summarized by occupation. Most listings include the average starting wage and the number of openings.

- Current unemployment rates for Minnesota and the United States.

- The Consumer Price Index for Minnesota and the United States.

- Unemployment insurance statistics.

- Employment data by industry for six labor market areas: all of Minnesota, Duluth, the Duluth-Superior Metropolitan Statistical Area (MSA), the Minneapolis-St. Paul MSA, the Rochester MSA, and the St. Cloud MSA.

- Employment projection files from 1989 to 1996.

- Data for areas such as business incorporations, building permits, retail trade, and average weekly earnings in manufacturing that are used to derive the Minnesota Economic Index. Data are available from 1970 to the present.

- Labor force data by county.

VITAL STATS
Data: 612-297-7343
Voice: 612-296-6546
Manual: INST_BBS.TXT

Nevada Labor Market Information System

Bureau of Research and Analysis
Nevada Department of Employment, Training and Rehabilitation
500 E. Third St.
Carson City, NV 89713

The Nevada Labor Market Information System offers labor market and industrial statistics, employer information, and wage data for Nevada. It's operated by the Nevada Department of Employment, Training and Rehabilitation, which receives substantial funding from the U.S. Department of Labor.

Here are some highlights of what's available:

- Current industrial employment, labor force, and prevailing wage data.

- Economic indicators for Nevada and the United States.

- Demographic data from the 1990 Census regarding the composition of Nevada's labor force.

- A database of Nevada employers that you can search to find names, addresses, industries, and locations.

- A bibliography of labor market information available from state and federal sources.

VITAL STATS
Data: 702-687-4194
Voice: 702-687-4550

NOICC Crosswalk & Data Center BBS

NOICC Crosswalk & Data Center
200 E. Grand Ave.
Des Moines, IA 50309

The NOICC Crosswalk & Data Center BBS offers information about how the federal government classifies occupations and how those classifications relate to each other and to training programs. The BBS has data from the Department of Labor, Department of Education, Department of Defense, the Census Bureau, and other agencies, and is funded by the National Occupational Information Coordinating Committee. The board also has employment projections by industry for 1992-2005 from the federal Bureau of Labor Statistics.

Almost all of the files are compressed in a self-extracting format that makes them unusable on most Macintosh computers.

VITAL STATS
Data: 515-242-4887
Voice: 515-242-4881
FedWorld gateway: 27

Region VIII Economic Data Service

Utah Department of Employment Security
140 East 300 South
P.O. Box 45249
Salt Lake City, UT 84145-0249

The Region VIII Economic Data Service has labor market information for Utah and Montana and limited census data for Utah. It's operated by the Utah Department of Employment Security, which receives major funding from the U.S. Department of Labor.

The board's operators hope to eventually provide data for Utah, Montana, North Dakota, South Dakota, Colorado, and Wyoming, but report receiving little cooperation from the other states.

VITAL STATS
Data: 800-828-5912
Voice: 801-536-7832

LAW AND JUSTICE

Appellate Bulletin Board System for the Second Circuit

Second Circuit Court of Appeals
Room 1702
40 Foley Square
New York, NY 10007

The Appellate Bulletin Board System for the Second Circuit provides opinions issued by the Second Circuit Court of Appeals, docket sheets, and the chief judge's order waiving fees for all BBS users. The opinions are posted daily before 11 a.m. EST. The board is also expected to offer a court telephone directory, local rules, forms and instructions, fee schedules, and court calendars.

The Second Circuit Court of Appeals serves Vermont, Connecticut, and New York.

VITAL STATS
Data: 212-385-6004 or
    212-385-6005
Voice: 212-791-0103
Login: **bbs**

Appellate Bulletin Board System for the Sixth Circuit

Sixth Circuit Court of Appeals
Room 524
Potter Stewart Courthouse
100 E. Fifth St.
Cincinnati, OH 45202

The Appellate Bulletin Board System for the Sixth Circuit has opinions issued by the Sixth Circuit Court of Appeals, in addition to information about the Sixth Circuit's electronic citation procedure, docket sheets, local rules and internal operating procedures, calendars of oral arguments, the court's order waiving user fees for the BBS, and related information.

The Sixth Circuit Court of Appeals serves Ohio, Michigan, Kentucky, and Tennessee.

VITAL STATS
Data: 513-684-2842
Voice: 513-684-2953

Court of Appeals for the Federal Circuit BBS (CAFC-BBS)

Court of Appeals for the Federal Circuit
717 Madison Place, N.W.
Washington, DC 20439

The Court of Appeals for the Federal Circuit BBS (CAFC-BBS) has opinions issued by the Court of Appeals for the Federal Circuit. It also offers instructions for citing from the BBS, a court calendar, a list of recently filed appeals, the Federal Circuit Rules of Practice, and a guide for pro se filings.

The Court of Appeals for the Federal Circuit has nationwide jurisdiction, and hears appeals from certain civil decisions of the district courts; appeals from decisions of the U.S. Court of International Trade, the U.S. Claims Court, and the U.S. Court of Veterans Appeals; appeals from administrative rulings by the Patent and Trademark Office, U.S. International Trade Commission, secretary of commerce, agency boards of contract appeals, and the Merit Systems Protection Board; and rulemakings of the Department of Veterans Affairs, among other types of cases.

VITAL STATS

Data: 202-786-6584 or 202-633-9608

Voice: 202-633-6593

FedWorld gateways: 95 and 121 (they are identical)

Electronic Dissemination of Opinions (EDOS)

Fifth Circuit Court of Appeals
Room 102
600 Camp St.
New Orleans, LA 70130

The Electronic Dissemination of Opinions (EDOS) BBS has opinions from the Fifth Circuit Court of Appeals for the past thirty days. It also offers an electronic version of the Federal Rules of Appellate Procedures.

The Fifth Circuit Court of Appeals serves Mississippi, Louisiana, and Texas.

VITAL STATS

Data: 504-589-6850 (9600 baud) or 504-589-6851 (2400 baud)

Voice: 504-589-2730

Login: **bbs**

Seventh Circuit Court of Appeals Bulletin Board

Seventh Circuit Court of Appeals
219 S. Dearborn St.
Chicago, IL 60604

The Seventh Circuit Court of Appeals Bulletin Board has opinions issued by the Seventh Circuit Court of Appeals. Docket information is also available, but only from 9 a.m. to 5 p.m. on business days.

The system's design is strange. For example, it frequently prompts "Main Board Command?" but doesn't give a list of options. In this situation, if you type **menu** you'll reach the Main Menu and then can proceed from there.

The Seventh Circuit Court of Appeals serves Indiana, Illinois, and Wisconsin.

VITAL STATS

Data: 312-408-5176

Voice: 312-435-5850

Note: You must register to use this system by leaving a message for the sysop on your first call. Usually, you'll be granted full access within 48 hours.

National Criminal Justice Reference Service (NCJRS)

Office of Justice Programs
U.S. Department of Justice
Box 6000
Rockville, MD 20850

Although the National Criminal Justice Reference Service (NCJRS) uses cumbersome software that died with the dinosaurs, it contains a vast amount of information about criminal justice. Files on the board are supplied by numerous agencies, including the National Institute of Justice, the Office of Juvenile Justice and Delinquency Prevention, the Bureau of Justice Statistics, the Bureau of Justice Assistance, the Office for Victims of Crime, and the Office for National Drug Control Policy.

If you use Windows, the NCJRS offers a free software program that's supposed to make the board easier to use. You can download the software from the board. If you don't do Windows, you're out of luck.

The file areas are called topics. They frequently have a series of subtopics, which in turn often have their own subtopics. Each of these topics or subtopics may have numerous files or databases. Navigating through all these layers to try to find what you want is a royal pain.

To access any topic or file, use your up- and down-arrow keys until you highlight the item you want. Then hit your Enter key. To go back one level, type **g**. To return to the main screen, type **h**.

Following are some of the major commands. In each case, you must hold down the Control key (Ctrl) at the same time you press the letter key:

VITAL STATS

Data: 301-738-8895

Voice: 800-851-3420 or
    301-251-5507

FedWorld gateway: 75

Login: **ncjrs**

Internet: telnet ncjrsbbs.
    aspensys.com

E-mail: askncjrs@
    aspensys.com

Ctrl-b   Jump to the bottom of the current screen.

Ctrl-n   Display next page.

Ctrl-p   Display previous page.

Ctrl-x   Cancel command or operation.

Here are some highlights of what the board offers:

- Background statistics on a wide range of criminal justice topics.

- A list of more than 2,000 street names used for drugs or drug activities.

- The text of criminal justice legislation being considered by Congress.

- Information about grants available from the Justice Department.

- Press releases from the Justice Department.

- Calendars of upcoming criminal justice conferences.

- Publication lists from various Justice Department agencies.

- Information about how to access criminal justice information on the Internet.

- The *State Drug Resources National Directory* from the Office for National Drug Control Policy.

- Extensive files about police equipment such as armor and body-worn transmitters.

- Contact information for state criminal justice councils.

- Information about criminal history records.

- Staff directories for selected Justice Department agencies.

- International criminal justice news.

- Reviews of books about law and politics.

- Country-by-country descriptions of criminal justice systems of Central America in English and Spanish.

NJS BBS

Naval Justice School
360 Elliot St.
Newport, RI 02841-1523

The NJS BBS, which is operated by the Naval Justice School, offers the full text of numerous books about military justice. Some of the titles available include *Environmental Law Deskbook, NJS Military Justice Study Guide, NJS Civil Law Study Guide, NJS Evidence Study Guide, NJS Procedure Study Guide, NJS Criminal Law Study Guide, Staff Judge Advocate's Handbook, Evidentiary Foundations, Commander's Handbook for Military/Civil Law,* and *Staff Judge Advocate's Deskbook.*

The BBS also has hundreds of utility programs for DOS and Windows computers, including archiving utilities, menu and editor programs, communications programs, and WordPerfect utilities, among others. However, almost all of the utility programs are several years old.

VITAL STATS
Data: 401-841-3990
Voice: 401-841-3800
File list: NJSFILES.ZIP

SEARCH-BBS

SEARCH

National Consortium for Justice Information and Statistics

7311 Greenhaven Dr.

Sacramento, CA 95831

The SEARCH-BBS provides the full text of Supreme Court opinions, dozens of software programs for various criminal justice agencies, selected documents from the Federal Bureau of Investigation, lists of job openings in criminal justice, and lots more. The board is operated by the National Consortium for Justice Information and Statistics, with funding from the U.S. Department of Justice.

Information on the board is divided into bulletins, files, publications, databases, and messages:

VITAL STATS

Data: 916-392-4640

Voice: 916-392-2550

Internet: See box, p. 304

File list: ALLFILES.EXE (compressed in a self-extracting format that makes it unusable on most Macintosh computers)

Time limit: 60 minutes per call

Bulletins The bulletins explain some of the board's functions, describe other criminal justice BBSs, and describe some criminal justice organizations. One bulletin contains the FBI's Internet posting about the UNABOM bombing investigation.

Files The board's files on both criminal justice and general computer topics are divided into more than a dozen file areas. To download a master file list, type **3** at the Files Menu. The file is compressed in a format that makes it unusable on most Macintosh computers.

The files area offers various software programs for courts, programs related to hazardous materials, dozens of programs for police departments, a legal spelling dictionary, several communications programs, database programs, a handwriting analysis program, and dozens of utility programs. Most of the files are for DOS computers.

Publications Here are some highlights of what's available:

- Supreme Court opinions, which are posted on the board the same day the Court releases them. The board contains opinions dating back to the beginning of the 1992 term. You can download entire opinions or search opinions by keywords.

- The monthly *FBI Law Enforcement Bulletin.*

- A publications catalog from the National Institute of Justice.

- The *Law Enforcement Management and Administrative Statistics* report, which contains data on more than 600 state and local law enforcement agencies that employ at least 100 officers. The files offer statistics on personnel, expenditures, salaries, equipment, drug enforcement activities, and other issues. The data are in Lotus 1-2-3 format.

- Several dozen publications from the U.S. Bureau of Justice Statistics on topics such as pretrial release, drugs, state and local police departments, recidivism, and drunk driving.

Databases   The board has seven searchable databases:

- *Automated Index*   The Automated Index of Criminal Justice Information Systems contains information about computer systems used by various agencies. You can search the database to identify systems that meet specific needs or to find out what systems other agencies are using.

- *Calendar of Events*   This database lists conferences, seminars, and training opportunities in criminal justice. You can search it by date, title, location, and sponsoring organization.

- *CJ BBS List*   This database lists other criminal justice BBSs nationwide. You can search it by area code, name fragment, city, or state.

- *Less than Lethal Weapons*   This database lists weapons such as chemical agents, stun grenades, mace, tasers, and rubber bullets used by law enforcement agencies in California.

- *NELS Employment Service*   This database contains national listings of job openings in criminal justice. It includes jobs in academia and research, community services and corrections, institutional corrections, and law enforcement and security. Each listing includes the type of position, job description, salary, qualifications, agency name, location, and closing date for applications. Jobs are arranged by category, and each category can be searched by job title, state, salary, agency, and closing date.

- *PALS*   The Planning Abstract Listing Service database provides information about innovative programs, policies, and procedures developed by law enforcement agencies nationwide. Each listing includes the project title, sponsoring organization, a brief project summary, and contact information.

- *Training Facilities*   This database contains descriptions of criminal justice training facilities. Each listing includes availability, contact information, computer systems available, instructional aids, type of organization,

Internet Access to SEARCH-BBS

Much of the information on the board is available through Internet e-mail. Files available through the Internet include all of the shareware, the Supreme Court opinions, and many of the publications.

To request a file, send an e-mail message to ftpmail@search.org. In the body of the message, type **get filename.ext** where *filename* is the name of the file and *ext* is the extension. To get a list of the available shareware files, send the message **get allfiles.txt**. To get a list of the Supreme Court files, send the message **get hermes**.

fees, and accommodations. The database can be searched by location, agency name, contact name, and computer equipment.

Messages   The messages area performs several functions. It offers:

- Forums for messages on law and policy, research and statistics, technology, training, vendors, and general topics.

- Access to some Internet mailing lists and Usenet newsgroups on information technology and criminal justice issues.

- Access to the FidoNet e-mail network.

- The ability to send messages to other SEARCH-BBS users.

SCIENCE AND TECHNOLOGY

Earth Science Branch Photographic Data Base

Earth Science Branch SN5
National Aeronautics and Space Administration
Lyndon B. Johnson Space Center
Houston, TX 77058

The Earth Science Branch Photographic Data Base has hundreds of digital images of Earth taken by astronauts. It has both hand-held color images and black and white electronic still camera images.

The site also has a searchable database that contains information about thousands of photos of the Earth taken during missions by Mercury, Gemini, Apollo, Skylab, the Apollo-Soyuz Test Project, and the Space Shuttle. The information available for each photo includes the frame number, geographical location, special features, center latitude and longitude, nadir latitude and longitude, percent cloud cover, and date and time of acquisition, among other data. You can order copies of photos that you identify through the database.

If you log into this site through the dial-in connection, you face a bit of an adventure. Here are the required steps:

1. Once you connect, hit your Enter key a couple of times.

2. The computer will prompt "ENTER NUMBER:," you type **sn_vax** and hit your Enter key.

3. The computer will say "CALLING 63109" (the number varies) and then say "CALL COMPLETE," after which you hit your Enter key a couple of times.

4. The computer will prompt "#," you type **j31x** and hit your Enter key.

5. The computer will prompt "Enter username>," you type **anonymous** and hit your Enter key.

6. The computer will prompt " Xyplex>," you type **c sseop** and hit your Enter key.

7. The computer will say "Xyplex -101 Session 1 to SSEOP established" and then prompt "Username," you type **photos** and hit your Enter key.

VITAL STATS

Data: 713-483-2500 (see the detailed login instructions)

Voice: 713-333-6663

Internet: telnet sseop.jsc. nasa.gov *or* ftp sseop.jsc.nasa.gov

Login (FTP only): **anonymous**

Password (FTP only): your e-mail address

Login (Telnet only): **photos**

Global Land Information System (GLIS)

U.S. Geological Survey
EROS Data Center
GLIS User Assistance
Sioux Falls, SD 57198

The Global Land Information System (GLIS) contains descriptions of land information that can be used in Earth science research and global change studies. The system has detailed references to regional, continental, and global land information. This includes cultural and topographic data, remotely sensed satellite and aircraft data, and land use, land cover, and soils data.

Scientists who find a data set they need can place a request for it online. The producing organization is sent the request and sends the researcher price and ordering details.

GLIS also has a gateway to numerous Internet sites that offer land data.

VITAL STATS

Data: 605-594-6888

Voice: 800-252-4547 or
605-594-6099

Internet: telnet
glis.cr.usgs.gov

E-mail: glis@glis.cr.usgs.gov

Note: Dial-in users may
need to experiment
with the terminal set-
ting in their communi-
cations program. A
setting of VT100 works
well.

Global Seismology and Geomagnetism On-line Information System

National Earthquake Information Center
U.S. Geological Survey
Mail Stop 967
Box 25046, Denver Federal Center
Denver, CO 80225

Both current and historical information about earthquakes is available on the Global Seismology and Geomagnetism On-line Information System. There are four ways to access the BBS:

1. **Toll-free telephone number** This method connects you directly to the BBS and you do not have to type a login.

2. **Toll telephone number** At the "GLDSV1>" prompt, type **c neis** and hit your Enter key.

3. **Internet** When asked for your user name, type **qed** and hit your Enter key.

4. **FedWorld** Because the communications settings for this BBS are different from those of most other boards, you can run into problems trying to access through FedWorld.

From the Main Menu, you can select from among three options:

Quick Epicenter Determinations Brief, technical descriptions of earthquakes that occurred anywhere in the world during the previous three weeks. For each earthquake, the BBS lists the date, time, latitude, longitude, depth in kilometers, magnitude, body wave magnitude, vertical surface wave magnitude, and the standard deviation from the arithmetic mean of residuals. Some listings provide additional information. You can search the database by date, location, and magnitude. Type **g** to have the entire list scroll on your screen. Type **e** to get an explanation of abbreviations used in the list.

Earthquake Lists Numerous nontechnical lists of earthquakes. The files list significant earthquakes of the world by year, significant earthquakes in the United States from January 1986 to June 1989, the most destructive earthquakes in the world, world earthquakes since 1900 that caused 1,000 or more deaths, the ten largest earthquakes in the United States, and the number of earthquakes per year since 1900 of magnitude 7 or greater. A file called Earthquake Facts and Statistics lists the average annual frequency of various magnitudes of earthquakes, the number of earthquakes in the United States since 1900 by magnitude and region, and the number of earthquakes worldwide from 1983 to 1992 by magnitude and year. It also explains the relationships between earthquake magnitude, ground motion, and energy release.

Geomagnetic field values   A database that provides values of the elements and parameters of the Earth's magnetic field. The values are estimates based on mathematical models. Values of the following elements and their rates of change are available: declination, inclination, horizontal intensity, north component, east component, vertical intensity, and total intensity.

National Earthquake Information Center (NEIC) BBS

U.S. Geological Survey
Denver Federal Center
Box 25046, Mail Stop 967
Denver, CO 80225-0046

The National Earthquake Information Center (NEIC) BBS is a great resource for amateur seismologists, but has little of interest to the general user.

The largest file directory is called AMSEIS, or Amateur Seismology. It contains a file called AMSEIS12.ZIP, which is a program that displays and prints seismograms from data files uploaded regularly to the directory. Seismograms graph the motion of the Earth's surface when waves caused by distant earthquakes pass by. The directory has dozens of data files to use with the program. The file called SEISBULL.TXT lists the data files that are available. The program can be used only with DOS computers.

The PDE file directory contains a file called QEDEVENT.DAT that lists epicenter information for recent earthquakes. The file is updated daily.

The BBS also has a database called Preliminary Determination of Epicenters that you can search by date, geographical area, magnitude, and depth. To access it, type **d** at the Main Menu, type **1** for the PDE search, and respond to the program's prompts until it's done. If you want to download the resulting file of earthquakes, go to the Files Menu. Once there, type **j** to reach the PDE directory and then type **d** to download the file called OUT.DAT. The database contains information about 250,000 earthquakes that occurred anywhere in the world from 1900 to the present.

VITAL STATS

Data: 303-273-8508

Voice: 303-273-8472

To access files: At the Main Menu type **f**

NOAA Environmental Services Data Directory

U.S. Department of Commerce
National Oceanic & Atmospheric Administration
1825 Connecticut Ave., N.W., Room 506
Washington, DC 20235

The NOAA Environmental Information Services system provides two searchable databases that contain information about oceanic, atmospheric, and related Earth science data available from the National Oceanic and Atmospheric Administration (NOAA) and other sources. It also has links to dozens of Internet sites that have related information. The system is easy to use because it transfers you into a Gopher rather than using a BBS interface.

If you access the system through a dial-in connection, three steps are required:

1. At the "Enter username>" prompt, type **guest** and hit your Enter key.

2. At the "Xyplex>" prompt, type **c esdim** and hit your Enter key.

3. At the "login:" prompt, type **gopher** and hit your Enter key.

To learn how to use the system, it's helpful to read the file called "How to Find, Order and Download Data from NOAA." It's item 2 on the main directory.

Following are the databases that you can search full text using keywords:

1. NOAA Environmental Services Data Directory (NOAADIR), which describes data sets available from NOAA relating to global change and other Earth science studies.

2. National Environmental Data Referral Service (NEDRES), which describes more than 22,200 environmental data sets available from federal, state, private, public, and academic organizations.

Here are some other highlights:

• A link to a NOAA Internet site that has a personnel locator and vacancy announcements.

VITAL STATS

Data: 800-722-5511 or 202-606-4653

Voice: 202-606-4548

FedWorld gateway: 66

Login (dial-in and Telnet only): **gopher**

Internet: telnet gopher. esdim.noaa.gov *or* gopher gopher. esdim.noaa.gov *or* http://www.esdim. noaa.gov

- Links to more than two dozen other NOAA Internet sites, including sites with images from satellites.

- Links to other Internet sites that have environmental data.

- Links to more than four dozen Internet sites that have weather information and images.

- Information about how to subscribe to various NOAA periodicals.

- A list of National Oceanographic Data Center publications.

U.S. Geological Survey Bulletin Board System

USGS National Center
Mail Stop 803
12201 Sunrise Valley Dr.
Reston, VA 22092

The primary features of the U.S. Geological Survey Bulletin Board System are conferences about geology and CD-ROM technology. The conferences contain messages and some files uploaded by users.

The board also has more than 100 shareware and freeware programs for DOS and Windows computers. These include communications and word processing programs, various utilities, and files to use with Lotus 1-2-3.

VITAL STATS
Data: 703-648-4168
Voice: 703-648-7300
FedWorld gateway: 48

EnviroNET

Mail Code 400.1
NASA Goddard Space Flight Center
Greenbelt, MD 20771

EnviroNET provides access to more than a dozen interactive computer models and two books about the space environment.

Logging into the board requires numerous steps:

1. After you connect, hit your Return key a couple of times.

2. At the "ENTER NUMBER:" prompt, type **sisc** and hit your Return key.

3. When the system responds "CALL COMPLETE," hit your Return key a couple of times.

4. At the "username>" prompt, type your name and hit your Return key.

5. At the "local>" prompt, type **c envnet.gsfc.nasa.gov** and hit your Return key.

6. At the "Username:" prompt, type **envnet** and hit your Return key.

7. At the "envnet's Password:" prompt, type **henniker** and hit your Return key.

The models, which you can access by typing **i** at the Main Menu, are primarily aimed at designers of satellites and space shuttle payloads. Callers use the models online, and can save any data generated during the session. You can obtain an extensive user's manual that explains all of the models by calling the voice number.

Two handbooks also are available on the board:

- EnviroNET Database—Natural and Induced Environmental Information: This book has information about the space environment and its effects on instruments and spacecraft. The chapters describe the space environment for the space shuttle and the space station, as well as for low altitude and high altitude satellites. There are chapters on thermal and humidity, vibration and acoustics, electromagnetic interference, loads and low-frequency

VITAL STATS

Data: 301-286-9000 (2400 baud) or 301-286-4500 (9600)

Voice: 301-286-5690

Internet: http://envnet. gsfc.nasa.gov *or* telnet envnet.gsfc.nasa.gov

Manual: Call the voice number to obtain the manual

Note: Your communications software should be set to emulate a VT100 terminal

dynamics, microbial and toxic contaminants, molecular contamination, natural environment, orbiter motion, particulate environment, and surface interactions.

- Spacecraft Environmental Anomalies Handbook: This book examines the adverse effects of radiation on electronics.

You can browse through both books online or download individual chapters. To browse, type **b** at the Main Menu. To download chapters, type **d** at the Main Menu.

JPL Info

Public Information Office
Jet Propulsion Laboratory
4800 Oak Grove Dr.
Pasadena, CA 91109

JPL Info, which is operated for NASA by the California Institute of Technology, contains images of unmanned spacecraft, images taken by unmanned spacecraft, publications for educators, and text files about spacecraft missions. It also has a few images taken by the Hubble Space Telescope.

The board has more than three thousand files. Here are some highlights of what's available:

VITAL STATS

Data: 818-354-1333

Voice: 818-354-5011

Internet: http://www.jpl.
nasa.gov *or* ftp
jplinfo.jpl.nasa.gov

Login (FTP only): **anonymous**

Password (FTP only): your
e-mail address

E-mail: newsdesk@jpl.nasa.
gov

- More than 100 pictures of celestial objects and JPL facilities taken by NASA/JPL spacecraft. Pictures are available of the Earth, a Jupiter moon, an asteroid, craters on Mars, various spacecraft and spacecraft launches, Saturn, Uranus, and Venus. A few of the images are animated.

- Images of the collision of fragments from Comet Shoemaker-Levy 9 with Jupiter in July 1994. The images were obtained from more than fifty observatories around the world.

- Numerous utility programs, including GIF viewers, decompression programs, an orbital tracking program, and a planetarium program. Programs are available for DOS, Windows, Macintosh, NeXT, Unix, Amiga, and Atari ST computers.

- Text files that include press releases, status reports, and fact sheets on spacecraft missions. There are files about missions by Galileo, Magellan, the Mars Observer, Ulysses, and Voyager, among others.

- NASA's budget request.

- Teacher materials provided by the JPL's Public Education Office on topics such as comets, convection, impact craters, eclipses, life in the universe, moon phases, the solar system, robotic spacecraft, the space shuttle, and sunspots, among others.

- Data from the TOPEX/Poseidon oceanographic mission.

NASA Spacelink

Mail Code CA21
National Aeronautics and Space Administration
Marshall Space Flight Center
Huntsville, AL 35812

Although NASA Spacelink is designed for teachers and students, it provides tons of valuable information for anyone interested in the National Aeronautics and Space Administration (NASA) and space exploration. It offers more than 4,000 files and computer programs on everything from unidentified flying objects to upcoming space shuttle flights.

If you tried using Spacelink in recent years and gave up because of the board's complexity, try again. NASA has totally redesigned Spacelink, transforming it from an ugly duckling into a beautiful swan. Now when you call the BBS, you are presented with a clean Gopher interface that is extremely easy to use.

Spacelink's only flaw is that it lacks a method for searching all of the files at once. Spacelink's thousands of files make such a feature essential.

Without writing a whole book about Spacelink, it's impossible to provide a complete description of everything it offers. Suffice it to say that any information you are seeking about space is probably available on Spacelink. Here are some highlights:

- Information about launch dates and payloads.

- Status reports about current NASA missions.

- NASA news releases.

- Congressional testimony and speeches by NASA officials.

- Extensive historical information about past NASA missions, starting with the beginning of the space program.

- Details about NASA's budget request.

- Information about newsletters, workshops, and other services for educators.

- Lesson plans for classes in science, math, engineering, and technology.

VITAL STATS

Data: 205-895-0028

Voice: 205-961-1225

Internet: telnet spacelink.msfc.nasa.gov or gopher spacelink.msfc.nasa.gov or http://spacelink.msfc.nasa.gov or ftp spacelink.msfc.nasa.gov

Login (dial-in and Telnet only): **guest**

Login (FTP only): **anonymous**

Password (FTP only): your e-mail address

Note: You must set your communications program to emulate a VT100 terminal

- Images of Earth taken from space.

- Astronomy, aviation, and satellite tracking programs for several kinds of computers.

- Information about NASA's facilities around the country.

- Information about NASA research projects.

- Biographies of all of the astronauts.

- Detailed information about every flight of the space shuttle, along with images from some flights.

- Background information about NASA's planetary probes, including images from the missions.

- Information about various satellites.

- Status reports, news releases, and images from the Hubble Space Telescope.

- Information about technology transfer.

NODIS

National Space Science Data Center
CRUSO
NASA Goddard Space Flight Center
Greenbelt, MD 20771

NODIS provides information about data and services available from the National Space Science Data Center (NSSDC) regarding subjects such as astrophysics, space physics, planetary science, Earth science, and life science and microgravity. The NSSDC is NASA's archive for planetary and lunar data in digital, document, and photographic formats.

Accessing the site requires a few steps:

1. After you connect, slowly press the Enter key several times until the "Enter Number" prompt appears.

2. Type **nssdca** at the prompt.

3. After a few seconds, the system will respond "Call Complete." Hit the Enter key again.

4. Type **nodis** at the "Username" prompt.

Primarily, NODIS offers catalogs of data available from the NSSDC. It also has information about CD-ROMs available from the NSSDC, copies of the NSSDC's newsletter, and links to other sites that offer space data.

VITAL STATS

Data: 301-286-4000 (see the detailed login instructions)

Voice: 301-286-6695

FedWorld gateway: 32

Internet: telnet nssdca.gsfc. nasa.gov *or* ftp nssdca. gsfc.nasa.gov

Login (FTP only): **anonymous**

Password (FTP only): your e-mail address

Note: Your communications software must be set to emulate a VT100 terminal, and your parameters should be set at 7 data bits, 1 stop bit, and no parity

Planetary Data System (PDS)

Mail Stop 525-3610
4800 Oak Grove Drive
Pasadena, CA 91109

The Planetary Data System (PDS) is a searchable catalog of more than ninety planetary science data sets. The system, which is operated by NASA's Office of Space Science and Applications, provides information about data available from past and active planetary missions, as well as from ground-based observations and experiments.

You can search the PDS by mission, target, spacecraft, and other variables. All of the data can be ordered online.

VITAL STATS

Data: 818-306-6914

Voice: 818-306-6130

Login: **pds_guest**

Internet: telnet jpl-pds.jpl.nasa.gov

E-mail: pds_operator@jplpds.jpl.nasa.gov

Space Environment Laboratory (SEL)

National Oceanic and Atmospheric Administration
U.S. Department of Commerce
325 Broadway
Boulder, CO 80303

The Space Environment Laboratory (SEL) offers current solar images, real-time data about the current weather in space, and a huge glossary of solar-terrestrial terms. When there's an eclipse of the sun, this is an excellent place to find images. The laboratory is operated by the National Oceanic and Atmospheric Administration.

If you use dial-in access, you connect to the SEL Gopher. This makes the site extremely easy to use.

VITAL STATS

Data: 303-497-7788

Voice: 303-497-5153

Login (dial-in and Telnet only): **gopher**

Internet: http://www.sel.noaa.gov *or* gopher gopher.sel.noaa.gov *or* telnet gopher.sel.noaa.gov *or* ftp ftp.sel.noaa.gov

Login (FTP only): **anonymous**

Password (FTP only): your e-mail address

E-mail: vhill@sel.noaa.gov

Discontinuance Notice Alert Bulletin Board System (DNABBS)

Defense Logistics Services Center
DOSC-SBB
74 N. Washington Ave.
Battle Creek, MI 49107-3084

The Discontinuance Notice Alert Bulletin Board System (DNABBS) helps manufacturers alert government agencies—primarily the Department of Defense—when they're about to discontinue production of parts used in government systems.

For each item, manufacturers post the Reference Number Data, the National Stock Number, the date of planned discontinuance or support, any replacement parts, and the manufacturer's technical point of contact.

VITAL STATS

Data: 800-305-8203 or 616-961-5193

Voice: 616-961-7472

FedWorld gateway: 141

Available: Monday through Friday only

Note: You must register online to access the system. Normally, it takes one business day to process your request. However, the sysop carefully screens new users, and you will not be granted access unless you have a legitimate reason for using the system.

Microcircuit Obsolescence Management (MOM) PC Board

Naval Air Warfare Center
Aircraft Division Code 7010 MS-38
6000 E. 21st St.
Indianapolis, IN 46219-2189

The Microcircuit Obsolescence Management (MOM) PC Board contains extensive information about obsolete microcircuits. The primary audience is people involved with the design, production, and support of electronic equipment who need to know whether a particular microcircuit is obsolete.

The board has two dozen bulletins, which you can access by typing **b** at the Main Menu. They explain how to use the board, describe how to use BBSs in general, and present news about defense microcircuit obsolescence.

Two databases are among the board's highlights. They allow users to search for obsolescence at the microcircuit level or by the type of equipment affected. You can accesss the databasess by typing **op** at the Main Menu.

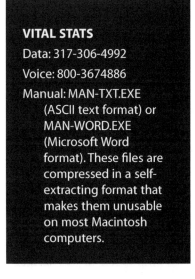

VITAL STATS

Data: 317-306-4992

Voice: 800-3674886

Manual: MAN-TXT.EXE
(ASCII text format) or
MAN-WORD.EXE
(Microsoft Word
format). These files are
compressed in a self-
extracting format that
makes them unusable
on most Macintosh
computers.

Telephone Time for Computers

U.S. Naval Observatory
3450 Massachusetts Ave., N.W.
Washington, DC 20392-5420

You can call Telephone Time for Computers to get the official time from the Naval Observatory's atomic clock. The service is similar to the National Institute of Standards and Technology's Telephone Time Service (see next entry).

Every second, the Naval Observatory's service provides the updated Universal Time Coordinated, previously known as Greenwich Time. The first five digits are the modified date under the Julian calendar. The next three digits are the day of the year. The last six digits are the time by hour, minute, and second. To figure your local time, subtract five hours for EST, six hours for CST, seven hours for MST, and eight hours for PST. You can use various shareware programs to call the Naval Observatory and automatically set the clock in your computer.

There are no files available for downloading.

VITAL STATS
Data: 202-653-0351
Voice: 202-653-1460
FedWorld gateway: 28

Telephone Time Service

NIST-ACTS
Time and Frequency Division
Mail Stop 847
325 Broadway
Boulder, CO 80303

The Telephone Time Service provides the official time from the atomic clock at the National Institute of Standards and Technology (NIST). The clock provides the Universal Time Coordinated, which previously was called Greenwich Time.

After you connect, the service will continually update the time. Within six seconds of connecting, type **?** to get a one-page description of the service. There are no files.

You can obtain free software that enables you to automatically set clocks on DOS computers by NIST's atomic clock. The software is available on the Internet from an anonymous FTP site at time_a.timefreq.bldrdoc.gov.

VITAL STATS
Data: 303-494-4774
Voice: 303-497-3198
E-mail: time@time.nist.gov

TRANSPORTATION

AEE BBS

Office of Environment and Energy
Federal Aviation Administration
AEE-120
800 Independence Ave., S.W.
Washington, DC 20591

The focus of the AEE BBS is controlling aircraft noise and pollution. However, the board is basically for internal use, and has little of interest to the general user.

The files area has a few policy and regulatory documents. The board also has eight conferences on such topics as hazardous materials, helicopter noise modeling, and air carrier economic costing modeling.

VITAL STATS
Data: 202-267-9647
Voice: 202-267-3559
FedWorld gateway: 98
Manual: BBGUIDE.TXT

Airports BBS

Office of Airport Safety and Standards, AAS 100
Federal Aviation Administration
800 Independence Ave., S.W.
Washington, DC 20591

The Airports BBS contains hundreds of technical files about airport safety and operations. It's aimed at airport operators and designers, officials in the Federal Aviation Administration's Office of Airports Standards, and others interested in airport issues. The board's primary role is to distribute Advisory Circulars (ACs), which provide guidance to airport operators.

The bulletins, which you can access by typing **b** at the Main Menu, provide general information about how to use BBSs, list upcoming airport conferences, and answer frequently asked questions about the FAA.

The files, which you can access by typing **f** at the Main Menu, provide the following types of information:

VITAL STATS
Data: 202-267-5205
Voice: 202-267-7669
FedWorld gateway: 101
File list: AIRPORTS.ZIP

- Dozens of Advisory Circulars, which provide guidance to airport sponsors and operators on everything from selecting architectural firms to how to conduct airport snow and ice control programs.

- A list of manufacturers that have obtained qualification approval for their airport equipment.

- Standards for construction of airports. Items covered include earthwork, drainage, paving, turfing, lighting, and incidental construction, among others.

- Extensive information about how to design airports to comply with the Americans with Disabilities Act.

- Dozens of engineering briefs about airport construction and maintenance issues.

- Computer programs for airport operators.

- A list of all public airports in the country, arranged by state.

- A list of all-cargo aircraft, with codes.

- Passenger statistics for selected airports.

- Selected FAA regulations.

Aviation Rulemaking Advisory Committee (ARAC) Bulletin Board

Federal Aviation Administration
Room 302
800 Independence Ave., S.W.
Washington, DC 20591

The Aviation Rulemaking Advisory Committee (ARAC) Bulletin Board has information about rules being developed by the Federal Aviation Administration. The following types of information are available:

- Notices of proposed rulemaking that are open for comment.

- Final rules that have been issued recently.

- Information about the Aviation Rulemaking Advisory Committee, its subcommittees, and its working groups. The files list upcoming meetings, describe each group's function, list members of each group, provide the status of recommendations to the FAA, and provide minutes of meetings.

VITAL STATS
Data: 800-322-2722 or
    202-267-5948
Voice: 202-267-3345
FedWorld gateway: 105

FAA Corporate Bulletin Board System

Federal Aviation Administration
Department of Transportation
800 Independence Ave., S.W.
Washington, DC 20591

The FAA Corporate Bulletin Board System is in limbo. It's still available, but little if anything is being added and virtually everything on it is seriously out of date. The BBS seemed to go into decline after the FAA turned over its operation to a contractor.

The BBS actually leads to three separate boards: SkyNet, Flight Standards, and Public Affairs. Each has its own bulletins, files, and e-mail system. SkyNet just has some freeware and shareware programs and utilities for DOS computers, so it's of limited interest. Flight Standards is eventually supposed to provide the full text of the *Airworthiness Inspector's Handbook,* the *Air Transport Operations Inspector's Handbook,* and the *General Aviation Operations Inspector's Handbook.* But for now, it just has bulletins associated with the handbooks.

That leaves Public Affairs, which would be a really interesting board if anyone ever updated it. When this book was being written, every file on the board was at least six months old. Here are some examples of what's available:

- A list of FAA publications.

- Speeches by FAA administrators.

- Files about civil penalties imposed against various airlines and people for violating FAA regulations.

- FAA press releases.

- Press releases about air travel from the Department of Transportation.

- Issues of a publication titled *FAA Aviation News.*

- Issues of a magazine called *Satellite Navigation News.*

- Data about aviation systems indicators such as accidents, incidents, efficiency, and forecasts. The files are compressed in a self-extracting format that makes them unusable on many Macintosh computers.

VITAL STATS
Data: 800-224-6287
Voice: Voice support is not provided
FedWorld gateway: 139

FAA New England

Federal Aviation Administration
FSDO-05
2 Al McKay Ave.
Portland, ME 04102

The FAA New England BBS contains Master Minimum Equipment Lists (MMELs) for dozens of types of aircraft and FAR Part 135 certification information. The MMELs list the equipment that must be operational on an aircraft before it can fly.

Several other FAA BBSs also have these lists, but usually they are in a self-executing format that makes them unusable on most Macintosh computers. This board, by contrast, offers the files in both uncompressed and self-executing formats.

VITAL STATS

Data: 207-780-3297

Voice: 207-780-3263

Manual: DUALINST.HLP
(a generic manual for
the BBS software)

To access files: At the Main
Menu type **f**

Time limit: 3 hours per call

FAA Pilot Examiner Section BBS

Federal Aviation Administration
Box 25082
AFS634
Oklahoma City, OK 73125

The FAA Pilot Examiner Section BBS is primarily designed for pilot examiners and certified flight instructors, although aviation safety inspectors and others interested in aviation safety are welcome to use it.

The board has several conferences, which you can access by typing **j** at the Main Menu. They serve as collection areas for messages about pilot examiners, ballooning, rotorcraft, and Federal Aviation Administration rules and regulations.

You can access the files by typing **f** at the Main Menu. Here are some highlights:

- Updates for the *Pilot Examiners Handbook.*

- A list of aviation-related BBSs.

- Details about ordering FAA publications.

- A list of phone numbers for FAA offices in Oklahoma City.

- A list of computer testing centers.

- A computer program called Know Your Aircraft.

- A weather analysis program.

VITAL STATS

Data: 800-858-2107 or 405-954-4530

Voice: 405-954-4753 or 405-954-6448

To access files: At the Main Menu type **f**

Time limit: 90 minutes per day

Note: You may need to experiment with the terminal setting in your communications software to access this board. A VT100 terminal emulation works well.

FAA Safety Data Exchange

Federal Aviation Administration
ACE-103, Suite 900
1201 Walnut
Kansas City, MO 64106

The FAA Safety Data Exchange, which is operated by the FAA's Small Airplane Directorate, features safety-related information about ultralight aircraft and other planes built by amateurs. The board's major function is to allow owners and pilots of amateur-built aircraft to learn about problems experienced by others and to report their own problems.

The BBS has seven areas, although there are no files to download. All information is displayed on your screen, and you can capture it using your communications software's capture feature. The three most important areas are numbers 2, 4, and 6:

2. Reports of aircraft problems filed by owner/pilots. All of the reports are filed anonymously, and they are not confirmed or verified by the FAA. You can search the report database by aircraft model or by system such as airframe, engine, or propeller.

4. Information about sources of metric hardware, a new sport aircraft builders BBS, and free aircraft-related software, in addition to questions about specific aircraft models.

6. A list of approved aircraft kits, manufacturer responses to reports, safety alerts, and technical articles. The list of approved aircraft kits lists manufacturers' addresses.

VITAL STATS

Data: 800-426-3814

Voice: 816-426-5954

FedWorld gateway: 58

Note: Your communications software must be set to emulate a VT100 or ANSI terminal. Also, your modem speed must be set at 9600 baud or less because the BBS's modem does not recognize higher speeds.

FAA-AFS 200 BBS

Federal Aviation Administration
Program Management Branch, ASS 260
800 Independence Ave., S.W.
Washington, DC 20591

The FAA-AFS 200 BBS has technical files that are primarily of interest to airlines and pilots. Many of the files are compressed in a self-extracting format that makes them unusable on most Macintosh computers.

Here are some highlights of what's available:

- Master Minimum Equipment Lists, which detail what parts or systems do not have to be operational for a particular kind of aircraft to fly. They also describe any restrictions in flying the aircraft with the broken parts.

- Flight Standardization Board documents, which describe the training that must be completed before a pilot can fly a specific type of aircraft.

- Advisory Circulars from the Federal Aviation Administration about topics such as weight and balance, crew resource management training, and ground de-icing training.

- Files about accident prevention.

- Selected safety recommendations from the National Transportation Safety Board.

- The FAA's policy about air shows.

- The full text of the Federal Aviation Act as amended.

- Selected FAA regulations.

- Selected FAA policy documents.

VITAL STATS
Data: 202-267-5231
Voice: 202-267-3764
FedWorld gateway: 96
Time limit: 30 minutes per call

Flight Standards BBS

North Florida FSDO-15
Federal Aviation Administration
9677 Tradeport Dr., Suite 100
Orlando, FL 32827-5397

The Flight Standards BBS is a gold mine for anyone interested in aviation. It has more than 1,000 files that offer information about accident prevention, flight planning programs, safety recommendations from the National Transportation Safety Board, and Master Minimum Equipment Lists (MMELs) for private and commercial aircraft.

Here are some examples of what's available:

VITAL STATS
Data: 800-645-3736 or
407-648-6309
Voice: 407-648-6956
File list: ALLFILES.ZIP

- More than 100 Federal Aviation Administration Advisory Circulars. Some sample titles include "Air Transportation of Mental Patients," "Cabin Ozone Concentrations," "Government Aircraft Operations," "The Ultralight Vehicle," "Extended Range Operation With Two-Engine Airplanes," and "Ground De-icing and Anti-Icing Training and Checking."

- More than a dozen accident prevention pamphlets. Some sample titles include "Preventing Accidents During Ground Operations," "Tips on Winter Flying," "All About Fuel," "Human Behavior: The No. 1 Cause of Accidents," "Balloon Safety Tips," "Medical Facts for Agricultural Aviation," and "How to Avoid a Midair Collision."

- Sample questions from tests for pilots, mechanics, and dispatchers.

- A publication called *General Aviation Airworthiness ALERT!*

- A list of local and national airshows.

- FAA regulations.

- A list of frequently requested FAA telephone numbers.

- A list of phone numbers and contacts for the Flight Standards District Office in Orlando.

- Numerous flight planning programs.

- A list of the three-digit codes that identify U.S. airports.

- A guide to FAA publications.

- A list of frequencies used by blimps.

- Descriptions of different types of helicopters.

- A list of other aviation-related BBSs.

- Master Minimum Equipment Lists for commercial and general aviation air-craft. The files, which are compressed in a self-extracting format that makes them unusable on most Macintosh computers, list the equipment the air-craft must have before it can fly.

- Reports and safety recommendations from the National Transportation Safety Board.

- Weather forecasts for Miami, Tampa, Jacksonville, and the state of Florida.

- More than two dozen news items from the FAA on such topics as pilot cer-tification, accident prevention, hot refueling, instrument flying, defensive flying, severe weather, thunderstorm hazards, and thin air accidents, among others.

Federal Highway Administration Electronic Bulletin Board System (FEBBS)

Information Systems Division (HMS-40)
Federal Highway Administration
400 7th St., S.W.
Washington, DC 20590

The Federal Highway Administration Electronic Bulletin Board System (FEBBS) is a mess—but a valuable mess. It's one of the worst-designed BBSs operated by any federal agency, yet it has tons of useful information about the federal highway and motor carrier programs. To make matters worse, many of the files are compressed in a self-extracting format that makes them unusable on most Macintosh computers.

After you connect, the BBS presents a series of announcements and then the Main Menu appears. New users have limited access to the BBS until they register. To register, at the Main Menu type **r** and then answer the questions.

Most of the information on FEBBS is organized by conferences, many of which represent the various program areas of the Federal Highway Administration. There also are conferences covering topics of interest to FHWA field offices and computer issues. Only registered users have access to all of the public conferences.

As you navigate through the levels, remember two commands: typing **+** returns you to the previous menu, and typing **-** returns you to the Main Menu.

Here are some highlights of what's available:

- An electronic version of 23 CFR, the section of the Code of Federal Regulations pertaining to highways.

- An electronic copy of the Federal Highway Administration's Federal Aid Policy Guide.

- Extensive information about transportation of disabled people under the Americans with Disabilities Act.

- A list of state fuel tax rates.

- Notices of Proposed Rulemaking.

- Traffic fatality summaries arranged by state.

VITAL STATS

Data: 800-337-3492 or
202-366-3764

Voice: 202-366-1120

FedWorld gateway: 20

To access files: At the Main
Menu type **c**

- Detailed information about the Intermodal Surface Transportation Efficiency Act, including a copy of the law.

- Copies of Federal Highway Administration orders, notices, and technical advisories.

- Information for contractors, including Requests for Proposals (RFPs).

- Lists of job openings in the Federal Highway Administration.

- A headquarters telephone directory for the Federal Highway Administration.

Federal Transit Administration Bulletin Board System

System Operator
DTS-38
U.S. Department of Transportation
55 Broadway, Kendall Square
Cambridge, MA 02142

The Federal Transit Administration Bulletin Board System has limited information about transit safety and security.

The board has a list of transit-related conferences and other events, a schedule of courses offered by various organizations, and a list of reports available from the Federal Transit Administration that you can order online (but which are not available on the board itself). The BBS also has message forums about drug and alcohol testing, bus safety, rapid rail safety, system safety, emergency planning, and related topics.

VITAL STATS
Data: 800-231-2061
Voice: 617-494-2108
FedWorld gateway: 94

Marine Data Computer Bulletin Board

NOAA/National Ocean Service
U.S. Coast & Geodetic Survey
1315 East-West Highway, Station 4746
Silver Spring, MD 20910

Databases available through the Marine Data Computer Bulletin Board list charts of U.S. coastal waterways that are prepared by the National Oceanic and Atmospheric Administration (NOAA). The BBS also has databases that list some sample airport charts and photos. The actual charts and photos are not available on the BBS.

You can reach the databases by typing **d** at the Main Menu. One of the most interesting databases lists shipwrecks and obstructions in coastal waterways. You can search the database by chart number or by latitude and longitude. The database supplies the latitude and longitude of each wreck and obstruction. Another database lists NOAA chart sales agents. You can search it by ZIP code or state.

The board also has a few files, which you can access by typing **f** at the Main Menu. They list NOAA products and services, NOAA contacts, marine pilots organizations, and other marine-related BBSs.

VITAL STATS

Data: 301-713-4573

Voice: 301-713-2653

FedWorld gateway: 112

Time limit: 60 minutes per call

Note: Your communications software must be set to emulate a VT100 terminal

MARlinspike BBS

U.S. Department of Transportation
Maritime Administration
400 7th St., S.W.
Washington, DC 20590

The primary audiences for the MARlinspike BBS are the U.S.-flagged shipping community and firms seeking contracts from the Maritime Administration, which administers laws and programs that are designed to help the U.S. merchant marine industry.

Here are some highlights of what's available:

- Information about bills introduced in Congress that affect the maritime industry.

- Reports about threats to shipping around the world, prepared by the Maritime Administration, the State Department, and the U.S. Navy. These include reports about piracy, among other threats.

- Numerous documents of interest to contractors, including Requests for Quotes, Invitations for Bids, and Requests for Proposals.

- Information for small and disadvantaged businesses.

- The Transportation Acquisition Regulations and the Transportation Acquisition Manual.

- Information about U.S. sanction and embargo programs from the Treasury Department's Office of Foreign Assets Control.

- Press releases from the Maritime Administration.

- Documents about the role of the Merchant Marine during World War II.

- A glossary of shipping terms.

- A calendar of market promotion activities.

- Sales leads.

- Information about cargo preference laws.

VITAL STATS

Data: 202-366-8505

Voice: Telephone support is not provided

FedWorld gateway: 72

- Information about the Ready Reserve Force and the National Defense Reserve Fleet.

- Announcements about trade fairs sponsored by the Department of Transportation.

- Bulletins of interest to shipyards.

- Bulletins and shipping schedules from various American shipping firms.

Navigation Information Network (NAVINFONET)

Defense Mapping Agency Hydrographic/Topographic Center
Attn: MCN/NAVINFONET
U.S. Department of Defense
Washington, DC 20315-0030

General users will find little of interest on the Navigation Information Network (NAVINFONET), which provides technical navigation information to professional mariners.

Logging into the board requires three steps:

1. After you get a connect message, hit your Enter key.

2. Type **login anms** and hit your Enter key. You won't be prompted to do this.

3. Type **pc 55** at the "Enter User ID" prompt.

NAVINFONET has the data used to produce the weekly *Notice to Mariners,* chart corrections, broadcast warnings, MARAD advisories, the Defense Mapping Agency list of lights, anti-shipping activity messages, mobile offshore drilling unit locations, corrections to DMA hydrographic product catalogs, the U.S. Coast Guard light lists, and Global Positioning System data.

Selection 5, Anti-Shipping Activity Messages, is interesting because it contains brief reports about pirate attacks against shipping around the world. It also lists ports where ships are at special jeopardy. For example, it reports that the Brazilian ports of Rio de Janeiro and Santos are among the most dangerous in the world. The report is updated weekly.

You cannot download files from the board. Instead, you can save the information in a capture file as it scrolls on your screen.

U.S. Coast Guard Navigation Information Service (NIS) Bulletin Board

U.S. Coast Guard ONSCEN
7323 Telegraph Road
Alexandria, VA 22310-3998

Information useful to recreational boaters, trucking companies, surveyors, and others is available on the U.S. Coast Guard Navigation Information Service Bulletin Board. Unfortunately, the board is badly designed and is harder to use than it needs to be.

Here are some highlights of what's available:

- Information from and about the NAVSTAR Global Positioning System (GPS), a satellite radionavigation system that provides position, velocity, and time information. There are real-time operational status reports about the satellites, descriptions of the orbit of each satellite, and data describing the orbit, health, and clock for each satellite.

- Information about other radionavigation systems involving the Coast Guard, including Omega, Loran-C, and DGPS.

- Notices to mariners, which are weekly notices that alert boaters about navigation hazards such as burned-out buoys, shipwrecks, and sailboat races.

- Limited information about boating safety.

VITAL STATS

Data: 703-313-5910
Voice: 703-313-5900
FedWorld gateway: 54
Internet: http://www. navcen.uscg.mil *or* gopher gopher. navcen.uscg.mil

APPENDIXES

APPENDIX 1

Boards Added Since the 1995 Edition

Bulletin Board	Sponsor	Page
AgEBB (Agricultural Electronic Bulletin Board)	Commercial Agricultural Extension Program, University of Missouri	44
Appellate Bulletin Board System for the Sixth Circuit	Sixth Circuit Court of Appeals	295
Aquaculture Network Information Center (AquaNIC)	Purdue University and the U.S. Department of Agriculture Extension Service	50
ASC-LMI	South Carolina Employment Security Commission	281
Automated Policy Issuance and Retrieval System (APIRS)	Administration for Children and Families	90
Automated Vacancy Announcement System (AVAS)	National Institutes of Health	269
BPHC ACCESS	Bureau of Primary Health Care	91
CapAccess	National Capital Area Public Access Network Inc.	29
CDC WONDER/PC	Centers for Disease Control and Prevention	241
Comprehensive Epidemiologic Data Resource (CEDR)	U.S. Department of Energy	243
Consolidated Farm Service Agency Bulletin Board System (CFSA-BBS)	U.S. Department of Agriculture	53
Court of Appeals for the Federal Circuit BBS (CAFC-BBS)	Federal Circuit Court of Appeals	296
CSMoS-BBS	U.S. Environmental Protection Agency	196
D.E.S. Data Center	Iowa Department of Employment Services	282
Department of Energy Home Page	U.S. Department of Energy	156
Department of Industry, Labor and Human Resources (DILHR) ON-LINE	Wisconsin Department of Industry, Labor and Human Resources	283
Department of the Navy Acquisition BBS	Department of the Navy	93

Bulletin Board	Sponsor	Page
Department of State Office of Small and Disadvantaged Business Unit Bulletin Board System (SDBU)	Department of State	94
Discontinuance Notice Alert Bulletin Board System (DNABBS)	Defense Logistics Services Center	322
Drinking Water Information Exchange (DWIE)	U.S. Environmental Protection Agency and West Virginia University	198
Earth Science Branch Photographic Data Base	National Aeronautics and Space Administration	306
Electronic Dissemination of Opinions (EDOS)	Fifth Circuit Court of Appeals	297
Energy Ideas Clearinghouse BBS	Washington State Energy Office and the U.S. Department of Energy	157
Enterprise Integration News BBS	Defense Information Systems Agency	215
EXNET	Cooperative Extension Service, Iowa State University	54
FAA Corporate Bulletin Board System	Federal Aviation Administration	331
FCC World	Smithwick & Belendiuk, P.C.	108
Federal Transit Administration Bulletin Board System	Federal Transit Administration	340
FedLink	Federal Reserve Bank of Chicago	80
FedWest Online	Federal Reserve Bank of San Francisco	82
GAO-OGC Decision Bulletin Board	General Accounting Office	97
GPO Access	Government Printing Office	25
HSTAT (Health Services/Technology Assessment Text)	National Library of Medicine	250
IDES LMI Bulletin Board	Illinois Department of Employment Security	284
Illinois Dialup Extension Access (IDEA)	Illinois Cooperative Extension Service	57
IRIS (Internal Revenue Information Services)	Internal Revenue Service	116
IRMa BBS	U.S. Department of Transportation	218
Liberty Link	Federal Reserve Bank of New York	85
LingNet	Defense Language Institute, Foreign Language Center	139
LMEA	Washington State Employment Security Department	285
LMI NET	Florida Department of Labor and Employment Security	286
LMI On-Line	California Employment Development Department	287
LMI ON-LINE	Michigan Employment Security Commission	288

APPENDIX 2

Boards Deleted Since the 1995 Edition

Bulletin Board	Sponsor	Reason
CAMEONet	National Safety Council	Defunct—Files moved to RTK NET (p. 182)
DoDIGNET	Department of Defense Inspector General	Defunct
Earth Science Data Directory (ESDD)	U.S. Geological Survey	No longer available to dial-in users
FAA Headquarters BBS	Federal Aviation Administration	Defunct—Replaced by FAA Corporate Bulletin Board System (p. 331)
Federal Deficit Reduction BBS	House Subcommittee on Information, Justice, Transportation, and Agriculture	Offline (at least temporarily)
Federal Jobline	Office of Personnel Management	Defunct
Fleet Imaging BBS	Naval Air Station Oceana	Defunct
ICAP BBS	Interagency Committee for Aviation Policy	Defunct
IMA BBS	Department of the Army	Defunct
INFOLINK	U.S. Department of Energy	Defunct
MASC Library RBBS-PC	Department of Commerce	Defunct
NGCR BBS	U.S. Navy	Defunct
NIST/NCSL Data Management Information Exchange (DMIE)	National Institute of Standards and Technology	Defunct
NIU-Forum Bulletin Board	National Institute of Standards and Technology	Defunct
OPM FedJobs Philly BBS	Office of Personnel Management	Defunct
PPCUG-RDAMIS	Pentagon PC User Group	BBS no longer public
PR On-Line	Stephen K. Cook and Company	Defunct
Small Computer Support Center	Malmstrom Air Force Base	Defunct
Surety BBS	Department of the Treasury	Defunct—Files moved to FMS Inside Line (p. 225)
Washington Area Service Network	Office of Personnel Management	Defunct—Merged with OPM Mainstreet (p. 274)

APPENDIX 3

Boards with Changed Names

Old Name	New Name
Air Transport Division BBS	FAA-AFS 200 BBS
Building and Fire Research Bulletin Board System (BFRBBS)	Fire Research Laboratory Bulletin Board System
Bureau of Mines Bulletin Board Network (BOM-BBN)	USBM-BBS
Defense Communications Agency Acquisition Bulletin Board System (DABBS)	DITCO's Electronic Bulletin Boards
Electronic Filing System (EFS) Bulletin Board	Centralized Electronic Filing Bulletin Board System
Information Infrastructure Task Force Bulletin Board	IITF (Information Infrastructure Task Force) Gopher
Library of Congress News Service	LC News Gopher
NIST Computer Security BBS	NIST Computer Security Resource Clearinghouse
NTIA Bulletin Board	NTIA Information Stores

GLOSSARY

ANSI graphics   A set of codes that control various features on a computer terminal. When you log into a BBS, you may be asked if your terminal supports ANSI graphics. If you aren't sure, answer "no" to the question.

ASCII   A plain text format that includes no coding. Many files on federal BBSs are in ASCII format because virtually every word processing program can read ASCII text.

Baud   A rate that indicates how fast a modem can transfer information. The higher the number, the faster the transfer.

BBS   *See* Bulletin board system.

Bulletin   A text file on a BBS that typically provides information about how to use the board or other news. Many boards display the Bulletin Menu when you log in, and you can reach it on other boards by typing **b** at the Main Menu. You can read bulletins online, and some BBSs allow you to download them to your own computer.

Bulletin board system (BBS)   A computerized system that users can access by calling with a modem attached to a computer. BBSs usually have text files and/or computer programs that can be downloaded. Most also have e-mail systems that allow users to send messages to each other and conferences where users can exchange messages on specific topics.

Capture feature   A feature in most communications software programs that allows you to "capture" in a text file the information that's scrolling on your screen from a BBS. After logging off the BBS, you can review the file with your word processing program.

Communications software   A software program that allows your computer to "talk" with a BBS.

Compressed file   A file that has been made smaller than its original size. Files are compressed so they download more quickly and take up less space. To use them, after downloading you must decompress them back to their original size, which usually requires a decompression program. However, some files are "self-executing," meaning you don't need a special program to decompress them. These files have an EXE extension on their names. For example, a self-executing file might be called BBSGUIDE.EXE. Self-executing files cannot be used on most Macintosh computers.

Conference   An area on a BBS containing messages about a specific topic. BBSs frequently have many conferences. On a few boards, conferences also have files. Some boards use other terms for conferences, such as forum or special interest group (SIG).

Decompressed file   *See* Compressed file.

Door   An area on a BBS containing a computer program you can use while connected. On federal BBSs, doors usually lead to searchable databases.

Download   To copy a file from a BBS to your computer.

Echo   The reposting of electronic messages written by users of one BBS on a second BBS. By "echoing" messages from other boards, a BBS allows its users to exchange messages with users of other BBSs across the nation or around the world.

E-mail   Electronic messages written by one BBS user to another. E-mail is basically private, although sysops can (and do) read messages to ensure the board is being used properly. On most federal BBSs, you can just exchange messages with other users of that board. However, a few federal boards also have "echoes" that allow you to exchange messages with users of other BBSs.

Emulate   A setting in your communications software that makes your computer act like it's another type of computer. When BBSing, it's common to make your computer emulate a VT100 terminal.

Extension   A three-letter code at the end of a file name that usually indicates what program was used to create the file. The extension is separated from the rest of the file name by a period. For example, on a file called BBSGUIDE.W51, the extension is W51 and indicates the file was created using WordPerfect 5.1. Sometimes the extension indicates which program was used to compress the file. For example, a file called BBSGUIDE.ZIP was compressed with the PKZIP compression program.

File   A document, graphic image, sound, or computer program. You can download files from a BBS to your own computer. On most BBSs, to reach the files you type **f** at the Main Menu.

File transfer protocol (FTP)   An Internet protocol used to transfer files from one computer to another. Most publicly accessible FTP sites on the Internet allow you to access them using "anonymous FTP." To use anonymous FTP, type **anonymous** when asked for a login and type your e-mail address when asked for a password. This procedure allows you to access selected files on the computer without being a registered user.

Forum   *See* Conference.

Freeware   A software program that you can use free of charge. Some federal BBSs have freeware programs that you can download.

FTP   *See* File transfer protocol.

Garbage   Nonsensical characters that appear on your computer screen when you connect to a BBS. They are commonly caused by noise on the telephone line or incorrect settings in your communications software.

Gateway   A connection that allows you to move from the BBS you are logged into to another computer system. A few federal BBSs have gateways to other federal boards or to the Internet.

GIF   *See* Graphics interchange format.

Graphics interchange format (GIF)   A popular format for compressing and storing graphic files such as photographs. You need a viewer program to de-compress and open the files.

Hacker   In common usage, a person who accesses a computer without au-thorization. Usually, a hacker improperly acquires passwords for a computer network and uses them to break into the network. Some computer insiders prefer to define *hacker* as a person who loves to explore the internal workings of computers and computer networks, and use the term *cracker* for those who illegally break into computers.

Home page   The opening screen at a World Wide Web site.

ID   The name you use to identify yourself when logging into a BBS. Most fed-eral BBSs require that you use your real name as your user ID.

Internet   A vast international network of computer networks. You can access some federal BBSs through the Internet, and a few BBSs offer Internet e-mail.

Login   A word or words you must type to access a BBS after connecting to it with your modem.

Menu   A list of options that outline how you can proceed on the BBS. The Main Menu is the heart of any BBS. It usually leads to other menus such as the File Menu, the Bulletin Menu, and the Message Menu, among others.

Modem   A piece of hardware that transforms data into electronic signals that computers can exchange over ordinary telephone lines.

Password   A private code that allows you to gain access to a BBS. You usu-ally choose your own password, although a few boards assign you a password and a few have universal passwords used by everyone. Various boards have dif-ferent rules about how long your password can be and what characters you can use. When choosing a password, you should avoid anything obvious like your name or the city where you live. Otherwise, a hacker may be able to guess your password and use it to access a BBS. For added security, some people create passwords containing a combination of letters and numbers.

Prompt   A message from the BBS asking what you want to do next. Many prompts present a list of options from which you can choose.

Protocol   The "rules" two computers must follow to exchange messages or files. For downloading files from a BBS, some of the most common protocols are Zmodem, Ymodem, and Xmodem. For the transfer to work, the BBS and your communications software must both use the same protocol. On the Internet, two of the more common protocols are File Transfer Protocol (FTP) and Telnet.

Shareware   A computer program you can try for free. If you decide to keep it, you must send the shareware fee to the program's author. Some federal BBSs have shareware programs that you can download.

Special interest group (SIG)   *See* Conference.

Sub-board   A second BBS that is a subsystem of the main board and that can be accessed from it.

Sysop   The person who runs the BBS. *Sysop* is short for system operator.

Telnet   An Internet protocol that allows you to connect to another computer and use it as if it were sitting on your desk. For example, you can use Telnet to access electronic card catalogs at libraries around the world.

Upload   To copy a file from your computer to another computer.

User   A person who calls and uses a BBS.

User ID   *See* ID.

Wildcard   A search capability available on some BBSs that is helpful if you don't know the full name of the file you're seeking. You can type a partial file name with wildcard symbols such as *, and the BBS will search for all files containing the partial name.

World Wide Web (WWW)   A hypertext-based interface to the Internet. Hypertext files have links to other, related files embedded within them. To access the related file, you click on the link.

WWW   *See* World Wide Web.

Zipped   *See* Compressed File.

INDEX

Abduction, 31
ABLEDATA database, 230, 231
ABLE INFORM BBS, 230–232
Access EPA, 174
Accessing Federal Data Bases for Contaminated Site Cleanup, 190
Access to federal bulletin boards, 22–28
Access to Internet. *See* Internet
Accounting machines, 74
Acetone, 110
ACF BBS, 219
Acid rain, 170, 172
Acquired immune deficiency syndrome (AIDS)
    alcohol and, 265
    bulletin boards list, 256, 260
    caregiver guidelines, 255
    clinical practice guidelines, 250
    comprehensive information, 3, 4, 241, 251–252, 255, 259–261, 264
    consumer information, 34
    FDA drug approval, 244
    HIV testing requirements abroad, 31
    1987–1989 mortality rates, 239
    nutrition and, 49
    Surgeon General's report, 256, 259, 260
ADA, The: Your Employment Rights as an Individual with a Disability (EEOC), 234, 278
ADA, The: Your Responsibilities as an Employer (EEOC), 234, 278
ADA Accessibility Guidelines (EEOC), 234
Ada programming language
    Ada Information Clearinghouse, 122
    Ada Technical Support Bulletin Board, 123
ADA Technical Assistance Manual (EEOC), 231
Administration for Children and Families, 90, 219
Administration on Developmental Disabilities, 219
Administration on Native Americans, 208
Administrative managers, 271
Adobe Acrobat Reader, 115, 116
Adolescents. *See* Children and families
Adoption assistance, 30, 31, 219

Advertising, 263, 265
Advisory Circulars, FAA, 329, 335, 336
Advisory Committee on Advanced Television Service Meetings, 107
Advisory Council on the NII, 38
AEE BBS, 328
Aeromedical Forum, 238
Aerometric Information Retrieval System, 170
Aeronautics and aerospace. *See* Space science and exploration
Africa, 31
African Americans, 42, 138, 265
AgEBB (Agricultural Electronic Bulletin Board), 44
Agency for Health Care Policy and Research, 250
Agent Orange, 255
Aging, 49, 265
AGRICOLA database, 46–49
Agricultural History Newsletter, 49
Agricultural Information Bulletins, 48
Agricultural Letter, 81
Agricultural Library Forum (ALF), 46–49
Agricultural Research Service, 48, 61, 258
Agricultural Trade and Marketing Information Center, 48, 49
Agriculture, 43–61
    aquaculture, 46, 47, 49, 50–51, 52, 204
    biological controls, 59–61
    biotechnology, 58
    bulletin board lists, 48
    California, employment and earnings, 287
    census data, 72, 73
    comprehensive information, 44–49, 54–55, 57
    economic and statistical data, 52, 53, 77, 78, 83, 84
    energy, 157
    farm safety, 277
    foreign trade, 48, 52
    hay locator services, 44, 56
    Internet sites, 49
    migrant and seasonal workers, 277
    technology transfer, 61

telecommunications systems and policies, 38, 39

trade information, 89

Commerce secretary, 296

Commercial fishing, 111

Commercial paper, 85

Commissioner's Annual Report (IRS), 118

Commission Issuance Posting System
(CIPS), 159–160

Commodity prices, 53, 54

Commodity specialists, 113

Common carriers, 108

*Common Groundwork: A Practical Guide to
Preserving Rural and Urban Land*, 200

Communications Act, 39

Communications sector. *See* Telecommunications

Communications software

DOS, Windows, and IBM-compatible,
48, 130, 150, 274, 301, 302, 313

information and purchase advice, 5, 6,
173

Macintosh, 6, 274

other or unspecified systems, 236

Community health centers, 239

Community Reinvestment Act, 82

Community Services, Office of, 219

Compensation. *See* Employment issues

Compensation Policy, Office of, 279

Compliance, Office of, FDA, 247

COMPLIance Information, 172

Comprehensive Epidemiologic Data Resource (CEDR), 243

CompuServe, 6, 12

Computer–aided acquisitions and logistic
support, 23

Computer–aided drafting, 157

Computers, 122–127

accommodation for disabled persons, 40,
217, 230

Ada programming language, 122, 123

Army data distribution systems, 125

foreign trade, 87

government acquisitions, 95, 100, 104

high performance computing, 103

industry data, 74

list of agency systems, 303

shareware. *See* Shareware and freeware

standards, 124

time services, 324, 325

viruses and other security issues,
126–128, 144, 236, 274

Computer Security Act of 1987, 127, 225

Condominiums, 74

Condoms, 34, 259, 260

Congress

bills, 25, 26, 35, 37

directories, 35, 70

Congressional Record, 3, 25, 26, 35

Connecticut, 85, 86, 294

Consensus Development Statements, NIH,
250, 256

Consolidated Farm Service Agency Bulletin
Board System (CFSA-BBS), 53

Constitution, U.S., 130, 144, 226

Construction. *See* Buildings and construction

Consular Affairs Bulletin Board (CABB),
30–32

Consumer Advocate, Office of the,
220

Consumer affairs

credit and finance, 80, 81, 84

information publications, 33–34, 200,
245

postal rates and services, 4, 67–68

Consumer Information Center (CIC) BBS,
33–34

Consumer price index, 79, 80, 278, 281,
282, 289

Consumer prices, 83

Consumer's Resource Handbook, 33

Contact lenses, 34

*Contaminants and Remedial Options at Pes-
ticide Sites*, 188

*Contaminants and Remedial Options at Sol-
vent-Contaminated Sites*, 188

*Contaminants and Remedial Options at
Wood Preserving Sites*, 188

Control Technology Center, 171-172

Convection, 316

Cooking programs, 144

Cooperative Administrative Support Program, 221

Eating disorders, 255

Eclipses, 316, 321

Ecology, 174

Economic Affairs, Office of the Under Secretary for, 73, 76

Economic Analysis, Bureau of, 72, 73, 75, 76, 86

Economic Bulletin Board (EBB), 72, 75–77

Economic Conversion Information, Office of, 64–65

Economic data, 72–86
  agriculture, 52, 53
  banking, economic, and financial data, 78–85
  census information, 72–74
  comprehensive information, 75–77, 277, 278
  defense conversion, 64–65
  energy, 158
  environmental preservation impact, 190
  international, 81, 82, 85
  Minnesota, 289
  Nevada, 290
  New England, 86
  South Carolina, 281
  Washington, 285
  water resources, 204
  Wisconsin, 283

Economic Development Administration, 64

Economic Research Service, 52

Economic Review, 82

Economics and Statistics Administration, 75

ED Board, 96

Editor programs, 301

EDRS Database Query System, 91, 262

Education, Office of, NIH, 141, 254

Educational Programs That Work, 144

Educational Research Improvement, Office of (OERI), 143–144

Education and training
  Ada and software engineering, 122, 123
  agriculture, 47, 59, 200
  aircraft pilots, 333, 335
  air pollution abatement, 171
  biomedicine, 141–142
  charter schools, 216

college costs and financing, 74, 144

comprehensive offerings, 138, 143–144, 236, 275

consumer information, 33, 34

criminal justice, 303

dental health, 253, 254

disabled persons, 235

emergency management, 150

energy, 157

environment, 185

ethics, 212

federal employment programs for students, 272, 273

financial assistance. *See* Government grants

foreign languages, 3, 139–140

hazardous materials response, 147, 148

hazardous waste treatment, 190

health and biomedicine, 216, 239–240

HIV/AIDS, 259

home schooling, 236

Iowa, 282

learning disabilities, 255

military personnel and veterans, 134, 278

minority colleges, 138

NSF documents, 103

quality of schools, 84, 216

science, 316, 317

South Carolina, 281

statistical data, 73, 143–144

student alcohol, tobacco, and drug use, 263–275

water pollution, 202

Education Department, 96, 143–144, 230, 235, 237, 291

Elderly people, 48, 74, 256, 263

Electrical equipment, 106–107

Electric power, 158–160

Electric vehicles, 157, 173, 216

Electronic Communications Privacy Act of 1986, 225

Electronic Dissemination of Opinions (EDOS), 297

Electronic equipment, 315, 323

Electronic Industries Foundation, 231

Electronic Information Dissemination Services, Office of, 35

Food stamps, 236
Footwear, 74
Forecast of Nationwide Contracting Opportunities, 105
Foreign Agricultural Service, 75
Foreign Assets Control, Office of, 342
Foreign investment, in energy sector, 158
Foreign language instruction, 3, 139–140
Foreign trade. *See* Trade and marketing
Forestry, 48, 49
Forms
    personnel office forms, 273, 274
    tax forms and instructions, 3, 22, 115, 116, 119
Fossil Energy Communications, Office of, 161
Fossil Energy Telenews, 161
Fossil fuels, 161
Foster care, 219
4-H programs, 55
France, 85
Fraud and waste, 212–213, 277
Freedom of Information Act, 39, 106
Freeware. *See* Shareware and freeware
French language, 139, 140
Fuel Economy Guide, 170, 172
Fuel prices, 158
Fuel tax rates, 338
Funerals, 34

Galileo spacecraft mission, 316
Games, 130, 151, 212
GAO Daybook, 29
GAO Office of Policy's BBS, 216
GAO-OGC Decision Bulletin Board, 97
GAO Watchdog, 213
"Garbage" characters, 13–14
Gardening, 47
Gas mileage guide, 34
Gasoline prices, 158
Gay men, 264
Gemini space missions, 306
General Accounting Office (GAO), 3, 25, 29, 35, 36, 97, 213, 216
General Aviation Airworthiness ALERT!, 336
General Aviation Operations Inspector's Handbook, 331

General Counsel, Office of (OGC), GAO, 97
General Services Administration (GSA), 33, 40, 100, 217, 221, 223, 224, 227
Genetic engineering/Biotechnology, 46, 58, 61
Genetics, and alcoholism, 265
Geographers, job openings, 271
Geography, 144
Geological Survey, 184, 204, 206, 268, 307, 308, 310
Geological Survey Bulletin Board System, 313
Geological Survey National Center, 313
Geology, 313
Geomagnetic field values, 309
Georgia, 26
Georgia Southern University, 26
Geriatrics education, 240
German language, 139, 140
Germany, 85
Gettysburg Address, 226
GIF viewers, 316
Glass industry, 74
Global change, 46, 103, 307, 311
Global Land Information System (GLIS), 307
Global Positioning System, 344, 345
Global Seismology and Geomagnetism Online Information System, 308–309
Goats, 47
Goddard Space Flight Center, 314, 319
Government Auditing Standards (GAO), 216
Government contracts
    appeals, 97, 296
    barred companies, 100
    construction criteria, 92
    contractors' discontinuance notice alerts, 322
    dental research, 253, 254
    education, 96, 138
    energy, 161, 209
    environmental research, 181
    GSA information, 217
    hazardous waste cleanup, 187, 189, 190
    mental health and substance abuse, 101
    Navy Dept., 93

environmental information, 206
FCC documents, 106
federal budget, 36
federal job information, 273–275
GPO Access, 25, 35
health policy and research, 250
HIV/AIDS, 260
Library of Congress resources, 42
NIH biomedical research grants, 99
shareware communications programs, 6
small business, 71
Supreme Court opinions, 36, 304
telephone time service, 325
Internships, 142, 272
Interview simulator, 271
Intext word processor, 139
Invertebrate pathology, 59
Investment information
energy sector, 158
investor publications, 22, 23
private domestic, 80
small business, 71
Iowa, 54, 80, 282
Iowa Department of Employment Services, 282
Iowa State University, 54
IRIS (Internal Revenue Information Services), 3, 116
IRMa BBS, 218
IRM Planning, Acquisitions and Security Service, 105
IRP-BBS, 117
Irrigation, 204
IRS Statistics of Income Division Bulletin Board, 118
Italian language, 139, 140
Italy, 85
ITC Chemicals BBS, 110

JAGNET Information Center, 130
Japan, 85
Japanese language instruction, 140
Jet Propulsion Laboratory, 316
Job issues. *See* employment entries
Johnson Space Center, 306
Joint Task Force on Postal Rulemaking, 220
Journal of Rehabilitation Research and De-

velopment, The, 135
Journal of the American Medical Association, 256
JPL Info, 316
Judge Advocate General's Information Network (JAGNET), 130
Judicial Conference of the United States, 4, 5
Judiciary
circuit courts, 4–5, 294–298
software programs, 302
Supreme Court, 29, 36, 302, 304
Jupiter moons, 316
Justice. *See* Law and justice
Justice Assistance, Bureau of, 299
Justice Department, 126, 183, 231, 233–235, 299–300, 302
Justice Statistics, Bureau of, 299, 303
Juvenile Justice and Delinquency Prevention, Office of, 299

Kansas, 54
Keeping Your Site Comfortably Secure: An Introduction to Internet Firewalls, 126
Kentucky, 79, 295
Keyboards, 230
Kidney stones, 255
Kidney transplants, 239
KIMBERLEY, 83–84
Know Your Aircraft computer program, 333

Labeling regulations, 244, 247
Labor Department (DOL), 276–278, 281–292
Labor issues. *See* employment entries
Labor News, 277–278
Labor Statistics, Bureau of, 73, 75, 76, 277, 282, 286, 288, 291
Lactose intolerance, 255
Ladybeetle Flyer, The, 59
Lakes and streams. *See* water entries
Landfills, 171, 180
Land Management, Bureau of, 268
Land resources, 307
Land sales, 224
Language instruction, 3, 139–140

INDEX

RTK NET, 4, 182–184
Rubber bullets, 303
Rugs and carpets, 74
Rules Committee, Senate, 36
Rural development and health, 46, 49, 185, 239, 264
Rural Health Research Center, 49
Rural Information Center, 49
Russia, 31, 42, 88
Russian language instruction, 139
Russian wheat aphid, 59, 60

Safety. *See* Crime and security; Health and safety; specific topics
Sailboat races, 345
Salaries. *See* Wages and salaries
Sales Bulletin Board Service, 227
Salmon farming, 47
Salmonella, 247
SAMHSA BBS, 101
Santa Claus's address, 68
Santos (Brazil) port hazards, 344
Saturn, 316
SAT verbal prep programs, 144
Savings deposits, 79, 83
Satellite design, 314–315
Satellite images, 23, 312
Satellite navigation, 345
Satellite Navigation News, 331
Satellite tracking programs, 318
Satellites, 318
SBA Online, 69–71
Scholarships. *See* Government grants
Schools and students. *See* Education and training
Science and technology
  career opportunities, 103
  documents database, 174
  manufacturers' discontinuance notice alerts, 322
  scientific integrity, 261
  technology transfer, 318
  telephone time services, 324, 325
  See also specific sciences and technologies
Science and Technology Information System (STIS), 102–103

Science and Technology Policy, Office of, 58
Scientific and Technical Information, Office of, 156
Scooters, 230
Seafood and shellfish, 47, 185, 247, 248
Search and rescue, 150
SEARCH-BBS, 36, 302–304
"Searching and Seizing Computers," 126
Seasonal affective disorder, 255
Seasonal farm workers, 277
Seat cushions, 230
SEC News Digest, 23
Second Circuit Court of Appeals, 294
Secretary, Office of (Interior), 268
Securities, 84, 85
Securities and Exchange Commission, 22, 23, 108
Seeds, 49
Seismology, 308–310
Semi-Annual Regulatory Agenda, 26
Senate, 29
Senior Executive Service, 272, 274, 279, 280
Service Contract Appeals Board, 276
Service Corps of Retired Executives, 70, 71
Seventh Circuit Court of Appeals, 5, 298
  Bulletin Board, 298
Sewage sludge, 203
Sexual harassment, 130, 132
Sexually transmitted diseases, 34, 260
Shakespeare, William, 225, 226
Shareware and freeware
  anti-virus utilities, 15, 274
  communication programs, 6, 130, 274, 313
  comprehensive offerings, 128–130, 208, 313, 331
  decompression utilities, 274
  DOS utilities, 279, 313
  education, 143–144
  emergency management, 150
  foreign language instruction, 139–140
  games, 130
  graphics, 130
  interview simulator, 271
  libraries management, 40
  nutritional content of food, 258
  small aircraft, 334

Washington Online

HOW TO ACCESS THE FEDERAL GOVERNMENT ON THE INTERNET

BRUCE MAXWELL

How to Access the Federal Government on the Internet 1996
Washington Online

By Bruce Maxwell

New Edition COMING SOON!

"This modestly priced book will be useful in academic, special, and public library reference collections as an aid to librarians and patrons, as a guide to creating "bookmarks" to specific Internet sites, and to individuals as a desk reference." *Library Journal*

A wealth of federal government information is available to the public for free on the Internet. Revised with the most up-to-date information available, this new 1996 edition provides detailed descriptions of nearly 300 Internet sites, mailing lists, databases, and other resources.

The book describes how to access:

- Speeches by President Clinton, the full text of bills being considered by Congress
- State Department travel advisories
- Census data
- Lists of federal job openings nationwide and overseas
- A wide range of information about AIDS
- Economic data
- Federal income tax forms
- Hundreds of thousands of images from NASA, the Library of Congress, and other agencies

- Electronic card catalogs at numerous federal libraries, including the Library of Congress and the National Library of Medicine, and the Environmental Protection Agency's library
- Mailing lists that automatically deliver news to your Internet account from NASA, the Census Bureau, and other agencies
- Searchable databases that track bills as they proceed through Congress, list all publications produced by the Government Printing Office, and provide access to hundreds of White House documents

How to Access the Federal Government on the Internet 1996 is written in easy-to-understand language that makes it useful to Internet newcomers and experienced pros alike. A glossary offers simple definitions of the language of the Internet, and an extensive index helps you quickly zero in on the information you're seeking.

Order Today!

☐ Yes! Send me _____ copies of *How to Access the Federal Government on the Internet 1996: Washington Online* at $24.95 each as soon as the book is available in June 1996. (Paperback. App. 420 pages. ISBN 1-56802-185-2.)

☐ Check enclosed for $_____ , payable to Congressional Quarterly (Free shipping in continental U.S. if you include payment).

☐ Charge my (circle one) VISA MasterCard in the amount of $_____. (Free shipping in continental U.S.).

Acct. #_____ Exp. Date_____

Signature_____

DC addressees add 5.75% sales tax; NJ addressees add 6%.
Prices subject to change.

Name _____

Phone (required) _____

Organization _____

Street address (required) _____

City _____ State _____ Zip_____

Mail to: **Congressional Quarterly Books**
Dept. V107
1414 22nd St., N.W.
Washington, D.C. 20037

or call toll-free to order **1-800-638-1710** • In Metropolitan D.C: call **202-822-1475** • Fax your order to **202-887-6706**

Congressional Quarterly Books
Washington, D.C.

V107